CAMBODIA
LAOS

First Edition
1994

TABLE OF CONTENTS

CAMBODIA

LIST OF MAPS

Note: The Cambodians and Laotians use ancient Indian scripts, from which it is impossible to establish a single, accepted spelling of personal names and place names. French, British and German experts have always used spellings, in their publications and maps, which correspond to the pronunciation of their own languages. Cambodians and Laotians, when using the Roman alphabet, have not adopted any one European spelling system consistently. In this book, the spellings most frequently used in Cambodia and Laos have been selected, and commonly encountered variants have been added in brackets. In certain cases the spelling of place names shown on the maps is not identical to that in the text. This is because the maps have been based on information supplied by the United Nations.

CAMBODIA / LAOS
© Nelles Verlag GmbH, 80935 Munich
    All rights reserved

First edition 1994
ISBN 3-88618-396-3
Printed in Slovenia

Publisher:	Günter Nelles	
Project Editor:	Annaliese Wulf	
Editor:	Dr. J.-Martina Schneider	
Picture editor:	Dr. Heinz Vestner	
Cartography:	Nelles Verlag GmbH	

Translation and
English editor: Angus McGeoch
Color separations: Priegnitz,
    München
Printing: Gorenjski Tisk

- 01 -

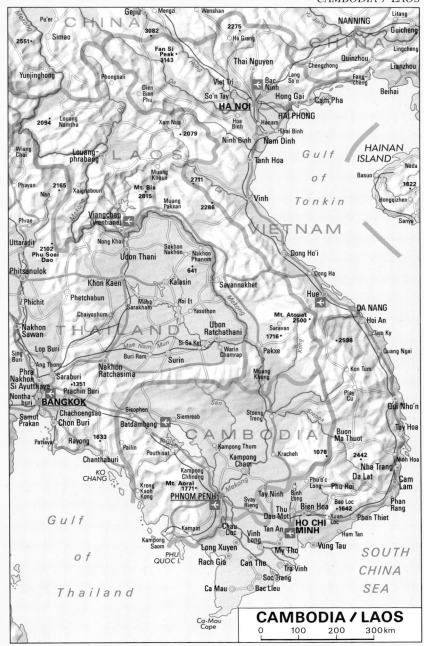

CAMBODIA / LAOS

0   100   200   300km

7

CAMBODIA:

LAND AND PEOPLE

Size and shape

Cambodia lies in that part of the mainland of Asia which is known as Indochina, and which, together with the Indonesian and Philippine archipelagos, forms the sub-continent of South-East Asia.

The land of the Khmer, as its main population group is called, has an area of 70,000 sq. miles (181,000 sq. km) and, apart from the city-state of Singapore and the Sultanate of Brunei, is the smallest country in South-East Asia. It lies south of the 15th parallel of latitude and is almost circular in shape, with its center near the city of Kompong Thom, east of the Great Lakes. Until the 15th century the Khmer empire stretched into southern Laos and to the Menam river in Siam (Thailand). For a time it included the kingdom of Cham in central Vietnam and controlled the Mekong delta and parts of the Malay peninsula.

About 5 per cent of present-day Cambodia consists of rivers and lakes. It has borders with Thailand to the northwest, with Thailand and Laos to the north and with Vietnam to the east and southeast. In the southwest its 200 miles (340 km) of coastline along the Gulf of Thailand give it access to the oceans of the world. The seaport of Kompong Som (Sihanoukville) was constructed in 1960 and freed Cambodia from dependence on the foreign ports of Bangkok and Saigon.

The plains of Cambodia are ringed by the last foothills of the Himalayas, the

Previous pages: Young monk and naga. (serpent god) Aspara dancers at Angkor Wat. Giant faces at the Bayon temple. Evening at That Luang, Vientiane. Left: A gamelan orchestra in Phnom Penh.

Cardamon range in the west, the Elephant or Damrei mountains to the southwest and the long chain of the Dangrek mountains to the north. The eastern frontier with Vietnam runs up into the high and inaccessible Moi mountains, which are only crossed by one international highway. Rising out of the plains, particularly in the north of the country, are ranges of hills and isolated mountains known as *phnom*. From earliest times these were considered to be seats of the gods. The people worshipped them and built settlements under their protective eye.

Even more important than the mountains are the rivers, traditionally the sites of settlement and culture in the South-East-Asian mainland. These rise in the Himalayas and flow southwards. The migrating Austronesian peoples followed their deep valleys and settled on the plains and deltas.

The Mekong river

The Mekong, which flows through the Cambodian plain, is one of the great rivers of the world and the third-longest in Asia. It has largely determined the way of life of the people and the history of the states along its banks. It rises 10,000 feet (3,000 m.) up in the plateau of Tibet and has carved a deep valley through the mountains of Yunnan (south China) and Laos. Before crossing the frontier into Cambodia it makes its way again through cliffs until it reaches the Falls of Khone, 50 ft (15m) high and 7 1/2 miles (12 km) long, which are followed by the Preaparat Rapids for a further 30 miles (50 km). Only then does the river, fed by numerous tributaries, settle down to flow slowly and majestically through the Cambodian plain. South of Phnom Penh it splits into two arms, the Bassac to the east and the lower Mekong to the west. In southern Vietnam it fans out into a broad delta and flows into the South China Sea through nine estuaries.

CAMBODIA

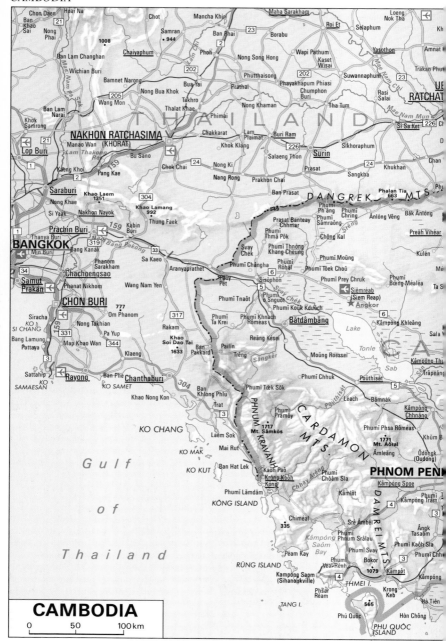

CAMBODIA

0   50   100 km

14

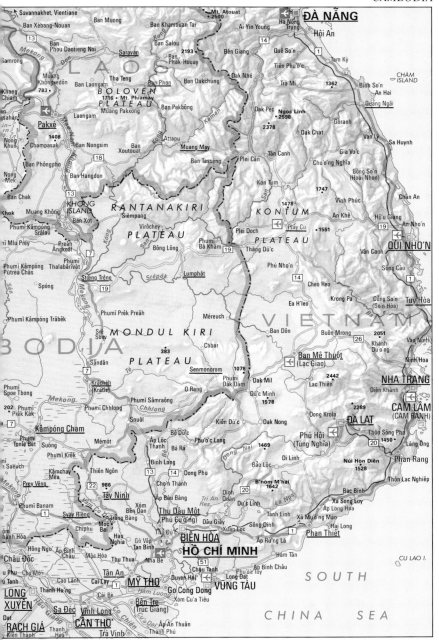

When swollen by the melting mountain snows and the monsoon rains – and also because of the destruction of vegetation by the mountain peoples – the river carries down masses of rich mud, deposits this as fertile alluvium in the valleys and is continually pushing the edge of the delta further out into the sea.

At the city of Kratie in northeastern Cambodia the Mekong is still 340 miles (550 km) from the sea, yet is navigable all year round. The regular rise and fall of the ocean tides is still quite perceptible, even this far inland.

Many thousands of years ago most of what is now Cambodia lay at the bottom of an arm of the Pacific Ocean, and its southwest coast was formed by the Cardamon mountains. But gradually the Mekong filled up the bay with its deposits and a fertile plain was formed, watered by rivers, or *stung*, and their tributaries, known as *prek*, which formed a natural

irrigation and drainage system. The rivers have built up high embankments of mud on either side, and even in the annual wet season, these prevent the surrounding land from being flooded. In parts of the plain the level of the land did not rise uniformly, and here large lakes were formed.

The civilization of Cambodia evolved here and, thanks to the work of the Mekong, became the largest and most fertile agricultural region in South-East Asia. The 60-mile (100 km) watercourse called the Tonle Sap, which links the Mekong and the large lakes of the same name, are relics of the former gulf.

However, for the civilization of Angkor to develop beside the Great Lakes, there had to be an additional climatic factor, namely the monsoon, whose rains fed the *baray*, the sophisticated irrigation system for the rice fields of Angkor. Without the monsoon it would be impossible to cultivate paddies where enough rice could be grown to support such a densely populated country.

Above: After the monsoon rains. Right: Jackfruit, related to the breadfruit.

The monsoons

Cambodia lies between latitudes 10°
and 15° north, in the tropical monsoon
zone. The monsoons divide the year into
two quite distinct seasons. The southwest
monsoon arises over the Indian Ocean
during the summer months and from June
to October brings the rains, which water
the rice paddies and fill the reservoirs. In
the winter months the northeast monsoon
forms over Siberia and blows over the
land mass of China, ushering in Cambodia's dry season. Then, in order to harvest a second crop of rice, the fields have
to be irrigated.

Flora and fauna

Cambodia's plant and animal life are
determined by the tropical climate and
geographic conditions. Seventy per cemt
of the country is covered with forests and
jungle. In the mountain forests hard-
woods, including teak and ironwood
trees, grow up to 100 ft (30 m) high.
Timber is one of Cambodia's most important resources. Lianas hang from the
trees and orchids grow in profusion. During the colonial period coffee, tea and
pepper were planted here, while in the
plain rubber- and cotton-plantations were
established. The mountain tribes sell
spices, medicinal herbs, fibers and resins,
in exchange for tools and equipment and
the much-needed salt which is mainly extracted from the sea near Kampot, on the
Gulf of Thailand. In the lowlands rice,
maize, vegetables, fruit and tropical nuts
all grow plentifully. The population
makes use of bamboo and palm products
at every stage of life. Cradles and coffins,
tools and domestic utensils, mats and
even houses are made from bamboo and
the wood and leaves of the palm tree.

The tropical fauna is rich in mammals,
reptiles and insects. Rare species have
withdrawn to remote habitats in the
mountain forests and the jungle. The

peasant farmer's most prized possession
is his waterbuffalo, the *zebu* (Indian
humped cattle), which is harnessed to a
cart or plough. He might also use a cow
instead, as a beast of burden, but milking
has always been unknown here, as in the
rest of southeast and eastern Asia. The
Cambodians are not great meat-eaters,
but although the Buddhist faith forbids
the killing of any living creature, a Buddhist may eat the meat of an animal that
has been killed by a non-Buddhist. Keeping pigs and poultry has up to now played
very little part in life. Hens were only
used as sacrifices in the cult of ancestor-
and spirit-worship. However, cock fighting is a favorite form of entertainment for
the Khmer. Cambodia's lakes and rivers
are more full of fish than almost any in
the world.

The population

The empire of the Khmer, or of the
Kambudja, sons of the legendary
Brahman Kambu, was known under

various names incuding, Kampucha, Cambodge and Cambodia. The Khmer Rouge named the country Kampuchea, but since 1989 it has reverted to Cambodia. The Khmer are a mixed race of Austro-Indonesian origin with unmistakably Melanesian features, but comparatively little of the Mongoloid character. They belong to the Mon-Khmer peoples, one of the oldest population groups of Indo-China. From Yunnan in southern China they followed the course of the Mekong, settled in the fertile plain south of the Laotian and west of the Vietnamese mountains, and founded the empire of Angkor, long before the Thai peoples moved into the valleys of the Menam and Mekong.There are many notable differences in appearance and still more in mentality, between the Khmer and their Thai, Laotian and Vietnamese neighbors.

The Khmer are seldom over 5 ft 6 ins (1.65 m) tall and can be either delicate or stocky in build; their skin is rather brown, their black hair is thick and wavy and their eyes dark bown and oval shaped. Some faces are soft and rounded, while others are flatter with pronounced, angular lower jaw and chin, such as are often depicted in the art of Angkor. The friendly, open and cheerful nature of the people points to an inner contentment.

Cambodian villages are very unlike the rigidly organized units that you find in China or Vietnam. This is partly to do with mentality and geography, but also with the distribution of land and methods of building and irrigation. On the other hand, the planting and harvesting of rice calls for planning, mutual help and community-based work. The Khmer live in extended families with an emphasis on the individual and a tendency towards passivity and stoicism. Competitiveness, business and trade mean little to them. Their thinking is influenced by their ani-

Right: A young Cambodian woman harvesting rice.

mistic beliefs and by their Buddhist faith, which is directed more toward the hereafter than the realities of earthly life.

In 1870 the population of Cambodia was between 6 and 7 million. There was massive loss of life caused by war and civil strife, particularly during the regime of the Khmer Rouge, from April 1975 to January 1979. Estimates vary widely, but the population must have been reduced by anything from 1 to 3 million. After 1979 the birthrate increased rapidly – in the years 1985 to 1987 it reached 5.7 per cent. According to the census in 1988 the population had reached 7,869,000. The density is only 111 inhabitants per sq. mile (43 per sq. km), and although the distribution is uneven, in normal circumstances there need not be any shortage of food. Three quarters of the population occupy half the land area, in the fertile regions between the Great Lakes in the northwest and the district south of Phnom Penh. Only ten per cent of Cambodians live in cities. Average life expectancy is 50 years, but infant mortality is very high at 16.5 per cent. In rural areas especially, there is a lack of doctors, hospitals and medical care.

About 90 per cent of the inhabitants are ethnic Khmer, which means that Cambodia has an unusually homogeneous population for this part of the world. There are ten minorities living in about one-tenth of the land area. Chinese account for 3 per cent of the population, and Vietnameses 4 per cent. Most of the Chinese live in the cities, fulfilling the trading function which the Khmer do not enjoy. During the colonial period they were employed by the French as middlemen and plantation workers. A few of the Vietnamese are also traders, but most of them live, like the Khmer, from farming and fishing.

Before 1970, the capital Phnom Penh had a population of 600,000, of whom 220,000 were Khmer and 380,000 Chinese and Vietnamese. And although

from 1970 onwards the non-Khmer were persecuted, killed or driven out, some have since returned.

The Cham and Malay minorities were appallingly persecuted by the Khmer Rouge on account of their Muslim faith. Today they live as farmers and fishermen in about 200 vilages on the Mekong or on the coast. They have their own mosques or prayer halls and the children go to Koranic schools. Togther with the few mountain tribes, the Pear, Puong, Styieng, Samré and Kuy, they number over 200,000. There is an unknown number of Thais and Burmese living in western Cambodia, near the Thai border.

Some 290,000 Cambodian refugees have been living in Thailand since 1975, while 100,000 have emigrated to America, Europe and other parts of Asia.

The economy

Cambodia used to be one of the most important rice producers in Asia. In the post-Angkorian era it was an agrarian nation, able to support itself from its own natural resources. During the colonial period, and up until 1970, rice, sugarcane, coffee and spices, as well as cotton and rubber, were grown and exported. But even today there are scarcely any processing-plants for handling agricultural produce and the rich fish catches.

Until 1989 Cambodia's most important trading partners were the states of the former East Bloc, but more recently their place has been taken by Japan, Thailand, Australia and western countries. In 1979, when the Khmer Rouge were push-ed back by the Vietnamese into the west-ern and northwestern parts of Cambodia, the east of the country and its capital, Phnom Penh were left in a state of total desolation. Of the original 600,000 inhabitants only 28,000 had remained in the capital. Those who had survived expulsion and forced labor on the land returned hesitantly and sought shelter in the abandoned and now scarcely habitable houses. Even at the beginning of the 1980s the Post Office had no stamps, and

the bank no banknotes. Pol Pot had, for a period of three years, eight months and 20 days, abolished money, destroyed industry and brought trade to a standstill. Food could only be obtained by barter or by paying in hard currency on the black market that flourished with neighboring Thailand. There were no medicines, clothes, building materials, transportation or communications. The intellectual class, as well as the Buddhist priesthood, had been practically wiped out, largely for reasons which simply defy belief. For example, anyone who wore glasses was considered an intellectual, and if they did not get rid of their glasses in time, they were killed.

Today, if you walk through Phnom Penh, a city where once again more than 700,000 people live, you can scarcely imagine the emptiness and misery which reigned here in the mid-1980s. Whatever one can say today about the rebuilding of

Above: Fishingboats near Phnom Penh. Right: Foodstalls in Tonle Bati, Takeo.

the economy refers to eastern Cambodia, the former People's Republic, but not to the so-called "democratic" Kampuchea of the Khmer Rouge. The part of the country that was controlled by the Khmer Rouge has been exploited and robbed of its resources of precious stones, from the area around Pailin, as well as of its hardwood forests. This is how the Pol Pot regime from 1979 onwards payed for the supplies and especially the arms, which they obtained from China and Thailand and, after the withdrawal of the Vietnamese army in 1990, also from the USA. It was Thailand and the Chinese living there who profited most from the unholy war in Indochina.

The economic recovery achieved by the People's Republic was remarkable, when measured against the shambles that they inherited in 1979. But from 1979 to 1989 the East Bloc states, especially the USSR, East Germany and Vietnam, were largely responsible for this success. The visitor cannot fail to notice the poverty of the people in town and country and the

lack of many of the essentials of life, but thanks to the rising output of rice, vegetables, fruit and fish, the rural population are not starving, whereas in the cities, unemployment, shortage of money and the ravages of inflation are clearly noticeable.

The proportion of the land area which is of agricultural value is 17 per cent, but today only 4 per cent is being cultivated, two-thirds of it with rice. The yields are poor. With more intensive methods of cultivation, irrigation, fertilizers, and bringing fallow land back into use, agricultural production could be increased significantly.

Another under-utilized resource is hydroelectricity. There are also worthwhile mineral resources waiting to be exploited, including phosphates (for fertilizer), bauxite, tin and copper. Since 1960, precious stones such as rubies, sapphires and onyx have been extracted at Pailin near the border with Thailand. However, at the moment this region is controlled by the Khmer Rouge. The suc-

cess of all the efforts in the economic sphere depends on political stability.

Food and diet

The basic element of every meal is rice, usually accompanied by vegetables or fish, but seldom meat, and often only by *prahoc*, a fish sauce without which no Cambodian meal is complete. Fish and crustaceans appear in many forms, as fish soup, crab paste (*kepi*), dried, boiled or grilled. Peasant families eat their meals squatting on a mat. They eat with their right hand from palm leaves, but the food is not cut up as small as in Chinese cooking. Hot spices such as chili, ginger and pepper are used generously and prevent the food from going bad in the hot climate. Essentially, Cambodian cooking is closer to Indian than to Chinese.

Clothes and housing

The women wrap a piece of cotton or silk cloth around their hips, to form a nar-

21

row, ankle-length skirt called a *sampot*. For everyday wear it is dark in color, with a small pattern, but on festival days *sampots* in brilliant colors are worn. The rather shorter sarong is still worn by men on formal occasions and in the country, where the peasants, when working, pull the corner of it between their legs to form a baggy pair of trousers. In addition the men wear a short jacket, the women a rather longer one. No traditional method of arranging the hair has been preserved. Straw hats are worn as a protection against sun and rain. The *krama* is a narrow cloth of cotton or silk, at least three feet (1 m) long and checkered in red or blue and white. It is used as headgear, shawl, scarf or belt, as well as for carrying babies or goods.

The Cambodian stilt house, or *pteah*, consists of corner posts and walls of woven matting or more solid material such as hardwood, depending on the

Above: Cambodian woman wearing a krama.
Right: The pteah, a house on stilts.

wealth of the owner. The roofs are made of straw or palmleaves, and increasingly today of tiles or corrugated iron. The *pteah* are built on platforms which rest on pillars of hardwood. The tree trunks from which they are made are left to lie in mud or water for several years before use, and this protects them for a long time against attack by termites. The rectangular houses are between 24 ft and 40 ft (7-12 m) wide. The entrance, in the middle of the long wall, traditionally faces east. The house usually has only two rooms with a covered verandah built in front. The kitchen stands outside the house on its own platform, and the buildings are grouped in the shade of palm trees or surrounded by low fence or hedge.

The Malayo-Indonesian style of building on stilts lets air into the rooms from all sides. The house is entered by a ladder which can be pulled up and which has 3, 5, 7 or 9 steps – an even number would bring bad luck. In the rainy season it is protected from the ground's dampness, and at all times it is safe from thieves, rats, snakes and, in remote areas, from wild animals. Livestock, carts, farm equipment and the women's looms can all be stored beneath the house. The peasants possess little furniture. They usually sit and sleep on mats.

Language and script

The language of the Khmer belongs to the Austro-Asiatic Mon-Khmer group. At the time of the Khmer empire of Angkor the Mon people occupied Indianized states in southern Burma and northern Thailand. They still live as minorities in both countries today. There are enclaves of Khmer speakers in Thailand, Laos, Vietnam, on the Nicobar Islands, and even some in India, so that in all the Khmer language is spoken by about 10 million people.

Some words in Khmer have the same root as Vietnamese, but the Mon-Khmer

languages were influenced by Sanskrit, the language of Hinduism, and are written in an ancient form of the Sanskrit alphabet of India. However, since the 14th century the Khmer language has taken a large part of its vocabulary from Pali, the language used in Hinayana Buddhism. The development of the Khmer language can be divided into three consecutive periods: Ancient Khmer (6th to 13th cent.), Middle Khmer (14th to 18th cent.) and modern Khmer, from the 19th century onward.

Unlike the monosyllabic, tonal languages of China, Thailand and Vietnam, Khmer lacks the tonal pitch which gives different meanings to the same basic word, and has words not only of one but also of two syllables, in which the stress is placed on the second syllable.

The 33 consonants of the Khmer language also serve as syllables, since the vowel *a* or *o* is always attached to them. According to the vowel used, the consonants are classified either in an a- or an o-register, though they can occur in both registers. A consonant written on its own can also signify a word. The consonant-registers determine the sound-value of the following vowel. Thus 16 vowel or diphthong signs can stand for 28 different sounds. The rules of pronunciation are highly complicated.

On the other hand Khmer grammar is simple. All words remain unmodified and their function can only be deduced from their position in the sentence. Complex forms such as the passive verb do not exist.

The normal word order consists of subject, verb and predicate. The plural, if used at all, is expressed by duplicating the noun or simply repeating its adjective. The verb never changes, and the different tenses are indicated by auxiliary verbs.

Literature and works of history from the pre-Angkorian and Angkorian periods were written on palm leaves and have not survived. Only the inscriptions of the kings, carved on temple walls and stone stelae have been preserved.

Khmer is the official language of Cambodia, but the second language of the educated older generation is French, while among younger people more English is spoken. The illiteracy rate is currently around 65 per cent.

Religions

Since earliest times the people of Cambodia have worshipped the forces of nature, the spirits of wind, water, earth and fertility, upon which the yield of their land and thereby their whole life depends. They offer them sacrifices from their harvest and their livestock, accompanied by the burning of incense. In former times they practiced human sacrifice. The greatest veneration is reserved for the earth spirits, *neak ta*, who may preside over a ricefield, a village, a region or even the entire country. Departed ancestors, especially chieftains, become

Above: Children selling josssticks at the temples.

guardian spirits, or *arak*, who attend to the well-being of their family and of the whole nation, from beyond the grave. They can be seen in the form of megaliths and menhirs, huge natural or roughhewn stones, which are worshipped as deified ancestors. The serpent, *naga*, is considered a symbol of water, and takes the form of a five-, seven-, or nine-headed cobra, which in Indian culture fulfils the same function as the Chinese rain dragon. At all levels of society the cult of the spirits of nature has remained alive right up to the present, and is also an element in the great annual Buddhist festivals.

From the 1st century AD Brahmaism came to Indochina, followed by the Hinduism which evolved from it. It became the religion of the kings and the foundation of god-kingship in Angkor.

Almost contemporaneously with the arrival of Brahmaism, Buddhist monks travelling between India and China spread the word of Mahayana Buddhism – as it was known in east Asia – to Cambodia. For a while this became the religion of the kings of Angkor, who saw themselves as the genuine incarnation of the Bodhisattva Avalokiteshvara.

The teaching of Buddha, the liberation from the cycle of reincarnation and an existence based on peace and harmony, also appealed to the common people. But it was the simplicity of Theravada Buddhism, based on the Hinayana teaching, which really captured their imagination and has remained the religion of the Khmer right up to the present. Theravada, or the Teaching of the Ancients, had evolved in Sri Lanka and reached Cambodia at the end of the 13th century, via Myanmar (Burma) and the Mon kingdom of Dvaravati.

Theravada Buddhism had not tried to close itself off from tradition. It was through tolerance that it achieved the variety, vividness and affinity with everyday life, which enabled it to capture the hearts of its followers. This faith became so deep-rooted in the people that it survived not only the passage of centuries but also the attempt by the Khmer Rouge to eradicate it, and the denial of all religion by the People's Republic of Kampuchea.

Until 1975 Buddhism played a large part in mass education and the elimination of illiteracy. Efforts to revive this activity can be seen today, and schooling is provided in monasteries that have survived or been rebuilt. But the terrible losses suffered by the monastic orders under the Khmer Rouge regime have not yet healed. Of the 60,000 monks alive in 1975, only about 500 survived, and most of the country's 3,000 temples and monasteries were destroyed. Since 1989 Buddhism has once more become the state religion, and the people find comfort from the hardships of life by contemplating the image of Buddha.

The Cambodian monastic orders in the 20th century modelled themselves on the Mahanikai and Thamayut orders of Thailand. They took part in political life, though not as actively as those in the neighboring country. In the central committee of the Khmer-Issarak, who from 1945 onwards fought against the return of French colonial power, 16 per cent of the members were monks. During the rule of Prince Norodom Sihanouk (1941-1970), when he was successively king, prime minister and state president, Buddhism was given the constitutional status of state religion in 1947. Two years later the Pali School in Phnom Penh was upgraded to a Buddhist university.

Buddhism meets the need of the Cambodians for inner harmony and strengthens the people in their self-sufficiency and patience in adversity. It relieves them of the anxieties of life in the present and excuses the inactivity which is inherent in their own mentality. Lying between two very active neighboring peoples, the Thais and the Vietnamese, this passivity has for centuries put the Khmer nation in a position of constant vulnerability.

At the court of the Cambodian kings, and during the rule of Norodom Sihanouk, Hindu ceremonies were performed for important state events and for the great festivals. However, at no time was Hinduism able to impose the Indian caste system on Cambodian society; the Brahmans did not enjoy any special social position as they did in India, though they did have certain privileges. Up to 1920 they were exempt from paying taxes, and until Buddhism became the state religion in 1947, they also had seats on the Crown Council.

Islam never gained a significant hold in Cambodia. Only the Cham and Malay minorities are Muslim. The Cham number about 190,000 and live in some 200 villages along the Mekong, north and east of Phnom Penh. Under the Khmer Rouge they suffered terrible persecution. Today some twenty mosques have been rebuilt and reconsecrated.

The Christian community of about 20,000 are mostly to be found among the Vietnamese minority.

THE HISTORY OF
CAMBODIA

The history and civilization of the Khmer began in the 1st century AD with its forerunners, the states of Fu Nan and Chen La. It reached its peak in the years 800 to 1471 with the empire of Angkor. Thereafter the Khmer empire went into a long and painful decline, which was only relieved by a glimmer of its past glory during the rule of Prince Norodom Sihanouk from 1941 to 1970.

To learn more about the kingdoms of Fu Nan and Chen La, historians turn to the Chinese annals. These were supplemented in the late Chen La and Angkor periods by royal inscriptions on temples and stelae, references in Arabic and Vietnamese texts and the rich evidence of the reliefs, especially those of the Angkorian epoch. No historical writings have come down from the people who lived before the Angkorian period, since they were written on palm leaves.

The frontier between the cultures of China and India runs down through South-East Asia. Cambodia lay within the Indian sphere of influence, though like its forerunners, Fu Nan and Chen La, it was bound to China through the system of tribute payments.

The religions and culture of India were spread by Brahmans who came to the royal courts with Indian merchants and were appointed to high office. From the 2nd to the 6th century, foreign trade provided a direct contact between India and the maritime nations of South-East Asia. But India made no attempt to exploit this politically, restricting itself to intellectual and commercial exchanges. In the 6th century, with the withdrawal of Indian

Left: Angkor Wat after its rediscovery in the colonial period.

merchants from the oceans of the world, the direct cultural influence of India also came to an end. The Indianized states of Fu Nan, Chen La, Champa and Khmer developed high cultures of their own, derived from Indian culture and indeed, particularly in the case of Khmer art, they surpassed their Indian exemplar.

The empire of Fu Nan

In the Mekong delta, in present-day Vietnam, the first Indianized empire arose, from the 2nd to the 6th century, in whose plains the few hills were worshipped as seats of the gods. The Chinese named this kingdom *Fu Nan.* (The Khmer word for mountain is *bnam* or *phnom,* and the Chinese transliterated this as Fu Nan). This term was applied to the land and its inhabitants. The reports of the early Chinese chroniclers were confirmed much later by the excavations of the French archaeologist L. Malleret in 1942-1944. At a place called Oc Eo, today in the Vietnamese province of An Giang, he discovered a port dating from the Fu Nan period.

The Fu Nan were seafarers and pirates, as well as merchants and farmers. In the Mekong delta they created a complex network of canals, linked with existing rivers, which were not only suitable for navigation but also irrigated and drained the land and its rice fields. The merchant junks that plied between Arabia and China were able to avoid the dangerous route round Cape Ca Mau and sail through the waterways of Fu Nan. From a helicopter one can still make out the canal system today. It is true that Malleret did not find any buildings, but he did locate the ancient foundations of brick-built temples, the wooden piles on which dwellings had been built, and an astonishing quantity of artifacts of all kinds, including coins and objects from the Mediterranean countries and the Near East, which bear witness to the economic

importance of Fu Nan as an international trading nation in those days.

Chinese travellers also gave accounts of the wealth of the Funanese population, mentioning precious metals, gold nuggets found in the rivers, and pearls; and they praised the handworking skills of the Funanese, especially in woodcarving. The people were described as crinkly-haired, dark-skinned, ugly and, in early encounters, unclothed. This leads to the conclusion that the population were mainly Melanesian.

Historical evidence about the last rulers is imprecise and full of gaps. It appears that the former vassal state, Chen La, in the hill country of present-day Cambodia, conquered and occupied Fu Nan in the 6th century. However, the territories of the Fu Nan on the coasts of Malaya and Indonesia were not claimed by the Chen La. It was the Buddhist king-

dom of Srivijaya in Sumatra which inherited Fu Nan's mastery of the sea and the coastal regions which they had controlled. Following Chen La's brief rule over the lowlands of Fu Nan, a large part of the Mekong delta fell under Khmer domination for several centuries, but gradually sank beneath the alluvial mud deposited by the Mekong river. Apart from some small Khmer settlements, which exist to this day in Vietnam, the rest of the delta was not returned to cultivation until the 17th century, when the region was occupied by the Vietnamese.

The empire of Chen La

The beginning and early period of the Chen La empire, from the 3rd to the early 7th century, are, like the end of the Fu Nan era, shrouded in darkness; all we know is what can be read in the Chinese annals or has been discovered by French archaeologists. The merging of the kingdoms of Fu Nan and Chen La is said to have taken place in 598 AD. In the 3rd

Above: A simple waterwheel provides irrigation. Right: Musicians in the temple of Ta Prohm (Tonle Bati).

28

century the capital of Chen La lay somewhere between Bassac and Roi Et. Then from 611 to 635, it was at Isanapura, 22 miles (35 km) north of modern Kompong Thom in Cambodia. Inscriptions in ancient Khmer, dating from the 7th century, indicate that there was a Khmer population in the territory of Chen La at that time.

From the 7th or 8th century onwards documentary evidence becomes more plentiful. There are Chinese reports of emissaries bearing tribute, and from these we learn of the name Chen La, though there is no explanation of it. The annals of China's T'ang Dynasty state that in the first decade of the 8th century Chen La split up into two realms, "Chen La of the Land" and "Chen La of the Water," which are also described as Upper Chen La, in the hill country, south of modern Phnom Penh, and Lower Chen La, in the Mekong delta.

The last mention of Upper Chen La in the Chinese chronicles is in 799; after that the Khmer empire began to arise in the country round Angkor. In the delta region many inscriptions have been found, dating from the years 681 to 716, according to which two dynasties, the moon dynasty of Aninditapura and the sun dynasty of Sambhupura, fought each other, but were then united through a marriage.

The Buddhist Shailendra dynasty in Java took the crown of the god-king of Fu Nan and further enhanced its prestige It also inherited the political power of Fu Nan and in the 8th century replaced the mighty Srivijaya empire as masters of the coasts of Malaya and the South China Sea.

The Khmer empire of Angkor

The founder of the empire of Angkor was Jayavarman II, a prince of of the Shailendra dynasty in Java, distantly related to an earlier Khmer dynasty, who returned from the court in Java around the year 790. Whether he voluntarily paid homage to the god-kings, or was compelled by them to do so as a vassal or prisoner remains unclear.

Upon his return he released himself from any such obligations by ordering a ceremony in which a Brahman made him a god-king and thus put him on an equal footing with the Shailendra of Java.

Attempts at apotheosis, the elevation of tribal chieftains and kings to the status of gods, can be observed in the nature-religions and empires in the ancient orient. The *devaraja*, India's god-kings, certainly provided the impulse for god-kingship in the Indianized states of what is now South-East Asia, but they never occupied a comparable position of power.

The Indian concept of god-kingship evolved from the god-kings of Fu Nan and the Champa empire, through the Shailendra of Java, culminating in the union of absolute religious and temporal power in the person of the god-king of Angkor. There is no doubt that this development was encouraged by the animistic concepts, deeply rooted in the philosophy of the Khmer, of a divine ruler as protector of the race, the country and the fertility of the fields.

Through his apotheosis the king possessed absolute and unchallengeable power. As an incarnation of God, the king of Angkor was the owner of the land and he alone could use it as he wished. He also had power over the water and thus procured the fertility of the soil, and the well-being of the country and of his subjects. In this way he controlled all the material and intellectual resources of the state and its population.

The god-kings of Angkor were not satisfied with being glorified during their own lifetimes; they wanted to assure their divinity after their death and so built temples with statues of themselves, which were to be worshipped in place of the living king. This desire to preserve their name and renown, as well as their memory, beyond the grave, was the driving force behind an extravagant spate of building activity, and consequently gave an impulse to the art of Angkor.

The cities inhabited by the people who built and adorned the temples, have vanished without trace. Where thousands once lived, silence and solitude reign. Only the walls and towers of temples, with the faces of dead kings, have survived, together with the reliefs which, like picture books in stone, show Angkor when it was one of the greatest cities and most importants empires of its age. Angkor grew up at the same time as the empire of Charlemagne in Europe.

The history of the kings is described in the chapter on art.

The post-Angkorian Khmer empires

In 1295 a Chinese traveler named Chou Ta Kuan could still describe Angkor as the richest city and the Khmer kings as the mightiest rulers in the region. But its decline could already be foreseen and many circumstances combined to make it rapid and inexorable.

The Cham, an Indianized race who lived in what is today central Vietnam, were anxious to avenge themselves for past invasions and the occupation of the country at intervals by the Khmer. They therefore conquered Angkor, put it to the torch and occupied it from 1177 to 1181. Although the Khmer kings subsequently defeated the Champa empire and occupied it once again (1190-1220), the capture and destruction of Angkor had shattered the faith of the inhabitants in the infallibility of the their god-kings. Buddhism had become the national religion. The kings attempted to take it over – they now saw themselves as the incarnation of Bodhisattva Avalokiteshvara – but did not succeed either in restoring their former position of power or in halting the

Right: Floodwater near Phnom Penh.

spread of Buddhism. The irrigation and drainage systems were neglected and began to silt up, so that malaria-carrying mosquitoes were able to breed in the murky waters.

The empire of Angkor owes its importance not only to its temples but also to its irrigation systems. The area round the Great Lakes was favored by nature through flooding and the depositing of fertile alluvium. By exploiting these phenomena and that of the heavy monsoon rains, the Khmer developed an elaborate irrigation and drainage system in which surplus water was stored so that it could be used throughout the year, making possible as many as four rice harvests. It was also a source of drinking water, thus promoting the growth of large cities.

Angkor was a culture based on water and rice. The worship of the earth gods and of the *naga*, or serpent, as a symbol of the powers of water, dominated the life of the Khmer.

Around 1353 came the first threatening incursions by the Siamese. The effect

of these is described in a Cambodian chronicle of doubtful authenticity. However, it is a fact that in the same year the Khmer helped the heir to the throne of Muong Swa (Laos) to take his rightful inheritance. Furthermore, the Chinese chronicles state that Khmer emissaries were still bringing tributes between 1371 and 1401.

Nevertheless, it may be supposed that until the final capture of Angkor by Siamese from the city of Ayuthia, in the year 1431, many attacks by the Siamese and counterattacks by the Khmer took place. There are reports that the Khmer kings dedicated themselves to battle in the temple of Baphuon in 1385, and that further skirmishes followed in 1394, 1401 and 1421. These disputes with Siam severely weakened Angkor and had the additional effect of bringing the Cham back into the fray.

Not until an attack by the Khmer on the Siamese capital of Ayuthia, did the Siamese invade Angkor. They wrought great destruction, plundered the royal

31

treasure houses and took prisoners, including craftsmen, artists and dancing girls from the temples. They then installed a Khmer prince as a vassal-king. It was not simply this destruction which caused the glory of Angkor to wither. The people abandoned the city and the rice fields when the water supply began to run short. They also fled from the forced labor for the gods of kings who were no longer theirs.

However, the end of Angkor was not the end of Cambodia, which remained an important and powerful state. In 1432 the king moved his court to Bassac, in the province of Srei Santhor, east of the Mekong. But in none of the later capitals can artistic achievement be seen that came near to matching that of the Angkorian civilization.

The period from the mid-14th to the end of the 15th century is covered by existing Cambodian chronicles, but these

Above: Guardian-figure at Wat Phnom Penh. Right: A Spanish ship from Manila.

were not written until the 19th century. There are also some Siamese records and a few inscriptions.

It appears that from 1467 until 1476 the kings once again ruled in Angkor. But around this time dynastic quarrels began, leading to rebellion, murder and usurpation which weakened Cambodia in the course of the following centuries to such an extent that it became a mere political football between its neighbors, Siam and Vietnam, as well as being a veritable playground for missionaries and adventurers from Europe.

The mightiest of the post-Angkorian kings was Ang Chan (1505 or 1516 to 1556), who had a fortified capital built at Lovek. A devout Buddhist, he founded many monasteries and stupas to mark his victory over the Siamese, not only in the capital but also in captured cities like Pursat and Udong. The Siamese were kept busy repelling attacks by the Burmese on Ayuthia, so that the Khmer were able to advance as far as the plateau of Korat.

No sooner had Siam recovered from the Burmese assaults, than it turned once again against Cambodia. The Siamese captured Siem Rap (Angkor), Bassac, Batambang and Pursat, and attacked Lovek. The king took refuge in Srei Santhor, was deposed and fled to Laos.

With the reign of king Satha (1576-1594) began an eventful but troubled period for Cambodia, which can only be described here briefly. As well as inscriptions we now have first-hand reports by Portuguese and Spanish missionaries. They describe the region round Angkor as well-populated at this time, with many great temples still standing.

The first missionary, who reached Lovek in 1555, was a Portuguese Dominican from Malacca, and others who followed him in 1583 were soon forced to retreat in the face of Buddhist opposition. Only a few, who enjoyed the favor of the king, were able to found a small

Christian community. The missionaries were followed by Portuguese adventurers from Malacca, one of whom, Diogo Veloso, was favored by king Satha, (also known as Chettha I). The king had hopes of being aided by them in his struggle against Siam. They surrounded him as a bodyguard and persuaded him to invite missionaries to his court and give them full freedom to spread the Christian faith. When it came to military assistance, however, Malacca possessed neither troops nor money. So the king turned to the Spanish who in 1571 had claimed the Philippines for themselves. In 1593, two Spanish adventurers appeared at court, named Blas Ruiz and Vargas. They arrived in Lovek shortly before a Siamese attack, tried to fetch help from Manila and, when this was not forthcoming, were taken prisoner by the Siamese. However, they were later able to escape.

After King Satha had fled to Vientiane in 1594, Cambodia was once again shaken by disputes over the succession. When the Spanish rescue fleet finally arrived in Lovek, having been decimated in a storm, it was met by a usurper, king Reamea Chung Prei. He banished the Spaniards to the foreign quarter of the city, where they fell to quarreling with the Chinese, pursuing the old enmity between the Spanish and the Chinese in the Philippines. When the Spanish wrought a terrible slaughter among the Chinese, the Cambodians, who took the side of the Chinese, exacted a bloody revenge. On the day after the murders, the Spanish general commanding the rescue fleet, which had been driven off course by the storm, suddenly reappeared. He found the royal court in uproar and confusion. Some leading courtiers offered the crown to the Spaniard, but he chose to return to Manila, taking the two adventurers, Blas Ruiz and Vargas, with him. However, they left the ship in a Vietnamese port and went off in search of King Satha. In Vientiane they learned that both the king and his eldest son were dead. So they made the second son king and forced him to ask Malacca, Manila and the Indian

colony of Goa to send missionaries to whom he would guarantee complete freedom to carry out their Christian work.

In Manila preparations were made for a Holy War, but once again the fleet was scattered in a storm. The Spanish adventure in Cambodia was brought to an end in 1599 by a Malay prince. The Spanish were heavily outnumbered and massacred. Velos, the Portuguese, and Blas Ruiz were killed, and very few escaped alive.

There was a rapid succession of occupants of the throne in Lovek, and help was sought again from the Spanish. But opposition to the Spanish grew, the court and nobility finally agreed that Prince Soryopor, who had fled in exile to Siam in 1598, should return with a Siamese army to Cambodia. He was crowned King Barom Reachea IV in 1603 and was

Above: The king performs the water ceremony at his coronation in Oudong. Right: Memorial at Wat Phnom Penh, recalling the treaty with France in 1866.

the first Cambodian monarch to reign as a vassal of Siam. In 1618 the Khmer attempted to free themselves from Siamese suzerainty and drove out the Siamese garrison.

In 1692 a South Vietnamese princely dynasty, the Nguyen of Hué, defeated the Cham and continued their march south. At that time the vast Mekong delta nominally belonged to Cambodia, but was settled by no more than 40,000 Cambodian families, whose villages still exist today. Cambodia had never suffered from a shortage of land, and the peasants were not greatly interested in cultivating the delta, which over the centuries had become covered with a layer of alluvial mud and forests of mangroves. The Vietnamese, by contrast, confined to the overpopulated north and a narrow coastal plain, were looking for new land to settle. In 1673 dynastic squabbles among the Khmer provided the Nguyen with a good opportunity to step in.

The Cambodian kings had transferred their capital to Udong. A rival king, Ang

Non, sat in Gia Dinh, the modern Saigon (Ho Chi Minh City). When his attempts to seize power in Udong failed, he called on the Nguyen for assisstance and thus fell under Vietnamese suzerainty.

Alarmed by the infiltration of the Mekong delta by Vietnamese settlers, and by the advance of the Nguyen princes, the Siamese also became involved in the succession disputes in Cambodia. Siam and Vietnam took turns to play the role of king-maker and exacted privileges in return for their support. While more and more of the the delta region fell into the hands of the Vietnamese, in 1793 Siam gained the western Cambodian provinces of Battambang and Siem Reap, which included Angkor.

Cambodia in the colonial empire of Indochina

In the 19th century the Vietnamese, still in permanent rivalry with the Siamese, annexed the whole Mekong delta and tried to tie the Khmer to Vietnam once

and for all by imposing Vietnamese culture and customs on the country. The great animosity felt by the Khmer towards the Vietnamese can be traced to this period.

Since 1847 France had been trying to open up Vietnam to trade and missionaries. When this operation met with resistance, a French expeditionary force advanced into the Mekong delta and in 1863 the region became the French colony of Cochin China. French gunboats steamed up the Mekong river into Cambodia, and in 1867, according to the French version of events, the king of Cambodia, who since 1866 had resided in Phnom Penh, asked the French for help against Vietnam and Siam. In 1884 King Norodom was forced to sign an agreement which left him with little more than his crown. Political power was transferred to the French Senior Resident. Below him, each province had a Resident responsible for its administration.

In 1887 the colony of Cochin China and the French protectorates of Annam

(central Vietnam), Tonkin (northern Vietnam) and Cambodia were combined to form the Union of Indochina, to which the protectorate of Laos was added in 1893.

Under the Treaty of Bangkok in 1907 the mainland of South-East Asia was divided up between Britain and France, with fixed borders drawn between the two colonial empires. By clever tactics, Siam succeeded in preserving its independence, though was obliged to return Cambodia's western provinces, and Angkor, to Cambodia, in other words to France. During the Second World War they fell once again under Siamese control, but after the war Cambodia got them back again and has retained them to the present day.

Sadly, neither Cambodia nor any other part of Indochina gained any economic benefit from colonization, nor did they enjoy any progress in administration,

education or healthcare. In the 1930s the French established large cotton- and rubber-plantations and brought in Vietnamese and Chinese laborers, since the independently-minded small farmers of Cambodia refused to act as day laborers. Up to that time, land had been divided up among many small proprietors; there was no leasing of land and no big landowners. Land-grabbing was unknown. Apart from cotton and rubber from the plantations, the country was not an important producer of raw materials. Cambodian peasants and fishermen were certainly not likely to be customers for French industrial products. But this enabled domestic Cambodian industry to survive. Not until the turn of the century did colonial policy take a new direction. France began to invest more in Indochina and Cambodia's economy improved slowly.

The Sihanouk era

Prince Norodom Sihanouk, of the Norodom dynasty, was born in 1922 and re-

Above: Prince Norodom Sihanouk as President of Cambodia's government in exile.

ceived his education from the French in Saigon. In 1941 he was summoned to Phnom Penh and made king in succession to his grandfather – bypassing his father – for the French believed they could control him. However, the 19-year-old king very rapidly developed diplomatic skills. He became a determined opponent of French colonialism and an adroit champion of Cambodian independence. In 1945 he accepted an offer of independence made by the Japanese, but Japan surrendered in the same year and Cambodia was occupied by French and British troops.

In 1946 King Sihanouk reached an agreement with France whereby Cambodia became a member of the French Union, but he saw this simply as a step towards full independence. In 1953 he succeeded in persuading France to grant him authority over the police, the judiciary and the army. In the following year, 1954, the French army was defeated at Dien Bien Phu, a supposedly impregnable fort in northern Vietnam, near the border with Laos. Soon afterwards, a conference on Indochina was held in Geneva, which among other things guaranteed the independence of Cambodia.

Since 1947 the restrictions of a constitutional monarchy had prevented King Norodom Sihanouk from active involvement in politics, and so in 1955 he abdicated in favor of his father, Norodom Suramarit. As prime minister, and later, after the death of the king in 1960, as head of state, Sihanouk tried to put into practice his idea of a "Socialist Buddhism." He saw this as a form of government which suited the mentality of the Khmer people, and as the only way of procuring social justice for all citizens. In the first free elections, held in 1955, the Sangkum Party, which Sihanouk had founded, gained 84 per cent of the vote and all the parliamentary seats. Its program was based on the tradition of the kingdom of Angkor, on Buddhism and

the peasant tradition of voluntary mutual assistance. Cambodia was the only one of the countries of Indochina to hold the elections which were called for by the Geneva Agreement.

Sihanouk the statesman proceeded to astonish the world just as Sihanouk the monarch had done. He was a charismatic personality who, through his unpredictable "see-saw" politics, became the terror of diplomats in East and West, whom he would often lecture on his notion of neutrality.

As a personality he was remarkable for his many artistic gifts and an obvious devotion to his country. His actions, which often seemed to run counter to convention, good sense and his own principles, were prompted by the desire, at all costs, to keep his country out of the second Indochinese war (1962-1975).

After the first American bombardement of Cambodian villages, he reproached the Americans with these words:" To you the Cambodians are just dogs and pigs. But to me they are all little Buddhas, and I will not see any of them die, except the communists who wish to kill Cambodia as an independent country." Yet his policies later led him to give in to the communists and make an alliance with the Khmer Rouge.

He took a lot of trouble to improve agriculture and spent many hours out in the fields himself, in an effort to urge the farmers into more activity and the adoption of modern methods. He was equally concerned to get industry moving and to improve opportunities for training and education.

He succeeded in doubling the number of primary schools from 2731 to 5857, he founded nine universities where previously there had been none and was able to make a substantial reduction in illiteracy. In 1955 there was only one hospital in Cambodia, a gift from the USSR, but by 1970 there were 43 of them, as well as 450 ambulances.

He sent the young elite to France to study and train. Among them was Saloth Sau, who later called himself Pol Pot, as well as Kieu Samphan and Ieng Sary, who became communists in Paris, and later led the Khmer Rouge. An academically trained work force grew rapidly, but so did their dissatisfaction, as Cambodia had no jobs to offer them.

For more than a decade Sihanouk tried to steer a neutral course for Cambodia between the divergent interests and flagrant intervention of the USA, the USSR, China, North and South Vietnam and the South Vietnamese resistance movement. This he did by exploiting their various mutual animosities. Since 1953 he had been accepting aid not only from the USA but also from the Soviet Union and China.

During the second Indochina war the Viet Minh of North Vietnam and the

Above: Girls on parade for the first anniversary of independence. Right: A soldier of the Khmer Rouge.

south Vietnamese Viet Cong frequently took refuge in Cambodian territory. Even if Sihanouk had wanted to stop them, he could not have done so. At the same time he was obliged to grant special rights to the United States. At the second Geneva conference on Indochina in 1962, he reported that the USA, Thailand and South Vietnam had infringed his land, sea and air frontiers in all over 300 times.

In 1963 the Sangkum Party decided that from then on they would accept no further aid from the United States. From May 1965 until June 1969 no diplomatic relations existed between Cambodia and the USA. They were restored again for a few months, after the US Air Force had launched "Operation Breakfast," the first phase of "Operation Menu." By May 1970 the USAF had flown 3,630 missions with B52 bombers. Their defoliation attacks destroyed rubber plantations in Krek, Mimot and Kompong Cham. The bombing raids did not end until 15th August 1973, after nearly 540,000 tonnes of bombs had been dropped on Cambodia – one and a half times as many as were dropped on Japan in the whole of World War II. It is believed that about 800,000 people died as a result. The departing US ambassador, Swank, said at his final press conference that the war in Cambodia had been "the most pointless war in Indochina." No amount of onslaughts by the Americans on Cambodia could have altered the outcome of the war.

Many of the decisions taken by Sihanouk as head of state can only be understood in the light of the internal situation in his country. In Cambodia there were many very different forces at work, and in conflict with each other. These crystallized into groupings, parties and militant rebel units, whose common purpose had once been the national struggle for independence from France.

As well as the Sangkum, Sihanouk's own party, there was a Liberal Party, a Progressive Democratic Party and an Anti-Monarchist Democratic Party. A decisive role was played by the Nekhum Issarak Khmer, a popular front and umbrella-movement which was open to non-communists and communists. The right-wing Khmer Serei split off from this group.

In the 1950s a regrouping of the communist parties in Indochina took place, from which both the Communist Party of Cambodia (also known as the Pracheachon) and the Khmer Rouge developed, the latter being founded in 1960. The situation in Cambodia reflected the ideological conflicts between the communist parties in the Soviet Union, Vietnam and China. The Khmer Rouge, who had a deep hatred of Vietnam and the Viet Minh, followed the Chinese road and tried, in the words of Zhou En Lai, "to travel it in a single step." Sihanouk attempted to achieve a balance by bringing politicians both of the left and the right into his government, such as Khieu Samphan and Lon Nol.

While Sihanouk was abroad, a coup was staged by Lon Nol, Sirik Matak and Cheng Heng (whom Sihanouk had nominated to deputize for him in his absence). The coup was supported by the United States, which recognized the new government two days later, on 18th March 1970. As the new head of state, Lon Nol established a military court which proceeded to pronounce death sentences on Sihanouk and his wife, revoke his Cambodian citizenship and sequester his property. The army was expanded three-fold, general mobilization decreed, the republic was suspended and a state of emergency declared. One newspaper reported this under the headline: "The second death of Angkor?"

A few days after the coup, US land forces crossed the Cambodian border, without the required approval of the American Congress. When the troops were withdrawn in June 1970, President Nixon anounced that the operation had been successful in killing 11,000 Vietnamese communists and sympathizers.

Even before the coup Lon Nol had arranged the assassination of the ambassadors of North Vietnam and of the provisional revolutionary government of South Vietnam. The Vietnamese minorities were massacred, and corpses, bound hand and foot floating down the Mekong became a common sight.

The rule of the Khmer Rouge

Among the population, 90 per cent of whom were peasants, there was still strong support for Sihanouk. The Khmer Rouge realized this and tried to win Sihanouk over to their ideas. He, for his part, certainly never had any illusions about their ideological standpoint. The fact that he nonetheless publicly declared his support for the Khmer Rouge, even abroad, must be taken as an attempt by him to prevent Cambodia from falling entirely into their hands.

On 1st April 1975 the Americans flew Lon Nol out of Cambodia, to Hawaii. The final evacuation of 276 foreigners and Cambodians who had gathered in the US embassy, took place on 12th April 1975. A few hours later the Khmer Rouge occupied the airfield and on 17th April they marched into Phnom Penh. Within four days, the city, where an unknown number of refugees had sought shelter, was evacuated. The Khmer Rouge were unable to maintain essential supplies and services to the city, but were afraid that any gathering of people in large numbers could provide fertile ground for counterrevolutionary cells and might spark direct resistance.

The political program of the Khmer Rouge consisted of a brutal restructuring of society on strictly Maoist lines. Their aim was to remove all differences between townspeople and peasants by destroying the centers of mercantile and

Right: Piles of bones in Siem Reap recall the massacres by the Khmer Rouge.

capitalist activity. Within two weeks of their seizure of power, whole populations of towns were forced out to the country to do slave labor in the fields. Money was abolished, to be replaced by barter trading. The darkest hours in the long and painful history of the Khmer people had begun.

The are no precise figures for the number of lives lost in "Democratic" Cambodia under the Khmer Rouge. The Foreign Minister, Ieng Sary, spoke privately of a figure of two million. The highest price in blood was paid by the officer corps, the intellectuals and priests of all religions. Anyone who spoke a foreign language or simply wore glasses was held to be a subversive or a parasite and ususally paid with their lives. It is hard to make any estimate of the numbers who died from hunger and disease.

In some parts of the country, for example in Siem Reap, there was frequent unrest. The Muslim Cham people also rebelled. But all resistance was bloodily put down by the Khmer Rouge. Their victims were often bludgeoned to death, in order to save ammunition.

In neighboring Vietnam, the long drawn-out war was in its final days. In January 1975 the North Vietnamese army started a final, massive offensive, capturing one city after the other. On 30th April Saigon surrendered and the last Americans were evacuated. The whole of Vietnam was now in the hands of a dedicated and powerfully armed communist regime.

In April 1975 Prince Sihanouk was living in Peking. Shortly before the Khmer Rouge marched into Phnom Penh, the Chinese had requested that he make contact with the United States. In a telephone conversation on 11th April 1975 the US government declared its willingness to hand over the leadership of Cambodia to "Prince Sihanouk and his partisans." However, the Khmer Rouge succeeded in preventing Sihanouk from returning to

Cambodia, by threatening to shoot down any aircraft that attempted to land there. At the beginning of September 1975 Sihanouk was finally allowed to enter the country. For three weeks he travelled around Cambodia, then he made visits to twelve countries in Europe and North America and gave a speech to the United Nations. He stated that he had been deprived of power in Cambodia. In December 1975 he returned once again to Cambodia, where he was given no official welcome, and was forced to grow vegetables in the grounds of his palace.

On 5th January 1976 a new constitution came into force. The country was now called Democratic Kampuchea, and there was no longer any role for Prince Sihanouk. In April 1976 he officially resigned as head of state and was put under house arrest. In the period that followed purges and internal divisions shook the ruling party. Many members of the old guard were liquidated. Pol Pot disappeared in September 1976, but a year later he was once again prime minister.

The quarrels with Vietnam became more acute and fighting broke out between units of the Khmer Rouge and the Vietnamese. There were also incidents on the border with Thailand. The Khmer Rouge lost all sense of reality and announced on Radio Phnom Penh: "For every Cambodian who dies, we will kill 30 Vietnamese. In order to exterminate the 50 million Vietnamese, we would only have to sacrifice 2 million Cambodians, and there would still be six million of us left." On 6th January 1979, after three years of house arrest, Sihanouk was flown back to Peking by the Chinese, and on 7th January the Vietnamese marched into Phnom Penh.

The People's Republic of Kampuchea

The People's republic of Kampuchea, or PRK, was established under the protection of Vietnam, with its capital in Phnom Penh. Heng Samrin, a member of the pro-Vietnamese group within the Khmer Rouge, was made head of the

41

government. He was one of the the three who had survived the attempted coup against Pol Pot.

Cambodia was bound to Vietnam by treaties of friendship, and nothing stood in the way of an alliance between the three states of former French Indochina, Laos being the third.

The Khmer Rouge, still supported by China, went underground in the region near the border with Thailand. Suddenly the old enemies of the west and the United Nations had changed: no longer were the Khmer Rouge despised. But Vietnam, who had tried to liberate Cambodia from the bloody and inhuman regime was now condemned by the west for its necessary invasion, and its attempt to combine the countries of Indochina into a single political and economic bloc. The UN called on Vietnam to withdraw its troops. The People's Republic of

China invaded Vietnam's northern province but described this operation as a punitive campaign of limited duration. At the UN a seat was reserved for the Khmer Rouge, and was renewed annually by a vote in the General Assembly.

The first dry-season offensives were successful for the Vietnamese, then their advance was halted and the battle front became fixed. On the Cambodian side a triple alliance, supported by the USA, was formed between the Khmer Rouge, Prince Sihanouk and the former prime minister, Son Sann, each with their own armies. Sihanouk did not want to hand over Cambodia either to the Khmer Rouge or to the Vietnamese.

Vietnam was suffering under the American trade embargo, the economic and moral pressure of the west, problems in obtaining supplies of any kind, and finally the drying up of aid from the East Bloc, which was itself facing ever greater economic problems.

The withdrawal of Vietnamese troops took place on the due date, and the last

Above: Government troops at Angkor Wat, which the Khmer Rouge used as an ammunition dump. Right: A relic of the war.

42

units left Cambodia at the end of September 1989. The government of Heng Samrin had not worked any miracles since 1979; Cambodia is still a poor country, but a number of small economic successes were recorded. It is to the government's credit that it recognized that the people rejected the communism which had brought them so much misery.

The State of Cambodia

On 30th April 1989 the People's Republic of Kampuchea had been given yet another constitution. The country was now to be called the State of Cambodia. However, the Cambodian Communist Party remained the leading political force. But according to the constitution the people were to be master of their own destiny and all power was vested in them. They would be represented by a National Assembly, whose delegates were elected by popular vote, as well as by other organs of the state. A new flag and national anthem were introduced, and the death

penalty was abolished. Four forms of property ownership were created. Buddhism once again became the official religion. There were also reforms in family law and administrative law and a new form of criminal hearing was enacted.

Far more sweeping changes were called for at the Extraordinary Party Congress held on 17th and 18th October 1991. A new party program was drawn up and new men appointed to the top posts. Heng Samrin, who up to now had been General Secretary, became Honorary Chairman of the party, and was replaced by Chea Sim, a politician who had risen very rapidly through the ranks.

Prime minister Hun Sen was elected Deputy Chairman of the party. The congress accepted Hun Sen's proposal that, at the next election to the office of State President, the party should back the candidacy of Prince Sihanouk.

The Revolutionary People's Party changed its name to the Cambodian People's Party, and its emblem was changed from the hammer and sickle to a sheaf of

43

rice and the five towers of the temple of Angkor Wat.

With the withdrawal of Vietnamese troops in autumn 1989, the resolution of the problem of Cambodia entered a new phase. Between 1979 and 1985 there had been no contact between the Vietnamese puppet-government (the People's Republic of Kampuchea) and the three-way coalition which opposed it (Khmer Rouge, Sihanouk and Son Sann). Between 1986 and mid-1989 the two sides got together at the Jakarta Informal Meetings (JIM) and the Paris International Conference on Cambodia (PICC).The French Foreign Minister, Dumas and his Indonesian counterpart, Mr Alata, played a major part in bringing these discussions to the desired conclusion: a peace treaty between the four parties in the civil war as the basis of a new political order in Cambodia.

Above: Prime Minister Hun Sen. Right: For the prince's return in November 1991 posters of the young Sihanouk are displayed.

From the autumn of 1989 the talks were held at more frequent intervals and on 9th and 10th September 1990, at the 4th session of the JIM in Jakarta, the four warring parties reached an agreement to form a joint transitional government, the Supreme National Council, in which all four parties would be represented.

The four groups are together usually given the acronym FUNCINPEC, which is based on the French words meaning National United Front for an Independent, Neutral, Peaceful and Cooperative Cambodia. Since Prince Sihanouk, as chairman of the Supreme National Council, could not hold any other office, he was represented in FUNCINPEC by his son, Prince Norodom Ranariddh.

The BLDP, the Buddhist-Liberal Democratic Party of the former prime minister Son Sann, is the party which seems to have had least impact.

The DK or Democratic Kampuchea of the Khmer Rouge is represented by the PKD, led by by Khieu Samphan, who bears less responsibility for the horrors of the Khmer Rouge than does Pol Pot.

The triple coalition was opposed by the Cambodian People's Party, the ruling party of the State of Cambodia.

At the second meeting of the Supreme National Council in Pattaya, Thailand, agreement was reached on an unconditional cease-fire and the ending of all foreign military aid. Surprisingly, the USA had already withdrawn their aid to the Triple Coalition in 1990.

The government of the State of Cambodia in Phnom Penh has repeatedly rejected any participation by the Khmer Rouge. For their part the Khmer Rouge took a long time to agree to allow UN peace-keeping forces into the country.

On 21st October 1991, after two years of negotiations at various levels between the Triple Coalition and the Phnom Penh government, and with the participation of the UN in Paris, a peace treaty was finally signed.

Subsequently UNTAC, a transitional authority of the UN, together with the Supreme National Council, the interim coalition of the four combatants in the civil war, under the presidency of Prince Sihanouk, were to take over control of Cambodia for 18 months, until a government chosen by free elections could assume power.

On 14th November 1991 Sihanouk returned to Cambodia, where he was greeted with jubilation and pent-up expectations. On the day of his arrival he was received by the prime minister of the Phnom Penh government, Hun Sen. When the emissary of the Khmer Rouge, Khieu Samphan, arrived in Phnom Penh on 17th November, he barely escaped with his life from an angry mob and had to leave the country. Soon afterwards, violent student demonstrations broke out in Phnom Penh against the government of the State of Cambodia.

The Khmer Rouge continued their attacks sporadically. These were aimed against villages and towns, and in par-

ticularly against the Vietnamese minority and the UN peacekeeping forces, when they attempted to carry out their patrol duties by entering or overflying areas occupied by the Khmer Rouge.

On 10th November 1991, the first units of UNAMIC, the UN Advanced Mission in Cambodia, under the overall command of the French general Michel Loridon, occupied key positions, and from 28th December they began carrying out inspection flights over Cambodia. They started to hold political negotiations, and at regular meetings with the four combatant parties, agreement was reached on 100 per cent disarmament of all forces, as opposed to the previously agreed level of 70 per cent. Finally, because the Khmer Rouge were opposed to disarmament and persisted with their attacks and engagements with the other troops, the full UN peacekeeping force was deployed at the beginning of January 1992.

On 9th January the Japanese diplomat, Yasushi Akashi, was nominated by the UN Secretary-General to be the UN Spe-

Above: Trucks fulfil the role of public transport vehicles (near Siem Reap).

cial Envoy in Cambodia, to supervise the full implementation of the peace treaty. Later on he was accused by the Khmer Rouge of lacking impartiality, and described as no better than the *yuon* – a rude name for the Vietnamese.

From March 1992 onward the UN peacekeeping force was built up to its maximum agreed number of 22,000 men, including a small number of civilians. They were distributed over 21 Cambodian provinces and cities.

The UN peace mission was responsible for supervising the cease-fire and the disarming of all four combatant forces. Three of the parties were willing but the Khmer Rouge refused, and could not be talked round at a conference in Peking in November 1992, since China let it be known that they wished the Khmer Rouge to have a part in the new government, as a counterbalance to Vietnam. China accused the Phnom Penh govern-

ment of holding on to power, when they should have made way for the Supreme National Council, but later China distanced itself from the Khmer Rouge.

The UN then voted on 30th November to impose economic sanctions against the Khmer Rouge. This met with a protest from Thailand, which did not want to lose its best customer. But Thailand was soon happily trading with the State of Cambodia. The refusal of the Khmer Rouge to disarm inevitably led to to the State of Cambodia continuing to keep its troops in battle readiness. UNTAC saw itself being attacked from all sides, since the peacekeeping troops had, by their behavior, forfeited much of the sympathy which the Cambodian people had initially shown them.

Another irritation to the Cambodians was the profit which the Thais, and mainly the Chinese minority in Thailand, were making by supplying the highly-paid UN troops in Cambodia.

Elections were set for the end of May 1993, which the Khmer Rouge tried to boycott. The reason for this, they claimed, was that there were still Vietnamese units fighting in Cambodia. After thorough investigation the UN were able to refute this. The situation is, on the contrary, that today only about 80,000 to 90,000 Vietnamese live in Cambodia, as compared to 500,000 at the beginning of the 1970s. They live as fishermen around the lakes, and on the banks of the Tonle Sap and the Mekong, or work in the rubber-plantations near Kompong Cham. The Khmer Rouge concentrated their attacks on the Vietnamese populations in these areas, creating panic and driving many out of the country.

The repatriation of 550,000 Cambodian refugees from camps in Thailand has been largely completed with the help of the UNHCR, the International Red Cross and a UN aid fund. This had to be preceded by an exercise by the peacekeeping troops to clear land mines away from the areas to be resettled.

By the beginning of 1993 the political line-up had been completed. Over 4 million Cambodians registered to vote in the elections at the end of May, for which 20 political parties were nominated. However, only four of them were known to the electorate:

The Cambodian People's Party (CPP), which was the ruling party of the State of Cambodia in Phnom Penh; Sihanouk's party; Son Sann's Buddhist-Liberal Democratic Party and a party founded in time for the election, the Cambodian National Union Party, with Khieu Samphan as its chairman – which then boycotted the election.

Every Cambodian over 18 was entitled to vote, and "Cambodian" meant being born in Cambodia or having at least one parent who was born there. However, someone with both parents born abroad, even with Cambodian citizenship, was disqualified from voting. This applied to many of the Khmer-Krom living in SouthVietnam, and also to Son Sann, the

former Prime Minister. The electoral law was passed in August 1992.

The Khmer Rouge played for time. The UN mandate was restricted to 18 months and the cost amounted to well over 2 billion dollars, borne mainly by the USA, Japan and Germany.

However, despite the boycott and threats by the Khmer Rouge, the elections were held according to plan on 23rd to 25th May 1993. 90 per cent of those entitled to cast their vote, made good use of their right. The results of the election provoked both amazement and, in some quarters, disappointment. Those who had expected a resounding victory for Sihanouk's party, saw it win with a modest 45.5% and 58 seats, closely followed by the Cambodian People's Party with 38.2% (51 seats). The Buddhist-Liberal Democrats only picked up 3.8% of the vote but it gave them 10 seats. Of the remaining 17 parties only the hitherto unknown Molinaka won a single seat.

The elected constituent assembly were in agreement as to the role which should be taken by Prince Sihanouk: on 14th June they elected him State President. After a great deal of horse-trading and power-broking, the formation of a government was finally announced on 1st July. The post of prime minister was to be shared by Prince Norodom Ranariddh and Hun Sen, and the same principle applied to several of the ministries.

In the meantime the new constitution for the nation was drawn up and passed by the assembly. Prince Sihanouk who is now in his seventies, was handed what might be considered a poisoned chalice: he was once again to be king in a constitutional monarchy. At first he refused to accept the post but finally relented.

With the withdrawal of the UN Peacekeeping Forces in October 1993, Cambodia was finally left alone, after more than two decades of civil war, and subversion, attack and occupation by foreign forces. One must hope for peace and stability.

THE ART OF CAMBODIA

No systematic research into the culture and art of the Khmer has ever been carried out. French scholars, archaeologists and art historians concentrated, during the colonial occupation, on the spectacular Angkor period from the 9th to the 13th century. Another focus of attention were the archaeological excavations in the Mekong delta, an area once occupied by the Fu Nan empire, also known as the Oc-Eo culture, after the place where the discoveries were made. It has not been possible to demonstrate a continuous development of Khmer art from the art of Fu Nan and Chen La, since we do not know enough about the origins and transitional phases of these cultures to piece the whole story together. Only French experts were involved in the researches in Cambodia. After the end of the colonial epoch, wars and otherwise extremely difficult social and political situations prevented the work from being continued.

Khmer art produced its most significant achievements in the field of architecture. Evidence of their remarkable skill as sculptors can be found in the reliefs, particularly the bas-reliefs of the Angkor period, as well is in many different forms of decorative art. The finest statues date from the pre-Angkorian epoch.

Building materials: For temple buildings and sculpture, wood and bamboo were originally used. These, of course, eventually rot and fall apart but are still used today even for general construction purposes. From the 8th century onward brick was used in sacred buildings, and from 925 AD, sandstone foundations are found, as well as laterite, a kind of red or yellow stone, in protective walls. But brick and

Left: Galleries and covered staircases at Angkor Wat.

sandstone buildings only came at the end of a long period of development. They appear as examples of a perfected art, and often imitate in stone the earlier styles of wooden construction, especially in doorposts, portals and baluster windows.

In the early brick buildings, figures and decoration were carved into the smooth and almost jointless masonry, which was laid without mortar, but possibly with intermediate layers of some organic material. The bricks were bigger than those we use today, well baked and with shiny surfaces. They were produced in local workshops.

Beside sandstone and brick, wood was still used for building in the 10th and 11th centuries. Both durable and less permanent materials were used in combination in the buildings of this period, so many of them did not survive the centuries so well.

During the post-Angkorian period the building of numerous temples by Jayavarman VII used up a great deal of sandstone. It became scarce and of poor quality, until finally the quarrries at Phnom Kulen were exhausted. After the end of his reign no more large temples were built of sandstone.

The sandstone came from Phnom Kulen, about 25 miles (40 km) northeast of Angkor, and floated on rafts down the river Siem Reap. From the bank, they were dragged to the building site using rollers and winches. In many of the stones one can see holes for wooden pegs, round which the tow ropes were tied. Large numbers of laborers were needed for this work. The square blocks of stone were stacked on top of each other without any form of cement, roughly dressed to begin with, then given their proper shape. Finally the smoothed surfaces were decorated with bas-reliefs and ornamentation. In some places, where the work was unfinished, one can still see the different stages of the process.

The sandstone, also called mudstone, *thma puok*, is a soft friable material

which can occur in various shades of color, from a metallic grey or blue-green, to red and yellow. For the foundations, laterite was often used. Called *bai riem* ("boiling rice") by the Khmer, this is a rough, porous, reddish volcanic stone that is found all over Indochina. It was laid in one or two courses on a layer of a concrete-like substance made of pebbles. Thick walls consisted of two layers of concrete with a layer of laterite in between.

Decoration of buildings: In all periods, wood was widely used for panelling, canopies, frames and roofs. Rough stone vaulting was clad with wooden roofs which have not survived to the present day. Very occasionally one can still find traces of paintings and gilding. There is evidence that sheets of gilded copper were used to roof temple towers, since the stone surfaces of these have not been dressed.

Above: The king's victory procession, a bas-relief at the Bayon temple in Angkor Thom.

Sometimes stucco was applied to pillars, door posts, lintels and brickwork, into which the decoration was carved as if it had been in wood.

The magnificent appointment of the rooms with carpets, silks, furniture, costly ornaments and statuary, can only be imagined. However, finds include pottery and ceramics which either came from China, or were made in Chinese workshops in Phnom Penh. Among these are elaborately decorated roof tiles, glazed terracotta and other ceramics used in building. Statues and figurines, jewelry, weapons and cult objects have been found, made from stone, bronze, silver or gold. Iron was used in the manufacture of spearheads, swords and other weapons. The National Museum in Phnom Penh holds valuable archaeological collections. However, the temples have been robbed of all movable ornaments, and their altars left bare.

The frequent variations in the form and decoration of lintels over windows and doors, of panels and door-posts, are evidence of a process of development and change and enable us to arrange the buildings according to the date of their construction. They are among the finest examples of the sculptor's art.

Religious art: The Fu Nan, Chen La and Khmer people created art for a privileged religious elite. It was used in the worship of the gods, Buddha and the god-kings, who saw themselves as the embodiment of the Hindu gods Shiva and Vishnu, of Bodhisattva, and also frequently as the *lingam*, the phallus of the god Shiva. It was the kings who endowed the temples. Not until near the end of the Angkor period did other members of the royal family, as well as nobles and Brahmans, put up stone shrines.

Inscriptions: Important evidence of the Khmer culture is provided by inscriptions in Sanskrit and ancient Khmer, later in Pali, the language of Theravada Buddhism. They tell in dramatic, allegorical and often mysterious language of the deeds and merits of the kings, and list the temples they endowed.

Architects and master builders: We know nothing of the master builders. While it is true that the Indianized states of Indochina did not adopt the Indian caste system, architects were nevertheless considered as artisans and therefore belonged to a lower order of society.

However, there were Brahmans and architect-priests who were no doubt initiated in the secrets of Indian architecture and made sure that the planning and execution of temple construction followed the immutable laws of the cosmos, and that the iconography was adhered to, without which no sculpture or relief could be contemplated. On the other hand, the artistic expression, the symbolism and stylisation were more strongly influenced by the Khmer tradition.

It took a great number of laborers, masons and sculptors to bring the material to the site, build the temples and carve the reliefs which were hundreds of yards long. Not all the craftsmen possessed the same degree of skill, and work of varying quality can be found in the same temple.

Themes: The reliefs contain scenes from Indian mythology, and from the great Hindu epics of the Ramayana and the Mahabharata. But they also glorify the battles and victories of the Khmer kings. Not until the post-Angkorian period do we find reliefs, such as those in the Bayon temple at Angkor Thom, depicting the everyday life of the people.

God-kings and temple mountains: When the Kings of the Mountain moved their realm down into the plains, the temples that had been built on isolated hilltops, or *phnom*, were replaced by temples built on artificial mounds of stone. These symbolized the *meru*, or mountain of the gods, which is at the center of Indian mythology.

From the beginning of the 9th century, the temples were used for the worship not only of gods but of the deified king, and only priests and temple servants were allowed into them. At great religious festivals there were processions in which, so Chinese travelers reported, the royal family took part. But even they were excluded from the ceremonies which took place in the inner sanctum. The ordinary people were not permitted to enter the temple at all. They continued to worship their fertility- and nature-gods, until Buddhism revealed to them completely new aspects of the relationship between man and god, and they turned away from their god-kings.

Angkor: In order to give a clearer understanding of the terminology, it must be said at the outset that the name Angkor is used today to describe several different things. The word "Angkor" is derived from *nokor* (*nagara* in Sanskrit), which literally means royal city or capital. But geographically "Angkor" refers to the plain between the Great Lakes (Tonle Sap) and Phnom Kulen, in which the realm and cities of the god-kings lay.

The name Angkor is also used to designate the period from 800 to 1431 AD, from the crowning of the first King of the Mountain, Jayavarman II, up to the conquest of the empire of Angkor by the Siamese from Ayuthia. In art history, "Angkor" stands for the Angkor style from 875 to 1175. The city of Angkor is the name given to the capital of Suriyavarman II, in the center of which rises up the finest temple in the whole of Indian culture, the Angkor Wat. Sadly, nothing remains of the city's thousands of wooden houses and the its royal palace. Only the Angkor Wat itself, built of sandstone, has survived war, conquest, the tropical climate and the encroachment of the jungle. The temple was built in honor of Vishnu, but perhaps also as a shrine and mausoleum of the deified king Suriyavarman II. In the post-Angkorian period it was used as a monastery.

Above: The Bayon Temple in an early 20th century engraving. Right: Stone carvings above a doorway in Banteay Srei.

Names of the kings and temples:
At the time of their construction, cities and temples bore the names of the kings who had built them, and of the gods to whom they were dedicated. The rulers changed the names frequently during their reign. They named themselves after whichever god they saw themselves as reincarnating.

The name Indravarman means: "he who enjoys the protection of the god Indra" (*varman*: "armored," "protected"). Other names refer to qualities of the king: Jayavarman, "protected by victory," Bhavarman, "protected by good fortune." In each case, French scholars reached agreement on the name by which a king was most often referred to in inscriptions, and added the numbers I, II etc. to recurring names.

The succession of kings to the throne was often disputed, and dynasties which survived for long are the exception in Khmer history. Over a period of nearly five centuries the kings built new capitals, with walls, ramparts and moats, with

the temple in the center. In later times, when space for cities and rice fields became scarce, new cities were built on the sites of old ones. Every new capital required the construction of a new, or expansion of an existing *baray*, or reservoir and irrigation system.

The ages of art

It is possible to distinguish three main epochs in the culture of Cambodia: Fu Nan, Chen La and Khmer. They evolved successively from the 3rd to the 13th century, in the region between the Mekong delta and the highlands to the north of the Cambodian plain.

Very probably the culture arose among peoples of different ethnic groups and traditions. But one thing they had in common was a remarkable knowledge of hydraulic technology, which was applied in various ways: the Fu Nan drained the marshland of the Mekong delta, and the Khmer irrigated the areas which had only one monsoon period. To achieve this re-

quired a strictly organized society under centralized leadership. This rice culture was the foundation upon which a very high level of Indian-inspired civilization could develop. It was based on Indian religions, of which Brahma-Hinduism had the strongest influence on their art.

French scholars have been able to subdivide these epochs into numerous different styles. These often overlap in time, may only be represented by one or a small number of buildings and in many cases only lasted for a brief period.

Each style marks a step forward in the field of architecture, relief, decoration and sculpture, and represents at the same time both the history of the kings and the succession of their dynasties. Often, nothing more is known about these kings than their contribution to art, which is documented in inscriptions put up by themselves or their successors.

However, the development of the art of relief carving added considerably more color and detail to our knowledge of the history of those far-off centuries.

EPOCHS OF ARCHITECTURE

PRE-ANGKORIAN ART

EMPIRE OF FU NAN:
Style of Phnom Da   514 - 539, 540 - 600

EMPIRE OF CHEN LA:
Style of Sambor Prei Kuk   c. 600 - 650
Style of Prei Kmeng . . .   c. 635 - 700
Style of Prasat Andet   . . . .   681 - 730
Style of Kompong Preah . . .   706 - 800
Style of Kulen . . . .   802 (825) - 875

THE ART OF ANGKOR

Style of Preah Ko . . . .   c. 875 - 893
Style of Bakheng . . . . . c. 893 - 925
Style of Koh Ker . . . .   921 - 944
Style of Pre Rup . . . .   947 - 965
Style of Banteay Srei . . .   965 - 1000
Style of Khleang . . . . . c. 965 - 1010
Style of Baphuon . . . . c. 1010 - 1080
Style of Angkor Wat . . c. 1100 - 1175

POST-ANGKORIAN ART

Style of Bayon . . . . .   c. 1177 - 1230

Archaeological discoveries of stone architecture and sculpture in the Indianized countries of South-East Asia indicate iconographic, technical and artistic skills and expressive power. We have some knowledge of the work in wood which preceded this, from the stelae of kings and from Chinese chronicles. The roots of this art lie in India, but it came to full flowering in the Indochinese empires of Fu Nan, Chen La, Khmer, and the neighboring Cham, in what is today central Vietnam.

In the 6th and 7th centuries, when Indian merchants withdrew from ocean-

going trade, direct contact between India and the Indianized states of South-East Asia was broken off. Only the Brahman priests stayed behind in the royal courts. The art of the Indianized states freed itself from its Indian exemplar and began to draw more strongly on its own tradition, symbolism and aesthetics. It followed the impulses of the religious and political changes taking place around it. In the 9th century the divinity of the king became the central idea of the state and its official religion. The apotheosis of the kings presented art with new tasks, leading it in new directions and enriching it.

A new and profound development is also seen to have taken place in the 12th century, when the kings adopted Buddhism. In place of shrines to the god and king, to which only the priesthood and temple accolytes had access, we now find large monastic establishments built to house great numbers of monks.

In the analysis of styles which follows, it has not been possible to describe the sculptures. Most of the important bronze and stone statues have disappeared from the temples. All that remain are a few Buddhist statues. However, these bear no relation to the history of the buildings. The National Museum in Phnom Penh possesses an excellent collection of statues, bronzes and ceramics. These exhibits are described in detail on p.80.

ART OF THE PRE-ANGKORIAN PERIOD

The style of Phnom Da
514-539 and 540-600

REIGNS: King Rudravarman (Fu Nan), 514-539 and *King Bhvavarman I* (probably Chen La), a grandson of Rudravarman who reigned around 550 AD. Rudravarman's capital is believed to have been at Angkor Borei on the hill of Phnom Da, about 37 miles (60 km) southwest of Phnom Penh. The location of Bhavavar-

Right: A brick tower in the Roluos Group. Far right: Gate of the Dead at Angkor Thom.

man I's capital has so far not been established.

RELIGIONS: Hinduism, Buddhism

EXAMPLES: Two groups of statues on the hill of Phnom Da. No definite examples of architecture, but foundations have been discovered at Oc-Eo and other places in the Mekong delta.

ARCHITECTURE: Though there is considerable debate on the matter, the small shrine of Ta Keo, also known as the Asrama Maha Rosei, or Hermitage of the Great Ascetic. is possibly the only building from the Fu Nan period that has been discovered intact. However, most art historians attribute it to a later period. The small structure of heavy basalt blocks admittedly shows signs of Indian influence, but it is similar to the Indian Pallava style, which never occurs again in the later architecture of Chen la and the Khmer. Nor does it show any resemblance at all to the brick architecture of Fu Nan, the foundations of which have been uncovered at Oc-Eo and other excavation sites in the Mekong delta.

**Style of Sambor Prei Kuk
around 600-650**

REIGN: King Isanavarman I (around 611-635). His capital of Isanapura, with its temple of Sambor Prei Kuk, was near the modern town of Kompong Thom in the hilly north of the country, on the Stung Sen, a tributary of the Tonle Sap. The empire of Chen La grew up on the high plateau, watered by the Se Mun river, in what is now southern Laos. On a hill beside the Mekong, where the Wat Phu is situated, near Pakse, the people of Chen La erected a shrine to Shiva containing a *linga*.

RELIGION: Hinduism, cults of Vishnu, Shiva and Hari-Hara.

EXAMPLES: Sambor Prei Kuk, Koh Kuk Krieng.

CHARACTERISTICS: Strong influence of Indian art. The design of large temple complexes remained largely unaltered, with minor modifications, for several centuries, but changed when Buddhism replaced Hinduism as the state religion.

55

With their central tower-shrine, surrounded by smaller towers, gated walls and moats, they recall the temple-cities of southern India. The small, square, windowless cells built from sandstone with overhanging, vaulted roofs, the blind windows set in pyramidal roofs, and the tripled-naved interior, or *mandapa*, with a flat roof – in all these north Indian influences can be recognized. But these quickly disappear, as do the octagonal towers, from the architecture of Chen La. Only the pyramidal roof reappears in the Angkorian style.

The arched window frames of sandstone were only installed after they had been worked on, and reliefs carved deeply into them, ending in *makara*, the heads of monsters. They developed from the simple wooden beams of Indian temples, on which garlands of flowers were hung. The medallions on the arches and walls are elegantly filled with decorative figures. Gates in the walls have been enlarged into small shrines with finely worked, vaulted ceilings of a beauty never again achieved in later periods. Garlands of leaves recur in many different forms. The pillars of the door frames are decorated with garlands and a ring and crowned with onion-shaped finials.

ARCHITECTURE: From the 7th century onward the development of art can be traced right up to the Angkor style. The temple of Sambor Prei Kuk is one of the most beautiful examples of pre-Angkorian architecture. The temple complexes of Chen La took shape around a *prasat*, or tower-shrine, which symbolized the *meru*, the mountain which Indian mythology places at the center of the universe, and on which the gods are enthroned. The god who is personally present in the temple is manifested in the divine image or *lingam*. The concept of god-kingship had not yet been introduced. The temple

was dedicated to the cult of the gods, and only the elite had access to it; it was not somewhere for the ordinary faithful to congregate and pray. The small, dark inner sanctum was always closed to all but the priesthood. The individual could not himself enter the presence of the gods, but could only let his sacrifice be carried out by the Brahman priests, who were there to fulfil his wishes.

The principal shrine was surrounded by secondary buildings, often constructed of wood, which were used for the worship of other gods and goddesses or as treasure-chambers.

This inner area was surrounded by a brick wall. The temple entrances faced east to the rising sun. Their gates, which themselves formed small shrines, were for the worship of the guardian gods and the beasts on which the gods rode, which were also held to be divine. Outside the walls lived the priests and temple servants, who included musicians, dancing-girls and slaves. This area was surrounded by a second wall beyond which lay a wide moat, fed by the river. Around the temples lay the cities, in whose center stood the seat of earthly power, the king's palace. In the days of Chen La and the Khmer, this would have been built of wood. In this respect the Indianized states of South-East Asia followed the example of the Indian priest-architects, who only permitted long-lasting materials like brick and sandstone to be used for the construction of sacred buildings.

The style of Prei Kmeng around 635-700

REIGN: Bhavavarman II, c. 635-656. We do not know where his capital was, nor what shrines he built, since there are no stelae extant bearing this information.
RELIGION: Shivaism is now the religion of the kings, but Hari-Hara, Vishnu and Hindu goddesses are also worshipped. As in the rest of Indochina statues of the

Right: From the archaeological collections in Siem Reap.

Buddha appear, since Mahayana Buddhism was widespread among the people.
EXAMPLES: Prei Kmeng, Phnom Bayang (Takeo), Phnom Preah Vihear, Han Chei (Kompong Thom).
CHARACTERISTICS: The styles of Prei Kmeng, Prasat Andet And Kompong Preah partly overlap in time. In all three it is possible to recognize influences of the styles of Phnom Da and Sambor Prei Kuk, in other words of Indian art. The brick-built tower-shrines have simple decoration on their doorframes. The *makara* were replaced by upward-curving spirals of leaves, and the medallions no longer have figurative decorations.

There is a profusion of foliage; only a few doorframes have reliefs of religious subjects. The pillars no longer have finials. Han Chei has the last little *cella*.

The style of Prasat Andet, 657-681

REIGN: Jayarvarman I ruled over large areas of present-day Indochina from 657 to 681. Despite many inscriptions, there

is still uncertainty about his capital. It may have been in the neighborhood of Angkor and now covered by the Western Baray, the great reservoir; or it might have been near Roluos and destroyed by a successor.
RELIGION: The worship of Shiva and the *lingam* had established itself as the religion of the kings. Among the people Mahayana Buddhism had lost some of its popularity.
EXAMPLE: Prasat Andet.
CHARACTERISTICS: In architecture the style of Prei Kmeng continues. Little innovation is to be seen in the decoration. What is noticeable is the frequent appearance of the *linga*.

The style of Kompong Preah 706-800

REIGN: Jayavarman I was succeeded in 713 by his widow Jayadevi. In the struggle over succession the country is split into two: Chen La of the Mountains and Chen La of the Water.

57

RELIGION: Hinduism.
EXAMPLES: Prasat Phum Prasat (Kompong Thom), Kompong Preah.
CHARACTERISTICS: The frames are now only decorated with leaves, and the pillars with narrow bands of flowers. Garlands of leaves wind round the large columns. Figurative decoration is absent. There is a certain impoverishment and lack of expressive power.

The style of Kulen
802-875

REIGN: Jayavarman II, from 802 to 850. After the fall of Chen La there was a political and cultural hiatus, which was eventually filled by the Buddhist empire of Srivijaya on Sumatra and the Buddhist dynasty of Shailendra, Kings of the Mountain. In about 790, Jayavarman II returned to Chen La from Java. His four capitals, from which he sought to unify

Above: Jungle scenery in northwestern Cambodia.

the country, were Indrapura, east of Kompong Cham (today called Banteay Prei Nokor), Kuti (Kutisvara) to the north of the Tonle Sap, Hariharalaya in Roluos and Amarendrapura near Ak Yum. In 802 he founded the new city of Mahendraparvata, on the hill of Phnom Kulen, in uninhabitable mountain country, about 25 miles (40 km) northeast of Angkor. He summoned a Brahman from India, to perform a ceremony by which he would be made a god-king and ruler of the universe.

From then on, the hill temple of Krus Preah Aram Rong Chen, atop the Phnom Kulen, represented the center of his empire. Its *lingam* was the symbol of the union between the god Shiva and the deified king. Afterwards, Jayavarman II returned to Roluos. He left behind no inscriptions; we learn of his deeds from the stelae of his successors. His son Jayavarman III (850-877) consolidated the empire and the divine kingship.
RELIGION: Hinduism, Shiva cults, Divine kingship.

EXAMPLES: Sambor Prei Kuk C1, Banteay Prei Nokor, the north tower of Prasat Prei Prasat (Roluos), Svay Pream, Prasat Kok Po and the second main tower of Trapeang Phong, as well as the temples on Phnom Kulen: Krus Preah Aram Rong Chen and Prasat Damrei Krap.

CHARACTERISTICS: The style of Kulen is described as a transitional style,which should be regarded as paving the way for the art of Angkor, and which many scholars do in fact class as Angkorian.

The simple towers, or *prasats,* were built on rectangular ground plans, with the doorway facing east and blind doors on the other three sides. The Indian style of dome was replaced by a multi-tiered roof structure. The temple of Krus Preah Aram Rong Chen on the Phnom Kulen hill shows an attempt at a stepped pyramid. Ak Yum, a three-storeyed stepped pyramid, was surmounted by five towers. The culmination of these attempts is reached with the towers of the Prasat Kok Po and the second tower of Trapeang Phong.

These established the concept of recreating in stone the Mountain of the Gods, the *meru* of Indian mythology. The artificial temple-hill becomes the basis of the architecture of Angkor.

In this phase of Khmer art close connections existed with the art of the neighboring empire of Champa, also influenced by India, in what is now central Vietnam. An element of the style of Kulen were the three-towered shrines, which rapidly disappeared again from Angkorian art, whereas they continued to be built in Champa until the end of its empire in the 17th century.

The decoration harks back to the style of Sambor Prei Kuk. The lintels again have arches, wrapped round with *makara.* An innovation are the horseback figures in the luxuriant foliage. In place of the *makara* one occasionally sees the heads of *kala,* sea monsters, which originated in Java. The doorways incorporate small, octagonal pillars, which also appear in later styles. The Khmer show themselves open to foreign influences. The pediments are harmoniously filled with figures of gods.

THE ART OF ANGKOR
875-1175

The style of Preah Ko,
around 875-893

REIGNS: Indravarman I, 877-889. A usurper who ruled large areas of Indochina. A highly educated Hindu philosopher, his teacher was the Brahman Shivasoma. His capital was Roluos. He dammed the river Roluos and, making use of a natural depression in the land, created Indrataka, the Lake of Indra, also called the Baray of Lolei. Over 2 miles long and half a mile wide (3.8 x 0.8 km), it provided water for the rice paddies and the city. He thus created the foundation of Angkor's wealth. *Yasovarman I,* 889-900, continued his father's work and later founded a new capital.

RELIGION: Hinduism in the form of a revived orthodox Brahmanism. Shivaism. Reaffirmation of divine kingship.

EXAMPLES: Preah Ko, Bakong, Lolei.

*CHARACTERISTIC*S: The style of Preah Ko still has an affinity with that of Kulen: the brick-built shrines stand together on a single base. Lintels, columns and blind niches of sandstone, cloverleaf-shaped pediments of brick. The arches are now only suggested by a tendril ending in a *naga*'s head. The external walls were covered in places with stucco, into which decorative leaves, lotus blossoms and circles were carved.

TEMPLE-HILLS: When the Khmer empire moved down to occupy the plains around Angkor, stepped pyramids were first built as artificial temple-hills. The substructure is built of laterite and the temples themselves of brick. The first of these is the Bakong in Roluos.

RELIEFS: Panels, on which the gods are represented standing side by side, are the first step toward the true art of relief. The first narrative representations appear on sandstone plaques set into the lower part of the temple walls. The Khmer developed bas-relief to perfection, while the neighboring Cham were masters of high relief. The artists of both peoples would continue to prefer relief to sculpting in the round. The narrative character of the work gave greater freedom for their powers of expression. For historians they opened up a rich new source of information, since later the lives of ordinary people were portrayed.

The style of Bakheng, 893-925

REIGN: Yasovarman I, 889-900, studied under a Brahman. His empire stretched from southern Laos to the Gulf of Siam.

Above: From the archaeological collections of Siem Reap. Right: The temple of Bakong in the Roluos group.

60

There was no room in Roluos to extend the rice fields.

Yasovarman I built his capital of Yasodhapura around a natural hill about a mile (1.5 km) from Angkor Wat. It was on this hill that he erected the temple of Bakheng. Making use of the Riem Reap river, he created the lake of Yasodharatataka, today called the Eastern Baray. Nearly 4 1/2 miles long and over a mile wide (7 by 1.8 km), it watered the rice fields as far as the Great Lakes.

No important temples are known to have been built by his sons who succeeded him, Harshavarman I, 900-921 and Isanavarman II, 922-928.

RELIGION: Hinduism, divine kingship. The beginning of the worship of the dead king. The first building of Yasovarman I was the temple of Lolei at Roluos, in honor of his father, Indravarman I. Monasteries were built for Buddhist sects.

EXAMPLES: Bakheng, Prasat Nan Khmau, Prasta Phnom Krom, Prasat Phnom Bok, Bakei Chang Krang.

CHARACTERISTICS: Temple pyramids on natural hills. The Bakheng was built in accordance with the laws of the cosmos. The five crowning temple towers were here built for the first time from sandstone.

Bricks were not used for building temples after 925; thereafter brick is only found in secondary buildings.

The foliage carved into the lintels reveals less figurative decoration than before. The columns are now decorated with a number of circles. The pediments filled with figures of gods, end in arches with *makara* heads.

RELIEF ART: The sandstone reliefs require new techniques and provide an opportunity for more sophisticated work.

The bannisters of the staircases are also decorated with figures. On the temple walls the figures are presented against a plain background. In this respect they anticipate one of the characteristic elements of the bas-reliefs of Angkor Wat.

The style of Koh Ker 921-944

REIGNS: Isanavarman II, 922-928, was toppled from his throne by a relative.

The usurper, *Jayavarman IV*, 928-942, founded a new capital with a temple-hill, at Chok Gargyar (later renamed Koh Ker), in barren hillcountry about 40 miles (70 km) north-east of Angkor.

His son *Harshavarman I*, 942-944, ruled from Koh Ker, but built several temples in Angkor, among them the perfect temple-hill of Baksei Chang Krang (Chamkrong).

RELIGION: Hinduism, cult of Shiva, *linga*-cults.

EXAMPLES: Koh Ker and Prasat Thom, Baksei Chang Krang, Prasat Kravanh, Prasat Neang Khmau.

CHARACTERISTICS: The temple-hill of Koh Ker anticipates the dimensions of later temples in Angkor. The building material is brick, since there was no sandstone in the vicinity of Koh Ker. In Angkor we also find brick temples, but these were the last to be built.

Notable features of Koh Ker are the porch built in front of the temple towers and the enlargement of the gate towers to sacred buildings in their own right.

The decoration becomes simpler, but on the lintels one still finds rich foliage ornamented with figures. The octagonal columns at the doorways are heavily decorated with circles and ornamental leaves.

It is in this period that we see galleries for the first time, on the Prasat Thom, the main temple of Koh Ker. These were to become an essential element in the design of the temples of Angkor.

RELIEFS: The reliefs which were created on the Bakong temple later fell into oblivion. In the Koh Ker style they are revived once again and are chiselled into the brick walls.

Reliefs are also found on the Prasat Kravanh at Angkor; but these are the last to be carved on brick walls. Traces of mural painting are found in the Prasat Kravanh and also in the Prasat Neang Khmau in southern Cambodia. With its

five *prasats* and tall brick towers its is the last Khmer temple to resemble the tower-shrines of the Cham.

The style of Pre Rup 947-965

REIGN: Rajendravarman II, 944-968, nephew of Jayavarman IV, who left Koh Ker and returned to Angkor. His capital is located to the south of the Eastern Baray. The Khmer empire develops continuously in the plains of Angkor.

RELIGION: Hinduism. Divine kingship and the worship of the dead king.

On an island in the Eastern Baray Rajendravarman II built the Eastern Mebon, a temple in honor of his ancestors. Pre Rup, orientated westward, is his own burial temple, which he himself erected.

Rajendravarman II was highly educated. The Brahman Yajnavaraha was his advisor, but his ministers also included

Above: Pre Rup, the mausoleum of King Rajendravarman II.

Buddhists. A number of monasteries of Mahayana Buddhism were built, such as Wat Chum.

EXAMPLES: Eastern Mebon, Pre Rup, Preah Vihear.

CHARACTERISTICS: The style of Pre Rup is a transitional style which puts the finishing touches to the foregoing elements of style and hints at architectural innovations to come. It is typified by stepped pyramids with lions as guardian-figures on the staircases and turrets built on to the parapets. Galleries built of stone imitate wooden construction and are roofed with wooden beams and tiles.

The decoration is simple. The lintels are still adorned with gods and fabled creatures nestling in luxuriant foliage.

The style of Banteay Srei 965-1000

REIGN: Jayavarman V. However, the builder of the Banteay Srei temple is not the king, but the learned Brahman Yajnavaraha, a grandson of king Harshavarman I and counsellor to his successors.

RELIGION: Hinduism, Shiva cult.

EXAMPLE: The little Shivaitic shrine of Banteay Srei, 20 miles (30 km) northeast of Angkor, often described as the most beautiful of all Khmer buildings.

CHARACTERISTICS: Building material, a reddish sandstone. The harmonious architecture is adorned with a wealth of decoration, which is rather untypical of the monumental and realistic art of the Khmer. The amount of figurative decoration is surprising, especially the female figures framed in foliage. Special attention should be paid to the tympana, or pediments above the doorways. The deeply carved reliefs look almost like sculptures and portray dance scenes. The style of Banteay Srei shows no innovation, either in architecture, decoration or iconography, but is the culmination of all previous creativity, the inimitable inspiration of an individualist, a masterpiece of the sculptor's art.

The style of Khleang 956(978)-1010

REIGN: Jayavarman V, 968-1001.
RELIGION: Hinduism.
EXAMPLES: Prasat Khleang, Cha Srei Vibol, Preah Vihear (Suriyavarman I).
CHARACTERISTICS: Both the architecture and the decoration are of equal importance. Nearly all the new stylistic elements can be identified in two small buildings, the Southern Khleang, and the Northern Khleang, which is older and whose design seems more perfect.

Temple pyramids continue to be built, and each tier is decorated with small towers and galleries running round it.

The decoration of the lintels appears simple. Out of the midst of rich foliage, which ends in a floral motif, a fabled animal rears its head.

The octagonal columns remain at the doorways, but they are now heavily dedorated with circles and small leaves. The pediments are also decorated with foliage, which has become the most com-

mon form of decoration. The workmanship of the decoration is finely detailed and appears to have been influenced by Banteay Srei. If any reliefs ever existed, none have survived.

The style of Baphuon 1010-1080

REIGN: Suriyavarman I (whose name means "protected by the sun") reigned, after a brief interregnum, from 1002 to 1050. His strong personality left its mark on the first half of the 11th century. As a prince of the empire of Tambralinga in Malaya, he had a claim to the throne of the Khmer on his mother's side, but had to fight a long civil war for the crown.

Chinese chronicles of this period attest to the splendor and power of the Khmer empire.

His son, Udayadityavarman II ("Protected by the Rising Sun"), reigned from 1050 to 1066, or according to some evidence, until 1080, and early on had to put down rebellions in his realm. The economic well-being of his capital and his government depended on the Eastern Baray, but he ordered the construction of the second, Western Baray, 5 miles long and 1 1/2 miles wide (8 km by 2.2 km). Using the natural slope of the land, this reservoir irrigated further land as far as the Great Lakes, so that double the area could be planted with rice. It also supplied the new capital with water. A 9th century city disappeared beneath the waters which rose behind the dam, and the temple of Ak Yum probably lies under the southern dyke of the reservoir. The Western Mebon temple stands on an artificial island.

The capital of Udayadityavarman II lies directly beneath the modern town of Angkor Thom, and part of it had already been built over by Jayavarman II in the 12th century. In its center was the badly damaged temple of Baphuon.

During the reign of his brother, Harshavarman III, Angkor was frequently at-

tacked, destroyed and finally occupied by the Cham (1177-1181).

RELIGION: Hinduism. Shiva cult.

Suriyavarman I tolerated Mahayana Buddhism, which slowly began to influence art. Even the *naga* cults of pre-Hindu times enjoyed a revival.

Udayadityavarman II only built temples to Shiva, although he allowed ample opportunity for the depiction of Vishnu myths. But he tried, probably without success, to suppress Buddhism.

EXAMPLES: The completion of Ta Keo and Phimeanakas. Wat Ek,Wat Basak. Western Mmebon. Baphuon.

CHARACTERISTICS: At the time of Suriyavarman I Malaya was under the cultural influence of the Khmer, so that his arrival in Angkor caused no interruption in the artistic tradition.

Suriyavarman I built stepped pyramids with five towers of sandstone, but also

Above: Stairs to the temple of Phimeanakas. Right: From a distance Angkor Wat appears to have only three towers.

shrines consisting of a temple at ground level with a central tower. Now, for the first time, court officials, members of the royal family and nobles built temples to local gods all over the country.

Udayadityavarman II created the Baphuon as the only temple-hill of its period. This masterpiece of Khmer architecture made use of lessons learnt from all the earlier styles, and in size and beauty is only surpassed by Angkor Wat, whose forerunner the Baphuon must be considered.

The Baphuon style is typified by the enclosing walls, the approach ways paved with stone slabs, causeways across the moats, vaulted galleries of sandstone with towers at each corner, eastern entrances with large vestibules, libraries and pavilions. The only building materials now used were stone and laterite. The use of wooden beams to support the vaulted stone roofs led to the early collapse of these structures.

The Baphuon already displays the three main elements of Khmer architec-

ture: long narrow interiors, galleries and towers with pyramidal roofs.

The decoration underscores the architectural form, without overpowering it. The figurative ornamentation is set off to full advantage against a plain background. Ornamentation is found on the pediments, walls, stairways, pillars, interior walls and threshhold stones. The towers have lotus-shaped finials.

According to Chinese travelers many of the temple towers were gilded, that is to say covered with gilded copper sheeting, and furnished with statues and a *linga* of pure gold.

A change of style in Khmer architecture can first and foremost be recognized in the decoration of the doorways and lintels. In the style of Baphuon these do not display any significant innovation, but revive motifs from the 8th century. Occasionally these spread to the pediments, with their rich, figurative decoration.

RELIEFS: On the long horizontal reliefs, there are depictions of scenes from the Indian Vishnu epics, the Ramayana and Mahabharata. These motifs, which recur again and again in Khmer reliefs, are also carried over into the panels.

The style of Angkor 1100-1175

REIGNS: Jayavarman VI, 1080-1107, was governor of a northern province, who usurped the throne and founded a new dynasty. Not being recognized by the south, he only reigned briefly from Angkor. The only buildings known to be his are in the north. He was succeeded by two of his brothers, who have no significance with regard to Khmer art.

Suriyavarman II, 1113-1150, was a distant relative. He conquered the empire of the Cham, advanced as far as Dai Viet, ruled over large parts of Malaya, invaded the Burmese empire, and reached the gates of Pagan, and Lopburi and Lamphun in the northern kingdoms of the Thai tribes. He was the first Khmer king to send emissaries bearing tribute to the imperial court of China. However, between 1149 and 1150 he lost his con-

quests again, the Cham were able to free themselves, and when he attempted to force his way through the Red River delta to Dai Viet, his army was defeated at the pass of Tranh Ninh and wiped out by disease. Not long afterwards, the king himself was dead.

Under his rule, however, Angkor achieved its political and cultural zenith. Suriyavarman II was the builder of Angkor Wat. *Dharanindravarman II*, 1150-1160, a cousin, succeeded him. That king's son, *Vasovarman II*, was murdered by a usurper in 1166. The Cham exploited the weak position of the Khmer empire and occupied Angkor from 1177 to 1181.

RELIGION: Hinduism. Jayavarman VI was a Shivaite. In his temple at Phimai Buddhist motifs were introduced here and there. Suriyavarman II was a Vishnuite. Dharanindravarman II was the first king of the Khmer to adopt Mahayana-Buddhism.

EXAMPLES: Jayavarman VI built the Wat Phu temple in southern Laos, the Phimai in northeast Thailand, and Preah Vihear on the border with Thailand. Suriyavarman was the driving force behind Angkor Wat, Beng Mealea, Banteay Samré, Thommanon, and Chau Say Tevoda, to name but a few. His successors were responsible for Preah Pithu, and Preah Palilay, and began work on the Preah Khan of Kompong Svay.

CHARACTERISTICS: Suriyavarman II led the empire of Angkor to its geatest artistic development. The style of Angkor is the classical epoch of Khmer art and the culmination of a long evolution, and yet it already gives us a glimpse of its coming decline and downfall.

The sheer vastness of Angkor Wat, one of the greatest temples in the world, is on a par with the pyramids of Egypt. At about this period in history, the cathedrals that were being built in Europe included Chartres, completed in 1130, and

Above: The terrace of the Leper-King, seen from the south. Right: From the collections of the Archaeological Institute, Siem Reap.

Mainz in 1137. The English cathedrals of Durham and York date from about that time, but Salisbury was only completed a hundred years later.

The style of Angkor Wat continues and perfects that of Baphuon without any further essential changes. The harmony and beauty of Angkor Wat derive from a complete mastery of the materials, and the varied, sometimes novel, application of all previous structural elements, experience and techniques.

Suriayavarman II created a three-tiered pyramid, of which the uppermost tier is surmounted by one principal tower and four smaller ones. The pillars, walls and panels are decorated with a wealth of ornament, tendrils and foliage, resembling the paintings on Chinese silk, with which the interiors were once furnished. Epics of gods and heroes are depicted on doorposts, lintels, and pediments. The friezes of the capitals and the ledges of the galleries are decorated with lotus flowers.

All the structural elements and decorative motifs assume a new importance in Angkor Wat. The roadways paved with large stone slabs, which cross the moats on pillars, become processional aveues. The tall plinths and lower walls carry reliefs and ornamentation, and the large porches become temples in their own right. Rearing serpents line the processional avenues, the staircases and ornamental pools, and many-headed *nagas* stand guard by the entrance gates. The walls are punctuated by pilasters, which allow a soft light to suffuse the interior. On the inside walls are carved, individually or in groups, some two thousand *devatas*, or goddessess, and *apsaras*, semi-divine dancing girls. In no later buildings do we find craftsmanship to equal the grace of these slender but full-bosomed figures, nor the fine work on their dress, jewelry and their elaborate, diadem-like coiffure.

A particularly attractive effect is achieved by the baluster windows. With

their seven twisted stone columns, which could not have been more finely carved had they been of wood, they adorn galleries and staircases. The fall of light projects their shadows on to the inner walls and the flagstones on the floor.

RELIEFS: The bas-reliefs at Angkor Wat, the finest in Khmer art, cover a total of nearly 22,000 sq. ft (2000 sq.m.) of sandstone walls.

Banteay Samré: among the buildings erected by Suriyavarman II in the style of Angkor Wat, is the temple of Banteay Samré. Art historians often describe this as the most beautiful Khmer temple to be built at ground level. Buddhist monks, who took possession of the abandoned temple, made some structural changes.

POST-ANGKORIAN ART

The style of Bayon 1177-1230

REIGNS: Jayavarman VII, 1181-1219, is not only the most interesting but also the most important of the Khmer kings.

At the time his father, Suriyavarman II, died, he was away fighting a campaign in Champa, and was denied the rightful succession to the throne. He then withdrew to the Preah Khan in Kompong Svay. When a rebellion against his half brother broke out in 1166, he arrived too late to save his kinsman's life, and once again had to cede the throne to a usurper.

The Cham twice attempted, in vain, to capture Angkor by land. Not until 1177 did they come up the Mekong and Tonle Sap in ships; they captured and destroyed the city, ransacked the temples and occupied the capital. The Khmer king died in battle. Jayavarman then took up the fight, destroyed the Cham fleet and put the enemy to flight. Later he ordered the story of the battle to be depicted in a relief in the Bayon temple. He also fought against Dai Viet, advanced into Laos as far as Vieng Chang (Vientiane) and

reached the borders of Burma. It is possible that his empire was even greater than that of his father, Suriyavarman II.

In 1181, at the age of nearly sixty, he ascended the throne as Jayavarman VII. He immediately had to put down a rebellion in the south of his country, then proceeded to wreak revenge on the Cham, by destroying their capital and occupying their territory.

The question as to why he twice renounced his claim to throne without a fight, gives rise to a number of theories, none of which can be proved. Was he a leper, who, having been miraculously cured, became a devout Buddhist? Was he already a devout Buddhist whose faith forbade him to shed blood? An inscription simply states that he returned in order to save his country.

Following the death of Suriyavarman II, Angkor fell into a long and gradual decline, both politically and culturally. Did Jayavarman VII realize this and attempt to halt the process? The divine kingship was based on Hinduism, especially the

Above: Giant trees threaten the temple of Ta Phrom (Angkor). Right: Head of Jayavarman VII, Preah Khan temple (Kompong Svay).

cult of Shiva. The apotheosis of the king, the unifying of god and king in the *linga*, the phallus of the creator-god, was the continuation of the pre-Hindu fertility cult of a rural society, which erected megalithic totems to the dead chieftain, as protector of the fields and harvests.

This symbiosis and symbolism was present in no other religion, not even in the cult of Vishnu, and so the Khmer rulers retruned again and again to Shivaism. In the course of their history, they had only known success in campaigns of conquest beyond their borders. But when the Cham fleet invaded Angkor and took possession of the city and temple of the god-king, and what is more, at a time when the people were already turning to Buddhism, the belief of the Khmer in the infallibility of their deified king and his gods, was inevitably shattered once and for all.

Did Jayavarman VII make one last, superhuman effort to save the divine kingship and thereby the empire? The pious Buddhist did not renounce his divine kingship. He made no changes to Hindu ritual, but ordained that he be worshipped as the incarnation of the Boddhisattva Avalokiteshvara, who was called Lokiteshvara in Cambodia. In feverish haste he rebuilt the Hindu temple that had been destroyed by the Cham. Did he hope thereby to restore the power of kingship? The Angkor Wat, which we see preserved to this day, is the version which was resurrected at his behest. He then began, with a restless speed, which is clearly visible in all his buildings, to surround his capital, Angkor Thom, with a protective wall, and to build gates, temples and terraces. On every available piece of land shrines to the new faith sprang up, and monasteries were built both to accommodate large numbers of monks, and at the same time as places in which to worship his deified ancestors.

By the end of his reign he had built more temples than all the rulers before

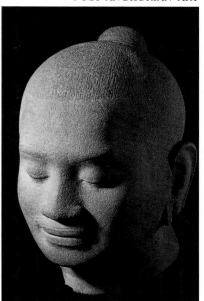

him, put together. The quarries at Phnom Kulen became exhausted. In the end he had to be satisfied with stone of poorer quality, and even made use of stone from ruined temples, something which would have been completely unthinkable in the Indian tradition.

Angkor Thom arose on the site of the capital of Udayadityavarman II, whose chief temple, the Baphuon, had been preserved. Jayavarman VII construcetd a further *baray*, 2 1/2 miles long and 660 ft wide (4 km by 200 m) and connected it to existing reservoirs by a series of new lakes and canals.

All over the country he built monasteries great and small, hospitals, resthouses and inns for pilgrims, whom he entertained generously. From the capital, highways led to all points of the compass, and he linked the temples by paths and canals. In all this he received support from his favorite wife, the pious and well-educated Jayadevi, who gave instruction in the teachings of Buddha in the monasteries. When she died, he en-

trusted the same educational responsibilities to her sister.

Accounts of his deeds are found in stelae and temple inscriptions. We know more about the man himself and his reign than we do about any other Khmer ruler. He even had his own thoughts chiseled in stone: "The misfortune which befalls mankind weighs heavily on the soul of the king, and is all the more painful since it is the people's sorrow which the kings can feel, and not their own suffering."

Nevertheless, there is much in his life which remains a mystery, and his personality is inaccessible and impenetrable. We do not know when he was born, but it is thought that he died bwteen 1202 and 1218. Many historians have sought to explain his tireless building activity by a fear of death and an obsession with saving his own soul, but such a theory seems to do less than justice to the man who was

Above: Giant faces in stone on the upper terrace of the Bayon temple (Angkor Thom).

the Khmer's greatest monarch. A more credible supposition, and one more appropriate to his great spirit and intellegence, is that he wanted to save the empire and the power of the kings by adopting the faith of the people. How else can the teaching of Buddha be interpreted as a legitimation of divine kingship, or its exhortation to self-denial as a means of holding on to power?

Do the gigantic faces of stone beside his temples and gateways represent the countenance of Bodhisattva, or did the king have his own image immortalized a hundredfold? Was he seeking to preserve his own life and that of his ancestors in the lifeless stones?

Two heads carved in stone, one which shows him as a fifty-year-old and the other a decade later, have been found in the Preah Khan at Kompong Svay, and in the Krol Romeas at Angkor. The serious expression on his face has been interpreted in very different ways. Should we read in it a scholarly nature or strength of will, kindness or harshness, ambition or arrogance? Are the eyes lost in mediation or do the betray madness? Was the king a mystic or a man obsessed with power? He refused to renounce his divine kingship and made no attempt to change the Hindu ritual. Hindu myths can be found mixed up with Buddhist themes. The Vishnu legend of the Churning of the Ocean of Milk by gods and demons is the motif of the city of Angkor Thom and of Bayon in its center, as a representation of the universe.

Indravarman II, his son, reigned from 1219 to 1243.

Jayavarman VIII, who was king from 1143 to 1295, may have been his grandson. He enjoyed a longer reign than any other Khmer monarch. Neither of the two had much merit either as rulers or as commissioners of building. They reverted to Shivaism, and Brahmans from India gained great influence at the court of Angkor. In the temples, many heads and faces on statues and reliefs were destroyed and Buddhas were replaced by Hindu gods. Neither king was able to prevent the rise of Siam to power. The attacks by the Siamese became more and more violent, leading to the collapse of the irrigation systems and the waning of Angkor's prosperity. The Hinduism espoused by the kings became an anachronism, since the people had long since turned to Theravada Buddhism.

Inscriptions give us the names of five kings who reigned after Jayavarman VII, then the chronicle of Cambodian monarchs, which was initially passed down orally, and only much later written down, comes to an end.

RELIGION: Jayavarman VII was a Buddhist and tried to combine divine kingship with Mahayana Buddhism. His successors reverted to Shivaism and court ceremonial was dictated by Indian Brahmans. The people adopted Theravada Buddhism, the Teaching of the Ancients, which was based on Hinayana Buddhism.

EXAMPLES: The completion of Preah Khan in Kompong Svay, the restoration of Angkor and other temples, the building of Banteay Kdei, Ta Prohm, Preah Khan, Neak Pean, Ta Nei, Ta Som, Krol Ko, Banteay Chmar, Angkor Thom and its five gates, de Bayon, the terraces and the palace quarter.

CHARACTERISTICS: The restorations and early original buildings of the period still lean toward the style of Angkor Wat. The architectural style of Jayavarman VII can be described as symbolism or even monumental symbolism. Innovations include the large monastic complexes built for communities of Buddhist monks in conjunction with places for the worship of the king's ancestors.

With the change to a new religion came a change in iconography. Buddhist themes come to the fore, even though Hindu legends are frequently depicted, such as the continually recurring motif from the Vishnu legend: gods and demons churning the Ocean of Milk, in order to produce *amrita*, the elixir of eternal life. The *naga*, or Serpent Queen, from pre-Hindu mythology, is a symbol of the rainbow and forms a bridge from the water up into heaven. The other completely new, and constantly repeated motif is the gigantic face, carved on a stone tower.

In the early buildings of Jayavarman VII, the integral sculptured elements are carefully worked. However, in the later buildings the execution becomes more sketchy, as if the sculptor, being constantly urged on to new assignments, was running out of time. The small columns in the door frames are no longer inset as separate components, but are carved from the stone, as are the blind windows. The last buildings of the period look as if they had simply been hewn out of a solid lump of rock.

With the death of Jayavarman VII the age of Angkorian and post-Angkorian art came to an end. Thereafter, no stone temple of any significance was built.

AWAKING FROM THE NIGHTMARE

PHNOM PENH
TOURING CAMBODIA

PHNOM PENH

The founding of the capital, Phnom Penh, and its name, are both said to date back to an event in the year 1327 which is related in the Cambodian annals translated by the French scholar George Coedes. There was at that time a prosperous widow, Don Penh, who lived on a hill near the banks of the river. In the mud left behind by a flood she found a tree and asked some fishermen to bring it ashore. In its branches she discovered five Buddhas: four of bronze and one of stone. It later turned out that these came originally from a pagoda in Laos and had been carried downstream by the flood. The five Buddhas were brought into the house of Don Penh with due ceremony. Later, with help from the villagers, the widow had the height of the hill increased and on the top of it she erected a small pagoda called Wat Phnom Don Penh, the Monastery on the Hill of Lady Penh. The news of the miraculous discovery soon spread throughout the whole land.

About sixty years later, when the existing capital, Angkor, had been captured by the Siamese, King Ponhea Yat

Previous pages: Fishingboats on the Tonle Sap, Phnom Penh. Left: A family riding in a bicycle-rickshaw.

founded a new capital in Chattumuk, on Don Penh's hill. The city was completed in 1434, the Year of the Tiger. It was soon abandoned again, however, and not until 1866, under King Norodom, did it finally become the capital of Cambodia. On the hill, whose summit was later raised even higher, the little pagoda was replaced by larger temples, built successively in 1806, 1894 and 1926.

In the 15th century, the main river flowing through this region was called the Tonle Sap. Today, this name is only given to the northwestern tributary of the Mekong, which flows for 80 miles (130 km) from the Great Lakes, to join the Mekong near Phnom Penh. South of the city, the Mekong splits into two arms, the Bassac and the Lower Mekong, so that one has the impression that the city lies on four rivers. Phnom Penh's original name, Chattumuk, means in fact "Four Rivers." Seagoing vessels can sail upstream as far as the harbor at Phnom Penh. River craft connect the Cambodian capital, via the Tonle Sap, with the area round Angkor, and ply further northwards along the Mekong towards Kratie, as well as southeastwards to My To in the Mekong Delta, only 50 miles (80 km) from Saigon.

In the second half of the 19th century Phnom Penh became a French colonial

PHNOM PENH

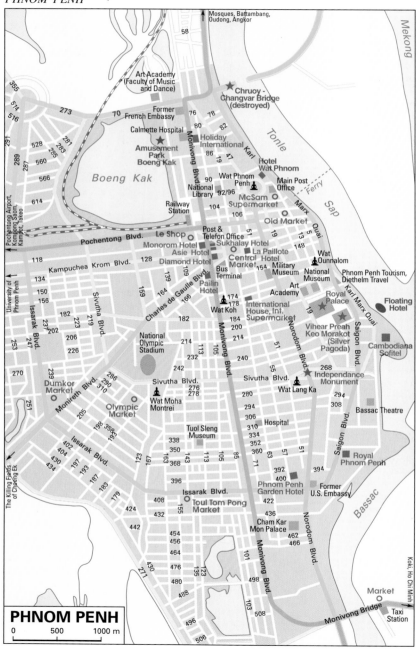

Mosques, Battambang, Oudong, Angkor

58

Art Academy (Faculty of Music and Dance)

Chruoy - Changvar Bridge (destroyed)

273

70

76 78

Former French Embassy

80 82

Calmette Hospital

Amusement Park Boeng Kak

86 19 47

Holiday International

Mekong

Tonle

Hotel

Wat Phnom

528
281
283
560
566
614

289
287

291

Boeng Kak

90

Wat Phnom Penh

Main Post Office

Ferry

Sap

92/96

National Library

104

Railway Station

McSam Supermarket

106

Old Market

Pochentong Blvd.

Le Shop

Post & Telefon Office

51

19

148

5

Monorom Hotel

Sukhalay Hotel

La Paillote

Wat Ounnalom

Asie Hotel

118

Kampuchea Krom Blvd.

128

Diamond Hotel

Central Market

154

Military Museum

National Museum

Phnom Penh Tourism, Diethelm Travel

134
150
156

139
109

Pailin Hotel

159
164
166

182

Bus Terminal

Art Academy

Royal Palace

Floating Hotel

182
202
206
226

219
223
237

174
178

Wat Koh

184
200
214

International House, Inf. Supermarket

214

Vihear Preah Keo Morakot (Silver Pagoda)

Cambodiana Sofitel

247
253

270

National Olympic Stadium

113
105

214
232

240

242

55

Saigon Blvd.

268

239

Dumkor Market

286
290
310

Sivutha Blvd.

276
278

51

Sivutha Blvd.

Wat Lang Ka

Independence Monument

251

205

198 192
358

Olympic Market

Wat Moha Montrei

338
350
368

280
294
306
310
334
352
360

Hospital

294

308

Bassac Theatre

123
167
163
143
113
105
85

Tuol Sleng Museum

63

57

71

Royal Phnom Penh

402
404
430
434

197
193
187
183
179

392
400

Phnom Penh Garden Hotel

394

Former U.S. Embassy

Bassac

408

Issarak Blvd.

424

155

Toul Tom Pong Market

422

432

442

436

Cham Kar Mon Palace

462
466

454
456
464
476

430

271

480

123
135

101

498

Norodom Blvd.

Koki, Ho Chi Minh

Market

488

508

Taxi Station

496

103

506

Monivong Bridge

PHNOM PENH

0   500   1000 m

76

city, with businesses, government offices, hotels and villas built in the colonial style. Broad streets, called boulevards, run east to west and north to south, linking the important parts of the city, but it is the riverside promenades, lined with palm trees, along the Tonle Sap and the Mekong, which give the city its special character. Here, beside the river, is where the life of the city takes place, especially in the evenings. In the villages to the north and south of the city, as well as on the opposite bank of the river, live the fishermen who supply it with fish and shellfish. Most of them belong to the Cham ethnic minority and live in impoverished settlements which have to be evacuated when the river floods.

Phnom Penh is divided into four administrative areas, or *khand*, and each of these is composed of a number of districts, known as *srok*. However, a visitor to the city will notice that it falls more naturally into three parts. In the north, between the Boen Kak Lake, with its leisure park and zoo, and the Tonle Sap river, lie some attractive residential areas. The hill of Phnem Penh, the main Post Office and a number of hotels, also belong to the European part of the city, which, with its ministries, banks and business houses, stretches southward as far as the confluence of the Tonle Sap and Mekong rivers. The large expanse of the European district is underlined by the broad, straight boulevards, the parks and green spaces, and a generous street layout, frequently interspersed with traffic roundabouts planted in the center with flowers. There is still a pleasant informality about the architecture in this part of town. There are no highrise buildings, only the hotels and public buildings are several storeys high and have a metropolitan look, but the face of the city is about to change very rapidly.

Where the Tonle Sap joins the Mekong, on Saigon Boulevard, the extensive grounds of the Royal Palace begin, and continue to the point where the Mekong divides into the Bassac, spanned by the Monivong Bridge, and the Lower Mekong. South of Phnom Penh Hill, the old heart of the city, around the covered Central Market, is like an island in the European city. Bounded in the north by the Boulevard USSR (whose name has not been changed), to the west by the Achar Mean Boulevard, and stretching east as far as the Tonle Sap river, it is an area of narrow lanes and little markets. Motor traffic, bicycles and rickshaws force their way between innumerable little shops, workshops, small hotels, restaurants, food stalls and street vendors. The colorful life of this typically oriental city is characterized by bustle, noise and a thousand strange and wonderful smells.

Today the city has more than 700,000 inhabitants, a number constantly being swollen by immigration, and most of them live in cramped conditions in the old town, in dilapidated properties which have somehow survived or been repaired in a makeshift fashion. Before 1975, Cambodians, Chinese and Vietnamese lived in separate streets, and different businesses and trades congregated in streets of their own. But after 1979, when the townspeople, who had been driven out by the Khmer Rouge, returned to the ruined city, and the peasant population fled to the capital to escape the continuing terror in the countryside, the boundaries between the various ethnic groups and trades became blurred.

With the reawakening of the city the old order returned. Once again there is a Street of the Basketmakers, a Street of the Jewellers, and streets for other occupations. Recently 184th Street, near the National Museum, has been nicknamed "English Street," because a rapidly growing number of private schools teaching English, and also a few teaching French, have been established there.

Knowledge of a foreign language improves people's chances of working for a

foreign company, where jobs are much sought after, as they pay princely salaries by Cambodian standards.

Since 1992 the Old Town, too, has been undergoing continuous and rapid change. As in other parts of the city, banks and businesses are springing up overnight. They are usually owned by Chinese, Thais, and less frequently, Vietnamese; but Japanese, French, Taiwanese and other Asian and European firms have also set up subsidiaries in Phnom Penh under the protection of the United Nations. A forest of hoardings display the names of world-famous companies, and extol products imported from all over the globe. Ever since the UN peacekeeping forces moved in, new hotels, restaurants, bars, nightclubs and discothèques have been opening every day. However, rural Cambodia has so far hardly been touched by this remarkable boom.

Above: Motorcycles in Phnom Penh. Right: Vishnu from the Prasat Damrei Krap, Kulen style (National Museum, Phnom Penh).

Available public transport is very far from adequate. Only a year ago traffic was brought to a temporary standstill by the huge number of bicycles, rickshaws – known here as *cyclos* – mopeds and motorcycles. Almost all of these are alarmingly overloaded, carrying familes with three or more children, or piled high with goods. Private cars and trucks used to belong almost exclusively to the government or the army. Now the traffic is dominated by vehicles marked with the large, white letters "UN." They have forced the rickshaws and cyclists into the gutter, since the former rule of the road, under which the more vulnerable road-users could count on consideration from motor vehicles, no longer holds good.

Pedestrians in Phnom Penh have to cover long distances through streets and squares which offer no shade. The temperature is constantly high, with the thermometer rarely falling below 26° C. Life comes to a halt during the midday heat, for two or three hours. *Cyclo* drivers offer their services to footsore walkers.

Up to now they have managed to man-oeuver their vehicles safely through the traffic – near-misses don't count – and those in the know will tell you that they only risk life and limb by cutting in on cars if they feel they are being pursued by a *kinoch,* or evil spirit. The hope is that if the spirit is hit by a car it will give up tor-menting the cyclo driver. Nowadays the cyclo drivers are chased less by *kinochs* than by the bonnets of the shiny new (mostly Japanese) cars belonging to the money-men.

Most of the streets in Phnom Penh, apart from the boulevards, are identified by numbers, albeit with some inconsist-encies, so that it is possible even for those unfamiliar with the Cambodian alphabet to get their bearings.

There is much to see in Phnomh Penh though few real tourist attractions. Never well-endowed with art treasures, those it had were mostly destroyed between 1975 and 1979. An exception is the National Museum with its fine collection of Cam-bodian art of the 6th to 13th centuries.

The National Museum

The National Museum (formerly the Albert Sarraut Museum), north of the Royal Palace on 13th street, was built of red brick by the French in 1917-1920, in a pseudo-Khmer style. It is a rectangle, 210 ft by 170 ft (66 m by 54 m), round a central courtyard. Until 1951 it was the responsibility of the French governor of Indochina, and was supported by French academics up until 1966. In the civil war, after 1970, local museums brought their collections here for safekeeping.

In 1975 the Khmer Rouge drove the museum's management out of Phnom Penh and the director was killed. The col-lections were decimated by the Khmer Rouge and left in total disarray. From the beginning of 1979 it was possible to carry out the most urgent repairs to the building and to rearrange the exhibits.

The museum was reopened on 13th April 1979, and despite still being in a poor state, it offers a good overview of Khmer scultpure and bronzes. In the temples of Angkor itself no statues are to be found.

Architecture, bas-reliefs, and the dec-oration of buildings are described in the chapter on the Art of Cambodia, p.54.

Further collections can be seen in the National Museum in Bangkok and in the Musée Guimet in Paris.

Tour of the museum: in the main building to the right and left of the ent-rance small objects, especially bronzes, are on display. **The statue collection**: The development of stone carving and the gradual emergence of three-dimen-sional sculpture, which began around the 6th century, can be easily traced through the well-chosen exhibits. The classifica-tion and description of the various styles was the work of French scholars.

These styles overlapped chronologi-cally, and can only be distinguished from one another by very minor details.

THE DEVELOPMENT OF FIGURATIVE ART IN THE NATIONAL MUSEUM

Style of Phnom Da 514-539

During the reign of King Rudravarman, the Fu Nan artists were already on the way to surpassing their Indian mentors, who had never created any Hindu sculpture in three dimensions.

In the 6th century the long road toward the creation of freestanding sculpture first began, with the detaching of the larger-than-lifesize sandstone statues from their stone backdrops and setting them in arched, and later pillared, niches. The careful modelling of the inward-facing parts of these figures shows clearly what was ultimately intended. The task of including all the accoutrements indispensable to the iconography of the work presented the artist with the additional problem of balance. The Hindu gods hold in their four or eight pairs of arms, outstretched to the sides, such symbols as a thunderbolt, a seashell, a discus or a lotus-blossom. The next step, if the iconography permitted it, was to support the lower pairs of arms on their weapons. The same supporting function, though hardly perceived as such, was sometimes served by the front of the loin-cloth, which acted as a third leg, since it hung down to the ground. The task of creating a freestanding figure was made easier, with statues of the Buddha, by his monastic robes falling down to the plinth.

The male statues are characterized by finely worked, round faces, with a gentle smile, hooked nose, and eyebrows which are drawn together to express strength and determination; no female statues were found on Phnom Da. The deity most frequently represented is Vishnu, who is recognizable by his conical crown, while the towering hair-arrangement of the god Shiva is formed by several plaits coiled up on the head.

Changes in hairstyle, but also a finer and more richly worked *sampot,* or loincloth, make the chronological classification of sculptures easier in subsequent periods. The early statues are presented without adornment. For ceremonies and festivals they were hung with expensive jewelry made of gold, precious stones and pearls from the temple treasuries.

A group of statues dating from between 540 and 600 AD, and attributed to King Bhavavarman I, are less carefully worked.

The early Buddhas are shown standing, the later ones seated. They exhibit the same sort of variations in artistic quality. Their faces resemble those of Hindu deities, and the hairstyle is composed of tightly rolled curls lying close to the head.

Style of Sambor Prei Kuk 600-650

In this period, female statues as well as male, are now found. The Hindu goddess Uma belongs to the northern group of the Sambor Prei Kuk, and a statue of Lakshmi comes from the Koh Kuk temple at Kratie on the Mekong. The voluptuous bodies of both are reminiscent of Indian female figures. Their skirts are held up by a belt and appear transparent. A straight pleat runs down from the waist to the gathered hem. The statue of Hari-Hara (one of the incarnations of Vishnu-Shiva), leaning against an arch, differs from the statues of Phnom Da in the well-modelled muscles of the body, a narrower face and more expressive features.

Style of Prei Kmeng 635-700

We now see major changes in the female figures, which have departed from the voluptuous Indian model and towards the delicate physical type of the Khmer womenfolk. A good example of this is the statue of Lakshmi from the Prasat Thleang.

Statues of Shiva, Vishnu and Hari-Hara have also been found in this style. But something new were the statues of the Hindu god Brahma, such as the Brahma of Sambor. From Ak Yum (Angkor) come the small bronze Buddhas and Bodhisattvas, which occur more often with the advent of Mahayana Buddhism.

The arch still remains to provide support for the figures, but the coiffure is stylized and simplified. The round faces are full of expression. The horizontal line of the heavily emphasized eyebrows is noticeable in the bronzes, something which is later also to be found on stone sculptures. New, too, are the simple thigh-length loincloths, fastened at the side with a clasp.

Style of Praset Andet 657-681

This is represented almost exclusively by sculptures of Hindu figures, in which a further step towards sculpture in the round is evident. Many statues still have an arch surrounding them as a support, others are supported by a stone plinth from which the feet have been carved.

The male bodies are less emphasized, only the shoulders seem broader. The men's heads are crowned with a mitre, which sits far down on the forehead and finishes above the tips of the ears. The faces are narrower and have moustaches. Short loincloths, *sampots,* such as the peasants still wear today, are drawn through between the legs. A bolder gathering of the material produces a bag-like fold on the left thigh, which is adopted by later styles in a modified form.

Female statues have narrower waists, full breasts and round, vacant faces. Their wide skirts have a vertical pleat at the front, diagonal folds over the thighs and, like the men, a bag or pouch below the waist. Sometimes the folds are merely hinted at by the carving.The jewelry is now carved into the stone.

The Hari-Hara of Prasat Andet is considered by many authorities to be the most beautiful sculpture in Khmer art or indeed in the whole of Indianized Asian art. It radiates harmony and beauty, and the depiction of the body's musculature, which is often rather carelessly done in statues of this style, here appears perfect.

Style of Kompong Preah 706-800

This is only represented by a few sculptures. In this style statues of Shiva were frequently replaced by depictions of the *lingam*. Now and again pillars replace the supporting arch.

The faces of the men are once again round, and as devoid of expression as those of the female figures, which have lost their freshness and their smile. The stylized arrangements of the hair are adorned with uniform cylindrical headgear. The pouches remain at the thighs, but the folds in the clothing are again just hinted at by roughly carved grooves. The art has become soulless and effete.

Style of Kulen 802-875

This ushers in a new beginning. The Khmer empire at this time stood as a symbol of the divine kingdom, and its kings moved from the mountains to the plains of Angkor.

There are no known female figures extant. The male statues are once again invested with energy. Initially they were still supported, like the Rup Arak Vishnu, on their weapons, then later the completely freestanding statue was achieved. Broad, very masculine faces were defined by the powerful, horizontal line of the eyebrows which are drawn together in a frown, and the faces still have moustaches. The hair reaches to the temples and covered with a mitre. Towards the end of this period the crown-like headgear makes its appearance and from now on becomes a feature of Angkorian sculpture. There is little change to the clothing, but the short *sampots* now have an overhang at the front.

Style of Preah Ko 875-895

This comes at the end of the period of development which began at Phnom Da and continued through the Che La culture. However, it is also the first of seven styles, from which the style of Angkor Wat, the classical period of the Khmer, later evolved.

The free-standing sculpture indicates bodily movement for the first time, by a slight tilt of the hips. Only the plump, sturdy legs still recall the earlier supporting pillars. The *garuda-naga* motif of Indian mythology, the pursuit of the snake by the mythical bird-man *garuda*, offers an opportunity to portray animals in motion.

The attempt to carry this feeling of motion over to the human body did not always succeed. One suc-

cessful example is a group comprising the god Indra with his two wives, in a small temple of the Bakong complex in Roluos. The innovation here is the representation of people in groups. It is presumably influenced by the emergence of sculpted reliefs in the same period. The things which the artists of the Preah Koh tried out, were later taken up again in the Koh Ker style.

The male statues look rather stocky but there is little that is novel about them. In addition to a moustache they now additionally wear long side-whiskers. The loincloth is smooth, but still has the pouch made from folds, and an overhang at the front. The women's clothing is richly adorned. Part of the dress is pleated and drops from the belt. Another part is coiled round the belt with its end on the left thigh. The depictions of the bodies are more voluptuous. The statues wear crown-like diadems.

Style of Bakheng 893-925

Here, the suggestion of movement is no longer present, and only reappears in the Koh Ker style. The statues are now presented from a strictly frontal viewpoint. The male figures are once again slimmer, the faces appear more severe, thanks to the accentuated horizontal line of the eyebrows. The loincloth has folds in it, some of which form a pouch, and the overhang in front is doubled. The women's clothing is also pleated and the diadem rests on a coiffure that is piled high on the head.

Style of Koh Ker 921-944

The statues of gods are very similar to those of the Bakheng. Their hair reaches the temples, the side-whiskers, moustache, and the straight line of the eyebrows remain unchanged. The dress of the male figures has a more stylized appearance and also has the double fall of material and the pouch on the left thigh. The figures are richly adorned with jewelry carved in the stone.

Something completely new and unique in Khmer art are the Koh Ker's groups of gigantic figures, human and animal, which have the common feature of being captured in lively movement. Good and evil demigods, called *yakshas*, act as guardians and make threatening gestures. Wrestlers, playfully squabbling monkeys, and the *garuda-naga* motif seem to have been chosen as subjects by the artists so that they can be completely liberated from the conventional, frontal pose. Thus the traditional rules of aesthetics and iconography, applying to all oriental art, are broken. This seems only to have been possible when dealing with non-religious themes and subjects, for the figures of gods remain untouched by this experimentation. Only the *garuda-naga* motif was adopted in later Angkorian art. The others remain confined to the experiments of the Bakong (Preah Koh) and Koh Ker styles.

Style of Pre Rup 947-965

This style evolved after the return of the kings from the north. Sculpture did not undergo any significant change. The animals sculptures, particularly those of lions standing guard on the temple terraces, are stylized and immobile.

Style of Banteay Srei 965-1000

This has only come down to us in one small shrine built by a Brahman. It essentially stands alone, without any connection with the art of the Khmer kings, which was increasingly taking on monumental dimensions. The basic elements of this style lie in the architecture, in reliefs and the decoration of buildings, and have a tendency towards fullness and exuberance. The attraction and appeal of this sculpture lie in its smiling naturalness, particularly in the female figures. All the foregoing styles are reflected in Banteay Srei. Taken as a whole, this is something new in itself, yet it does not add any new elements to Khmer art.

A tympanum in the Banteay Srei style gives an impression of the art in relief form. The sculptures are small, suiting the modest dimensions of the temple. The hair, clothing and adornment are similar to earlier styles.

Style of Khleang 965-1020

Few changes in these areas were introduced in this style either, if one is to judge from the small number of sculptures that have been found. The clothing of the male figures is simplified, the overhang of the material has disappeared. The skirts of the women begin below the navel but are higher at the back, and are turned up at the front.

Style of Baphuon 1010-1080

Sculpture in the round reaches its zenith in this style and from now on will take second place to the bas-relief carving preferred by the Khmer sculptors. Harmony and completeness are the basic characteristics of the Baphuon style, which is comparable only with the style of Angkor Wat.

The free-standing sculptures radiate an uninhibited naturalness. The figures are slim and graceful, their faces are round, smiling and finely chiselled. The clothing of the male statues is simpler, finely pleated and elegant. The back of the loincloth now sits higher and the front leaves the navel bare. The clothing of the female figures is similarly carved, but they have an overhang at the front and a knotted belt.

Parts of a huge statue reminiscent of the Koh Ker style, were found in the Western Mebon temple at Angkor. The reclining bronze figure of Vishnu must have been about 13 ft (4m) long and cast in several sections. Only the head and a portion of the torso have been found. These show how the artist broke with convention by giving an impression of movement and expressiveness

Style of Angkor Wat 1100-1175

It is here that Khmer art reaches the summit of its perfection. Its highest achievements are in architecture, the ornamentaion of buildings and reliefs. Sculpture in the round is subordinated to these – perhaps the sculptors wished it so. In fact we only know of the sculpture from a relatively small number of examples. No statues have survived from the Main Temple of Angkor Wat. It must be remembered that the important deities, who were represented in bronze and precious metals, were often stolen by temple-robbers. However, we can see from the materials and inscriptions available to us, that the statues were carved in a formal and rigid frontal pose with faces almost devoid of expression.

The hair is drawn into a knot, called a *mukata*, at the neck, or tied into a *jata-mukata*, a double-knot, coiled on the head and adorned with a crown.

The *naga*-Buddha is frequently found among the many representations of Buddha. Its iconography relates to a legend according to which, when deep in meditation, he was borne through the surging waters by the King of the Snakes, who coiled himself around the Buddha and protected him with his outspread hood. The *naga*, which originated in early nature cults, appears frequently in Shivaism and Vishnuism. It also found its way into the Buddhist faith of Indianized Asia.

Style of Bayon 1177-1230

The Buddhist phase of Khmer art extended its iconography, with out abandoning Hindu motifs. The stone sculpture falls into line with the monumental style of Jayavarman VII, is the inspiration of enormous statues and finds expression in the towering human faces of the Bayon style, at the gate of Angkor Thom and other temples, as well as in the giant figures of deities and demons which stand before the gates of Angkor Thom.

Jayavarman VII. drove his building projects, especially the later ones, along at such a pace that the quality and detail of the workmanship inevitably suffered.

Among the most beautiful creations of this style is a Lokiteshvara from the Preah Khan Temple which probably represents the king's father. The blissful peace which emanates from its features is also to be seen in other works commissioned by Jayavarman VII. The predilection for depicting the *naga*-Buddha remains. Few of the great number of bronze statues have been preserved.

After Jayavarman VII, Khmer art had exhausted its inspiration. Even after the fall of Angkor, sculptures made from various materials were produced in other leading towns in Cambodia. They include some works worthy of attention, but even these bear no comparison with the great Khmer art of Angkor.

The Royal Palace
and the Silver Pagoda

One block further south on Saigon Boulevard, which runs parallel with but inland from the Tonle Sap, stands the Royal Palace. The present-day buildings were constructed earlier this century on the site of the Banteay Kev, a citadel built in 1813. The ground plan and style of the palace buildings, and of the temple area which is separated from them by a wall, are strongly influenced by the Royal Palace and the Royal Temple in Bangkok. The palace in Phnom Penh was taken over in 1970 by the rebels during General Lon Nol's coup d'état. During this time valuable objects were lost. Between 1975 and 1979, the Khmer Rouge era, the palace grounds were left to run wild and it became known as the "palace of the birds." The roofs were damaged, doors broken in and windows smashed. From

Above: The royal palace in Phnom Penh.

1979 onward the palace was open to the general public as a museum. Since Prince Sihanouk's return to Phnom Penh in November 1991 the palace has once again been closed. Its most important buildings are: the **Chan Chhaya Pavilion,** which was built in 1913 by King Norodom in the style of an earlier wooden structure. It serves as a venue for musical and dance performances on special occasions and was used by the king and head of state as a platform for speeches on days of national remembrance. The pavilion overlooks the main entrance to the palace grounds and can be seen from Saigon Boulevard.

The **Throne Hall of Prasat Tevea Vinichhay**, in the center of the palace site is about 330 ft long and 100 ft wide (100 m by 30 m). It was built in 1913-1917 under King Sisowath by the Khmer architect Oknha Tep Nimit Mak, and replaced a wooden palace dating from 1869. Its *prasat,* or tower, is 190 ft (57 m) high, and it was used for the coronation of the kings and now for official

receptions and traditional ceremonies. In the center of the hall stands the golden throne, a symbol of the monarchy. With seats for the king and his queen, it is surmounted by a seven-tiered canopy. At the sides of the hall are seats for the court officials. Many objects of value were destroyed by the Khmer Rouge, but murals on the walls and ceiling, depicting the epic of Ramayana, have survived. In processions, the monarchs rode in the **boskot**, a carved and gilded wooden chariot, which is on display. It is shaped like a ship resting on a dragon.

Samran Phirum, "sound sleep," is the name given to a smaller building to the north of the throne hall, where the traditional musical instruments were kept. It was later also used by the king and queen for mounting their elephants. The elephants' stables were also within the palace precincts.

Above: To learn Cambodian dancing, you have to start young. Right: A mural in the gallery of the Silver Pagoda.

The extensive **Khemarin** palace itself was built in 1930 as the king's residence.

The **Sahametrei**, or Officers Club, is a pavilion built in 1958 for the officers of the royal guard. After the death of King Suramarit, his wife, Queen Kossomak, mother of Prince Sihanouk, left the Khemarin palace and used the Sahametrei as her residence.

The Buddhist temple of **Vihear Suor** was built by the royal family in 1930. Its name derives from a statue of Buddha, which King Monivong brought to Phnom Penh from Vihear Suor in the province of Kandal.

The **Phochani Hall**, dating from 1913, is used as for royal audiences and for performances by the royal ballet.

The **Napoleon Palace** or **Iron Palace** was presented to King Norodom by the Emperor Napoleon III in 1869, and is built in the French style.

The **Royal Offices,** dating from 1948, stand to the rear of the Napoleon Palace and were also used as a residence by the Regent.

The **Vihear Preah Keo Morakot,** commonly known as the **Silver Pagoda,** stands in its own walled grounds beyond the southern wall of the palace, and separated from the palace by a narrow walkway. (The entrance is by the north gate, situated on this path). On the left near the entrance is a library (*mondap*), which once contained priceless manuscripts on palm leaves. The stupa which stands behind it was built by King Norodom (1859-1904), the first king of the Norodom dynasty, to which Prince Norodom Sihanouk aslo belongs. Next to it there is an equestrian statue of the king. On the right, in the corner, is a bell tower built on a high plinth. In a covered gallery right round the inside walls there are huge murals, painted around the turn of the century, which have been restored by experts from the Polish State Heritage Department. The depiction of the Indian Ramayana epic begins at the east gate and runs in a clockwise direction. Next to this entrance stands the stupa of King Ang Douong (c.1841-1859), and beyond

it, near the south wall, a small temple built over a footprint of Buddha. Another of Buddha's footprints, in bronze, from Sri Lanka, is housed in the **Phnom Mondap,** a round stupa built on a small artificial hill, named Kailasa Parvata after the sacred mountain in the Himalayas. There are two other stupas, built by the Norodom family, and a pavilion used for religious ceremonies.

The **Silver Pagoda**, or **Vihear Preah Keo**, was built in 1962 to replace a wooden temple dating from 1900. It owes its name to the 5,000 tiles, each made from 2 lbs (1 kg) of silver, which cover the floor of the *vihear* or *vihara*, the room containing the image of Buddha. (Shoes and cameras must be left at the entrance, reached by a staircase of Italian marble.) The interior furnishings were plundered by the Khmer Rouge, but they left some statues of Buddha made from precious metals, a collection of valuable dance-masks, ritual artefacts and items from the royal collection, which are exhibited in glass cases.

The most valuable statue, to the right of the altar, is a life-size Buddha made of solid gold and weighing 165 lbs (75 kg). It is inlaid with 9,584 precious stones, including diamonds as large as 25 carat. It was created in 1907 in the royal workshops. Its companion pieces on the left are a silver Buddha and a bronze one weighing 176 lbs (80 kg). The small stupa made of gold and silver in front of the golden Buddha contains a relic from Sri Lanka.

On the altar is enthroned a replica of the Preah Keo (Emerald Buddha) from the royal pagoda in Bangkok. Preah Keo played an important role in Laotian and Siamese history, and so King Norodom had this replica made from crystal.

The marble Buddha behind the altar was a gift from Myanmar (Burma). Beside it is a litter used for coronations, in which the king was carried by twelve men.

Above: National Museum in Phnom Penh.
Right: The Wat Botum Vadel.

Towards the back of the *vihear* are displayed the coronation apparel, and further gold and silver works including two gold Buddhas, weighing 10 lbs and 3 1/2 lbs (4.5 kg and 1.5 kg) and inlaid with precious stones.

The Silver Pagoda has been undergoing restoration since the beginning of 1993 and it is not known when it will be open to the public again.

The **Wat Botum Vadei** is situated south of the Vihear Preah Keo. The *vihear* is surrounded by a garden of remembrance for the royal family, whose ashes are interred in the small memorial stupas.

The **Academy of Art** (Ecole des Beaux-Arts) was set up by the French at the same time as the National Musuem, and is situated just behind the museum. Its reconstruction was completed, with modest success, about ten years ago. Adjoining it is an exhibition of works which are for sale. The Department of Music and Dance is located in the north of the city, near the Boeng Kak lake.

The Wat Phnom Penh

The Wat Phnom Penh, visible from far around, is situated on a tree-covered hill approximately 100 ft (30 m) high, in the northeast of the city, not far from the bank of the Tonle Sap, where Tou Samuth Boulevard and 47th Street are joined by a number of sidestreets. It is surrounded by an extensive park. A flight of steps which are guarded by stylized lions and flanked by a *naga*-(serpent) balustrade leads from the east side to the *vihara*. The reliefs on the stairway come from Angkor.

The city's oldest shrine looked neglected up until a few years ago, but since Buddhism has once again been declared the state religion the faithful bring flowers and incense here. Many people again come here to pray for protection on a journey, success in examinations and healing from sickness; and they bring offerings in gratitude for the answering of their prayers. Another temple that has been renovated and is now visited by many people, is the one dedicated to the earth spirits, who are the guardians of the city. It is supposed to bring luck if one feeds the monkeys which romp about in the trees, or if one buys the freedom of the birds shut up in little cages, though they are quickly captured again afterwards. Even the draw for the state lottery occurs in this place of good fortune, every Thursday at 10 o'clock.

The ashes of the first king of the post-Angkorian period, Ponhea Yat, who made Phnom Penh his capital, are said to lie in the stupa which stands close to the *vihear*. On the way to the stupa is a pavilion containing a statue of Don Penh, the founder of the shrine.

Chinese and Vietnamese residents have erected a small temple to Thien Hau Tanh Mau, the Daoist goddess of the sea and the guardian goddess of fishermen, whom they worship. She is flanked by her two helpers – Thien Ly Than, who

can see for a thousand miles, and Thuan Phong Nhi, who can hear from a thousand miles away – and they tell her if a ship is in distress.

There are elephants on which visitors can ride around the hill, except in the midday sun. These come from the **zoo** at the foot of Phnom Penh.

In the **Main Post Office** on 98th Steet, with its entrance on 13th Street, collectors can purchase specially issued stamps – at collectors' prices.

Monasteries and mosques

Phnom Penh was once rich in Buddhist monasteries. Many were destroyed between 1975 and 1979 and are being rebuilt in a modern idiom. The Cham and Malay minorities possessed several mosques which were similarly damaged or detroyed by the Khmer Rouge. The largest of these was the An-Nur Mosque, built in 1901. Beside the new building erected in 1981 in Chraing Chamres, 3 3/4 miles (6 km) from the city center, is a

Koranic school, known as the Medrese, from the Arabic word *madrassa*. In the larger communities along the Mekong and the Tonle Sap, in which the Cham and Malayans live, Friday prayers are still held in small prayer houses, and the children are taught in makeshift Koranic schools.

Wat Ounnalom, the monastery situated on a large open square on Lenin Boulevard, was founded in 1443. More than forty buildings were attached to the Wat, all of which were damaged or destoyed by the Khmer Rouge, including the irreplaceable Buddhist library. The *vihara* and a few monastic buildings were restored and are today occupied by about forty monks – before 1975 there were more than 500.

The leader of the Cambodian Buddhists of the Mahanikai sect resides here.

Above: Photographs of victims of the Khmer Rouge in the Tuol Sleng Museum. Right: Wat Ounnalom, seat of the religious leader of the Cambodian Mahanikai Buddhists.

On the ground floor of the three-storey building a marble Buddha from Myanmar has been preserved; it was smashed by the Khmer Rouge and pieced together again after 1979. On the second floor, too, the memory of Pol Pot's reign of terror lives on. The statue of Samdech Huot Tat, the revered fourth patriarch of Cambodian Buddhists, which was made in celebration of his eightieth birthday in 1971, stands beside the alter. Huot Tat was murdered by the Khmer Rouge and his statue thrown into the river, but it was found again in 1979. A few books which were also saved, are on display and are intended to form the nucleus of a new Buddhist library. The statue of a patriarch of the Thammayuth sect was also saved. On the third floor there is a Buddha, which was robbed of its silver mounting by the Khmer Rouge. The *Jakatas* on the walls, stories from the Buddha's previous lives, date from 1952, and the stupa in the garden behind the *vihara* is said to contain a relic of the Buddha. There is a school in the monastery grounds.

Wat Lang Ka, on Sivutha Boulevard, was similarly rebuilt in a contemporary style after 1979.

Wat Koh, on Achar Mean Boulevard, is said to date from the mid-15th century. Work has started on its restoration. Nearby is an obelisk in memory of the victims of the Khmer Rouge.

Wat Moha Montrei, the Monastery of the Great Minister, is situated near the Sports Center on Sivutha Boulevard. The building was sponsored by one of the ministers of King Monivong. Its concrete tower, 115 ft (35 m) high, was completed in 1970. During the Pol Pot regime the monastery was used as a grain store and that is why it was not destroyed. The wall-paintings and statues in the *vihara* are of more recent date. A school is run by the monastery.

Other sights of interest

Visits to places dedicated to the memory of the victims of the murderous Pol Pot regime are not, of course, obligatory for foreign tourists, but they do help one to understand the unforgettable horrors of the years from 1975 to the beginning of 1979, and the fear that one day the Khmer Rouge may return.

The Tuol Sleng Museum is located in a densely populated part of the city, to the west of Achar Mean Boulevard on 350th Street, with its entrance in the narrow 113rd Street. In 1975 the Tuol Sleng High School was taken over by the Khmer Rouge and turned into a prison for the state security service, known as S-21. It was surrounded by a high fence and the houses facing it were evacuated. The methods of torture, extraction of confessions and killing are reminiscent of the worst excesses of the German Gestapo. The prisoners – men, women and children, and foreigners among them – were stripped of their possessions, (some of these have been found and are on display), then registered and photographed

with a number branded on their chest. Many of the photographs on display testify to the terror and suffering of the victims. Prison cells and the apparatus of torture have been preserved. From lists of prisoners that have been found for the year 1977, it is known that up to 100 people a day were brought into S-21. In the last stage of the terror, torturers from the ranks of the Khmer Rouge were themselves put to death.

When the Vietnamese army arrived in 1979 there were only seven people left to be liberated. Fourteen others had been tortured to death at the last minute and are buried in the school yard.

The notorious extermination camp of **Choeng Ek** is situated on a continuation of Pokambor Boulevard, about 9 miles (15 km) southwest of the city. It became known to the world as *The Killing Fields*, through the American film of that name. At least 17,000 people, men, women and children, many of whom had first passed through the Tuol Sleng prison, were beaten to death with cudgels and rifle

butts. The Khmer Rouge needed to economize on ammunition. The dead were thrown into 129 mass graves, of which 43 have since been opened. The bones, divided into skulls, arm- and leg-bones, were until 1988 put in simple wooden sheds between the open pits and the still unopened graves. These simple memorials had a greater impact than the glass tower which stands there today as a kind of stupa containing the bones. On 9th May, known as the Day of Genocide, commemorative ceremonies are held every year at Choeng Ek.

The **Independence Monument**, erected in 1958, later became a memorial to Cambodian soldiers, and wreath-laying ceremonies are held here. It towers over the intersection of Tou Samuth and Sivutha Boulevards, like a Cambodian version of the Arc de Triomphe in Paris.

Above: The Chruoy Changvar Bridge was destroyed in 1975. Right: The Market Hall in the heart of the Old Town.

The Chruoy Changvar Bridge over the Tonle Sap was blown up by the Khmer Rouge in 1975, at the city end. Provided the elections turn out favorably, the Japanese propose to repair the bridge, which has also become famous through *The Killing Fields*. Enterprising owners of food and drink stalls exploit the fondness of many young Cambodians for an evening stroll down to the ruined bridge.

The National Library on 92nd Street was built in 1924 and used by the Khmer Rouge as stables. Some of the books, which had been hurled into the street in a mindless orgy of destruction, were gathered up and later returned, thus providing the basis of a new library in 1979.

The Cham Kar Mon Palace on Tou Samuth Boulevard, once the temporary residence of Prince Sihanouk, is used today as a government guest house.

Markets and market halls are to be found in every part of the city. A visit to one of these gives a wonderful opportunity to become acquainted with the produce of the country – vegetables, fruit,

and spices – and also to purchase textiles, examples of local craftsmanship and folk-art, antiques, and gold and silver jewelry. Many goods are imported, or more often smuggled, from Thailand and are considerably cheaper here than in the country of origin. Markets also offer the best oppprtunity to sample Cambodian food, which in restaurants – if indeed it is offered at all – tends to taste no different to Chinese cuisine. The best places for shopping are these:

The **Central Market Hall,** also called the Great Market, is in the center of the old town. It boasts the fifth largest dome in the world. Four halls lead off the central circular area, to the northeast, northwest, southeast and southwest. Countless stalls offer fabrics, textiles, jewelry (priced according to the weight of its gold or silver content), books, stationery and so forth. Round the market hall are flower and food stalls, shops and a wide choice of restaurants.

The **Toul Tom Pong Market** in the south of the city is a veritable treasure-trove for antiques, statues of the Buddha, temple bells, silver vessels and much else. To make a sensible purchase here you only need to be aware that by no means everything is antique. You can also buy textiles, books, jewelry, cosmetics, luggage, shoes, and food from the many stalls.

The country round Phnom Penh

Boat trips on the Tonle Sap and the Mekong take you to the fishing villages on the opposite bank of the Tonle Sap and to silk-weaving villages on the Mekong. The harbor is also used by ocean-going vessels.

The **beach at Koki** is the most popular destination for weekends and Sunday outings. About 7 1/2 miles (12 km) beyond the Monivong Bridge, on the National Highway 1 to Saigon, a road turns off towards Koki. In this watery world of rivers and lakes, holidaymakers from Phnom Penh can rent a house built on piles at the water's edge.

TOURING IN CAMBODIA

South and southwestwards from Phnom Penh

Before the wars in Indochina, the beautiful, hilly landscape between Phnom Penh and the Gulf of Siam was much visited for its mountain spas and seaside resorts, which had grown up during the colonial period. Most of these were destroyed by the Khmer Rouge and are only now gradually coming back into use again. On the way there are several sites of archaeological interest.

From Phnom Penh three National Highways, numbered 2, 3 and 4, and all in poor condition in places, lead southward towards the beautiful coast of the Gulf of Siam, with its many cliffs and offshore islands. It is best to visit the coast in the winter months because during the summer it is swept by the southwest monsoon.

Kompong Som (or **Saom**), was built as a port in the early 1960s when it was called **Sihanoukville**. With the return to political normality, it is to revert to its original name. It lies at the end of the 140-mile-long (230 km) National Highway 4, which was built at the same time as the port. There is also a railway line linking it with the capital. A branch of Highway 4 leads to the port of Phsar Ream, further to the east, which was eclipsed by the larger Sihanoukville.

From Highway 4, about 28 miles (46 km) before reaching Kompong Som, a road, currently in poor condition, branches off to the east and takes you through a charming coastal landscape with views of the sea, as far as the idyllic fishing port of **Kampot** at the mouth of the Preak Thom River. (Kompong Som – Kampot: 60 miles / 100 km). The extensive pepper plantations were laid out by the Chinese. The region is also known for durian fruit. The fishermen of Kampot are for the most part Vietnamese or Cham.

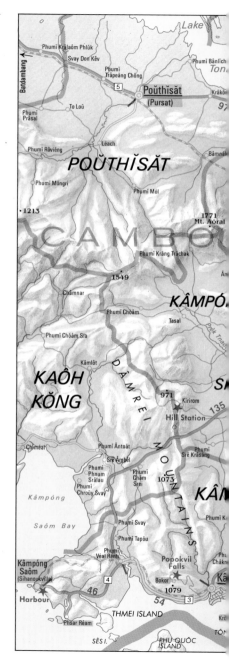

SOUTHERN CAMBODIA

0   25   50km

93

Highway 3 also terminates in Kampot, but it is in a very poor state (Phnom Penh – Kampot 92 miles / 148 km). It runs almost parallel with Highway 2 and is connected to it by several sideroads.

Krong Keb, 107 miles (172 km) from Phnom Penh, was founded at the beginning of the present century. It lies on the sea, southeast of Kampot, and during the colonial era was a favorite bathing resort with its beach shaded by palm trees. However, it was destroyed by the Khmer Rouge. There are many islands off the coast, of which **Koh Tonsay** is particularly well known.

The **mountain village of Bokor**, 116 miles (187 km) from Phnom Penh, lies at a height of 3,500 ft (1080m) in the coastal mountains, 25 miles (41 km) from Kampot. It can only be reached by a rough and twisting road.

Bokor was once a favorite holiday resort, but since 1975 it has been forgotten. It was known for its mild climate, for the **Popokvil Waterfalls**, and for the wide panorama over the Gulf of Siam.

Ta Khmau, Tonle Bati, Phnom Chissor and **Phnom Da** can be reached by National Highway 2, which runs from Phnom Penh to Takeo (Takev). It continues into the Mekong Delta as far as Vietnam. Tourists are not allowed to cross the border.

Phnom Khmau lies about 2 1/2 miles (4 km) from Ta Khmau on Highway 2. On the 330-ft-high (100 m) hill are the remains of a temple, **Prasat Nankhman** (Bakheng style, 898-925 AD). The site can be reached either by way of a steep flight of steps or by an easier but longer path. The view from the top alone makes it worth the effort.

The **Ta Prohm Temple** at **Tonle Bati**, in Takeo province is only 19 miles (30 km) south of Phnom Penh, on a by-road which leads off Highway 2, to the right.

Right: A colonial-style house in the little port of Kampot.

Near the temple area, which also includes the Yeah Pean Temple and a Buddhist monastery, a peninsula runs out into the river Bati. This is a favorite spot for excursions for families who come from Phnom Penh with their picnic baskets, and with their bicycles and motorbikes piled high with their belongings.

There was a shrine on this site as early as the 6th century, but the construction of the Ta Prohm temple is usually attributed to King Jayavarman VII, who ruled in Angkor from 1181. But whether he or someone else was its architect remains to be proved. The temple was renovated and altered several times, and so does not have an integral appearance. Its oldest parts probably date from the 10th and 11th centuries; and its most recent modification may have taken place in the 17th century. A stele from the 16th century has survived. The large rectangular grounds were designed as a Hindu shrine. It is surrounded by a substantial wall, and the gates at either side have large porticos. The main entrance faces east. The central shrine is surrounded by courtyards and consists of a portico and two main temples which are linked together by passageways. A further passage leads to the western gate. To the right and left of the east gate are the so-called libraries. The reliefs repay close inspection, since some of them represent graphic scenes from everyday life. The Khmer Rouge, alas, did their worst here too.

A legend has grown up around the Ta Prohm temple and the small Temple of Yeah Pean, which stands about 100 yards away from it, and contains a statue of Buddha and one of Yeah Pean, the fishergirl. A king of Angkor is said to have fallen in love with the beautiful Yeah Pean, the daughter of a fisherman. When he left her he gave her a ring with instructions that she should send the child she bore him, whether a son or a daughter, to Angkor with the ring. The lovely Yeah Pean obeyed the wish of the king. When her

son, whom she had named Prohm, presented the ring in Angkor, he was given a welcome and an education in his father's palace. Later the king sent him back to the province of Takeo as governor. Prohm administered the province well and built a temple like those he had seen in Angkor, which was named Ta Prohm after him. For his mother he erected the little Yeah Pean temple.

The **monastery of Tonle Bati**, next to the Yeah Pean temple, damaged by the Khmer Rouge, has since been restored

Phnom Chissor lies about 38 miles (62 km) from Phnom Penh, 13 miles (21 km) south of Tonle Bati and a short distance to the left of Highway 2. Two temples and a water cistern are to be found at the foot of the hill. On the eastern side steps lead up to the hill shrine, which is sited in line with the temples in the valley and has a gallery all round it. The building dates from the Angkorian period (11th century) and is reminiscent of the Khmer temple of Wat Phu in southern Laos. Laterite and brick were

used in its construction and the lintels of the windows are of sandstone. The temple has been altered several times and the original Hindu shrine was subsequently converted into a Buddhist monastery from which a few statues of Buddha have been preserved.

Phnom Da is situated 12 miles (20 km) east of Highway 2 and the provincial capital of Takeo. The modern village of Angkor Borei is thought to have been the site of Vyadhapura, the last capital of the kingdom of Fu Nan. The statues which were discovered by French archaeologists in the caves at Phnom Da can be seen in the National Museum in Phnom Penh. The Phnom Da style is the first recognized stage of pre-Angkorian art. A small building constructed of heavy basalt blocks stands on the hill. This is **Ta Keo** or **Asrama Maha Rosei**, the Retreat of the Great Ascetic. The influences of the Indian Palava style can be seen here, but its chronology is disputed.

Takeo (Takev), capital of the province of the same name, is on Highway 2, 47

miles (76 km) from Phnom Penh. The town lies to the south of Lake Takeo and has little to offer the visitor. Its pagodas were destroyed by the Khmer Rouge. South of Takeo lies Phnom Bayang.

From Phnom Penh to Saigon

Highway 1 links Phnom Penh with Ho Chi Minh City (formerly Saigon) in Vietnam, a distance of 148 miles (238 km). It can be used by tourists with Cambodian and Vietnamese visas, in which entry is recorded. The driving time by private car or minibus is at least 6 hours on a generally good road, but one also has to cross the Mekong by ferry at Phumi Banam and this can involve a lengthy wait. However, there is the compensation of the colorful comings and goings on the river.

The Mekong delta is sparsely populated on the Cambodian side, and the un-

Above: In the Ta Phrom temple (Tonle Bati).
Right: Sunrise at the confluence of Mekong and Tonle Sap in Phnom Penh.

cultivated land is punctuated only by the occasional rice field. Tall, slender sugar palms (from which betelnut is obtained) rise up from this flat landscape. Over the border in Vietnam no sugar palms are grown. In the densely populated Vietnamese part of the delta every inch of land is devoted to growing rice and vegetables.

The largest Cambodian town on this route is **Svay Rieng**, capital of the province so named. The distance to the frontier at Moc Bai is 117 miles (188 km)

The northeast

The Chen La came from the mountainous north and it was not until about AD 800 that they moved down to the plain. At the moment it is not possible to visit the north and northeast regions, nor is there any information available about the state of archaeological sites and temples known to be there.

Highway 5 on the west bank of the Tonle Sap is being improved. Highway 6 branches off to the northeast 3 miles (5 km) before Oudong. In Prek Kdam, 20 miles (32 km) from Phnom Penh, the river is crossed by a ferry. At Skon (Skun), Highway 6 swings in a wide arc towards the northwest.

Highway 7, which runs up into the northeast of the country, starts at Skon and goes east via Kompong Cham towards the Vietnamese border. The road forks at Phumi Krek; one branch leads southeastwards to Tay Ninh in Vietnam, but tourists are not allowed to cross the frontier.

Before the war, Highways 6 and 7 provided the quickest route between Angkor Wat and Saigon, avoiding Phnom Penh. Today the roads and bridges have been destroyed and even the most basic tourist facilities are lacking; most importantly, the safety of tourists is not guaranteed.

Air trips to Stung Treng and boat trips on the Mekong to Kratie (Kracheh) will be possible long before road journeys are feasible again.

Oudong (**Udong**), 24 miles (38 km) north of Phnom Penh, can be reached in a half-day excursion via Highway 5 along the Tonle Sap. The road and bridges were damaged but are being repaired.

Most of the fishing villages along the Tonle Sap are Cham settlements. The Khmer Rouge killed many members of the Muslim minority and their mosques and medresas (Koranic schools) were destroyed, but after 1979 simple prayer-rooms and schools were opened again.

King An Chan (early to mid-16th century) was the most powerful ruler after the fall of Angkor. He governed from Lovek, but had stupas and temples built in Oudong as well. In the mid-17th century Oudong was the seat of the Cambodian kings, who did not move their capital finally to Chattamutuk (Phnom Penh) until 1866.

The Khmer Rouge occupied Oudong and Lon Nol bombed their hideouts, with the result that almost all the buildings of

the former royal city were flattened. It lay between two parallel mountain chains running from the northwest to the southeast along the Mekong. Walking over these mountains gives one many beautiful views of the river landscape, but sadly the ruins that remain give scarcely any idea of the city's former splendor.

At the foot of the hill is a pagoda that is much visited at weekends. There is a flight of some 240 steps climbing the hill from the south. A legend about the Chinese temple on the hill tells that in the pagoda on the south slope, some monks had reared an *a mao*, a black dog, and after its death they buried it on the hill. Many years later the Emperor of China began to suffer from incurable headaches. When his doctors were unable to help, he consulted magicians who discovered that in a previous life he had been an *a mao*, and that it was buried in the middle of a hill in Cambodia. It seemed that tree roots were growing down into the grave and causing him the pain. He would have to remove the roots from the grave. The emperor believed the magicians and sent a delegation to Oudong.

Sure enough, when the roots had been removed, he recovered. He had a temple erected in Buddha's honor on the site of the grave. But the Cambodians believe that the Chinese knew that the grave of the *a mao* lay at the entrance to a dragon's cave and that the dragon gave its power to the kings of Cambodia. In building the temple they sealed up the dragon's lair and broke the power of the Kings of the South.

The Cambodians like to carry their legends into the present, and they are convinced that General Lon Nol, who had abolished the monarchy, ordered the bombing so as to slay the dragon and thus prevent the return of the kings. The bombardments have left only a few pillars of the temple standing

In 1992 the government in Phnom Penh resolved to restore the stupas in which the ashes of some of the kings were interred. The Ta San mosque, which had been destroyed, is also going to be rebuilt.

The remains of a shattered and mutilated Buddha and the ruins of the Preah Vihear Chaul Nipean offer a depressing spectacle. All that is left of the Temple of Preah Ath Roes, built in 1911, and its 30 ft (9 m) high Buddha, are broken fragments and the ruins of walls and pillars.

Along the way a few small and somewhat better preserved temples like the Preah Ko, the Temple of the Sacred Cow, and the Preah Keo, the Temple of the Emerald Buddha, are a reminder of the Hindu-Buddhist period. Three stupas have survived, in which the ashes of the king were interred.

There was a prison at the foot of the hill, and a memorial to the victims of the

Khmer Rouge was erected there in 1982, in which torture apparatus and bones from the mass graves are on display, and drawings on the walls are a reminder of the hideous deeds of the Khmer Rouge.

Qudong is a favorite place for locals to go for picnics at weekends.

Lovek, the seat of the kings of Cambodia from the end of the Angkor empire until the mid-17th century, was destroyed by the Siamese. No ruins worth visiting have survived.

National Highway 7 to Kratie and Stung Treng

Kompong Cham, capital of the province of the same name, lies on the west bank of the Mekong and is known as a green and pleasant town.

Rubber is grown in the rich, red earth of this province.The plantations were laid out during the colonial era, but the trees had become too old after the wars and yields declined. From 1979 onward, aid from Bulgaria and the former USSR helped to increase production again.

The hills of **Phnom Tet Srei** (660 ft/ 200 m) and **Phnom Bos**, lie 22 miles (35 km) northwest of the town, close to Highway 21, which links Kompong Cham with Kompong Thom. At the foot of Phnom Bos there are mass graves of people slaughtered by the Khmer Rouge. They repeatedly attacked Kompong Cham because of the Vietnamese minority among its plantation workers.

At the end of the 8th century Banteay Prei Nokor, or **Indrapura**, to the east of Kompong Cham, became the first capital of King Jayavarman II, who in 802 established divine kingship at Phnom Kulen, and is considered to have been the founder of the empire of Angkor.

Wat Nokor, a monastery of Mahayana Buddhism dating from the 9th century, lies 1 1/2 miles (2 km) from the town. It was taken over and restored by the Theravada sect in the 16th century.

Right: Transport ancient and modern on the National Highway near Siem Reap.

A ferry crosses the Mekong to Phumi Tonle Bet, from where Highway 7 traces a wide curve through the red-earth region to Kratie (Kracheh).

Kratie (Kracheh) lies on the east bank of the Mekong, 214 miles (345 km) from Phnom Penh, and in the mid-1960s had a population of 15,000. The Mekong is navigable all year round as far up as Kratie. Roads lead out from here into the Mondulkiri highlands.

In the 8th century the empire of Chen La broke up into two states. Chen La of the Land, which the Chinese called Wen Tan, had its capital at Sambhupura (Sambor), near Kratie, with its Koh Kuk Krieng temple (style of Sambor Prei Kuk). In 722 and 750 AD Chinese annals report that delegations brought tribute from this state to the Chinese imperial court. An inscription was found in the ruins of Preah Theat Kvan Pir in Kratie province, which gives the earliest indication of the deification of a ruler.

Not far from Kratie is the monastery of **Wat Phnom Sambok**.

Stung Treng is 87 miles (140 km) north of Kratie, also on the east bank of the Mekong. It is about 300 miles (485 km) from Phnom Penh and 135 miles (217 km) from Pakse in Laos. From Stung Treng to the Laotian border is only 30 miles (50 km).

Ships can only ply between Kratie and Stung Treng from September to January; for the rest of the year the water level is too low. Stung Treng can also be reached by air from Phnom Penh.

The rapids and waterfalls upstream from the town make it impossible to travel into Laos by boat. The river Kong flows in from the east, joins the Srepok and San rivers, and together they form a tributary of the Mekong.

For the foreseeable future the plateau of Ratanakiri will not be accessible from Stung Treng. Roads and bridges have been destroyed. It can only be reached from Pleiku in the central Vietnam highlands. (This route is closed to tourists).

Two roads lead out of Phnom Penh towards Angkor: National Highway 6

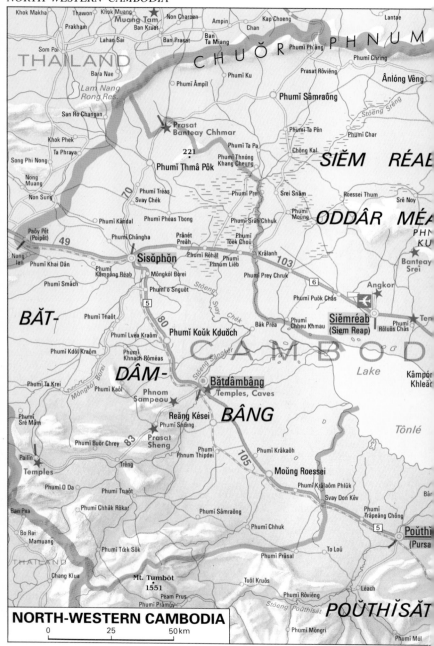

NORTH-WESTERN CAMBODIA

0   25   50km

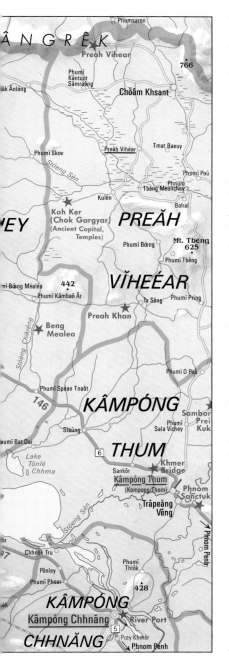

along the north shore of the Great Lakes, and Highway 5 along the southern shore. The southern route is in better condition and, given the more stable political situation, will soon be open to tourists.

The northwest and west (National Highway 6)

Before the wars it was possible to reach Siem Reap and Angkor Wat by private car along the well-maintained National Highway 6, in six or seven hours. The road branches east off Highway 5 just outside Oudong. It goes to the ferry at Prek Kdam and then runs north through the province of Kompong Thom, to the capital of the same name.

Prasat Phum Prasat lies not far from the road between the kilometer marks 138 and 139. It is a brick building in the style of Kompong Preah with a richly worked, foliated lintel. The two heavily carved supports on each side of the door have also been preserved.

Kompong Thom (Kompong Thum) is 104 miles (167 km) from Phnom Penh. Phnom Sanctuk, a monolithic building, stands on a small wooded hill, over which a few statues lie scattered.

Kompong Thom is the starting point for a visit to a number of ancient capitals and temples, which have played a significant part in Khmer history, but which at the time of writing are not accessible to tourists: Sambor Prei Kuk was the principal temple of Isanapura, the city of Isanavarman I which was the capital of the Chen La empire in the seventh century. The temple groups in the style of Sambor Prei Kuk (600-650) represent the earliest stage of Chen La art.

The temples have been severely vandalized. They comprise a northern and a southern group, both facing the rising sun and surrounded by ramparts and moats. Beyond these lay the city. A brick wall, inset with medallions, in which figured jewelry was found, survives from the

101

southern temple, which dates back to Isanavarman I. The east gate is dedicated to
the bull Nandi, the deified steed of the
god Shiva, and has the most beautifully
designed ceiling of the Chen La period.
The main tower, a shrine ro Shiva raised
on a high base, was surrounded by five
octagonal towers, a design element
which was to continue unaltered into
Angkorian art.

Of the northern part, only foundations
and towers of various periods have survived. The central shrine, surrounded by
four towers, also dates from Isanavarman's reign. A small *cella,* a square windowless building of sandstone slabs, with
a vaulted, overhanging roof and blind
skylights, is reminiscent of earlier buildings in India.

The vast laterite and sandstone temple
of **Preah Khan**, 65 miles (104 km) north
of Kompong Thom, is situated in the

town of Kompong Svay, in the southwest of the province of Preah Vihear,
which is in the very north of Cambodia,
on the border with Thailand. Construction of the temple was begun in the
middle of the 12th century by King Suriyavarman II, the architect of Angkor
Wat. It was built in the style of Angkor
(1100-1175) and was completed by
Jayavarman VII some time before 1181.

Koh Ker, north of Preah Khan in the
province of Preah Vihear, has given its
name to the pre-Angkorian style of Koh
Ker (921-944). Jayavarman IV made
Koh Ker his capital and built the temple
of Prasat Thom there. The great brick
building has been severely damaged.

Beng Mealea, west of Preah Khan in
the province of Siem Reap, was built by
Suriyavarman II in the Angkor Wat style.

Preah Vihear is a temple-city 2,400
feet (730 m) up in the Dangrek Mountains, right on the border with Thailand.
This region has frequently been fought
over and up to the present is still claimed
by Thailand. However an international

Above: Going to market in Siem Reap.
Right: Village children near Siem Reap.

ruling has assigned it to Cambodia. The temples date from different periods. Jayavarman VI, the governor of a northern province, who usurped the throne of Angkor, built himself a temple here in the 11th century, in the style of Koh Ker. In 1160 another temple was built in the post-Angkorian style of Bayon. For tourists, Preah Vihear can only be reached from Thailand.

In **Kompong Kdei**, on the way from Kompong Thom to Siem Reap, the road passes an old Khmer bridge, with a *naga* balustrade, across the River Praptos. This is one of the few stone bridges dating from the Angkorian era.

In **Roluos**, 15 miles (24 km) before you come to Siem Reap, there are three important temples to be seen: Lolei, Bakong, and Preah Ko.

Siem Reap (Siemreab), the capital of Siem Reap province, is the starting-point for the visit to the temples of Angkor and Roluos.

Sisophon lies 64 miles (103 km) east of Siem Reap at the intersection of National Highway 6 (Phnom Penh to Sisophon 257 miles / 414 km) and National Highway 5 (Phnom Penh to Sisophon 230 miles / 372 km). The latter runs round the south of the Great Lakes. It is a further 30 miles (49 km) to the Thai border at Poipet.

Prasat Banteay Chhmar (which means Tower of the Small Citadel) is 44 miles (71 km) north of Sisophon. It was one of the capitals of Jayavarman II (802-850), the founder of the empire of Angkor. At one time the city was surrounded by a massive defensive wall, 5 1/2 miles (9 km) long. In the 11th century there was a large Buddhist monastery here. The city was badly damaged by marauding Thai tribesmen.

Poipet (Paoy Pet) is a town on the Thai border. It is 262 miles (421 km) from Phnom Penh via Highway 5, and 288 miles (463 km) via Highway 6. There is also a railway-line of 239 miles (385 km) from Phnom Penh to Poipet. The border crossing is not open for tourists. Even before the war the frontier was closed fre-

quently due to the 500-year-long owner-ship dispute between Cambodia and Thailand over the provinces of Battam-bang, Pursat and Siem Reap. These were not returned by Thailand to Cambodia until after the Second World War. Travellers have to walk over half a mile (1 km) across no-man's-land. From Aranya Prathet, the town on the Thai side of the border, you can reach Bangkok by rail (149 miles / 239 km) or road (165 miles / 265 km).

National Highway 5
Phnom Penh – Angkor

National Highway 5 runs from Phnom round the south side of the Great Lakes, through Oudong and Lovek.

Kompong Chhnang, 56 miles (90 km) from Phnom Penh, is an important fish-ing port on the Tonle Sap river, close to where it leaves the Great Lakes. The

Above: A damaged bridge on National Highway 5.

town and its surrounding area are famous for their pottery. The Babaur Pagoda dates from the 17th century.

The Phnom Penh-Battambang-Poipet railway does not pass through Kompong Chhnang, but the town is linked with Phnom Penh by boat services on the Tonle Sap.

Pursat (Phouthisat) has a train station and is capital of Pursat province. A temple and a monastery were built during the post-Angkorian era. The moun-tainous province is famous for its pink marble, from which artefacts are carved both for practical and decorative use. The jungle regions of the province are roamed by herds of elephants, up to fifty strong, as well as wild boar, tigers, gibbons and other wildlife. In the mountain villages around **Leach**, 4 miles (6 km) south of Pursat, wild elephants are trained to work in the teak forests. After a year's training, they are capable of pulling a load of timber equivalent to half their own weight, over 15 miles (25 km) of moun-tainous terrain, day after day.

Pursat province is one of the regions which, since the 1980s, have been systematically plundered by the Khmer Rouge for the hardwood which they sell to Thailand to finance their civil war.

Battambang is Cambodia's second largest city and capital of the like-named province, which is famous as a rice-growing area and is also under the influence of the Khmer Rouge. Before the Second Indochinese War approximately 350 sq. miles (900 sq. km) in this under-populated province lay uncultivated; two-thirds of it is suitable for rice growing, and the rest for planting rubber, coffee and fruit.

Claims that the Khmer Rouge are pursuing a policy of deforestation, in order to prepare the land for the resettlement of refugees from camps in Thailand, are not accurate. Cambodia may suffer many deprivations, but it is not short of land for building. It is nonetheless true that extensive tracts of land have to be cleared of mines before they are fit for habitation.

As the most westerly province of Cambodia, Battambang was the last province to be given back to Cambodia, or rather to the French colonial administration, under the treaty of 1907 between France and Siam, as it was known then. It was annexed again by Siam between 1941 and 1947, when after 500 years it was finally returned to Cambodian possession.

The town of Battambang is 181 miles (292 km) from Phnom Penh on Highway 5, and 80 miles (129 km) from the border at Poipet. It is also the most important station on the rail line between Phnom Penh and Poipet, and is 170 miles (274 km) by rail from the capital. Before the war, people arriving here by train could continue their journey to Siem Reap (Angkor) on a fast road via Sisophon (50 miles / 80 km).

Currently the road is in a poor state of repair. For security reasons tourists will only allowed to use it when the political situation is stabilized.

Battambang was founded on the banks of the Stung Sangker river in the 11th century. It has palm-lined treets and was once famous for its temples. Next to the **Wat Po Veal** (Pothiveal) is a museum with displays of Khmer art, although in 1970, on the outbreak of the civil war, some of the exhibits were taken to the National Museum in Phnom Penh. On the east bank of the river lie **Wat Kandal**, **Wat Po Khnong**, **Wat Bopharam** and **Wat Sangker**. On the west bank is the modern town with its station, government buildings, shopping streets, hotels and restaurants as well as the **Wat Piphit** and the **Wat Damrei Sar**, which also has a museum attached to it.

Wat Kampheng, **Wat Sla Ket** and **Wat Kdol**, 2 miles (3 km) outside the town, were built as recently as the 18th century but possessed some 100 statues of Buddha dating from the 13th century onwards, and were surrounded by ancient stupas. **Wat Ek**, 5 miles (8 km) north of the town, built in the 11th century Baphuon style, was used by the Khmer Rouge as a prison. Eight miles (13 km) north of Battambang is the **Wat Tuol Baset** (Wat Prasidhi), similarly dating from the beginning of the 11th century, but with foundations that go back to the 7th century. It has reliefs taken from the Indian Mahabharata epic.

Before 1975 Battambang had a number of industrial companies, cotton mills, textile and jute factories, and a university. On the east side of town there was a small enclave of the Muslim Cham minority, with a mosque.

On the way to Pailin, 8 miles (13 km) southeast of Battambang, is a well-known place of pilgrimage, **Phnom Sampeou**, with a Buddhist cave-temple.The **Prasat Sheng**, 14 miles (22 km) from Battambang, has three brick and one sandstone tower, and reliefs depicting scenes from Hindu mythology.

Pailin lies 50 miles (80 km) from Battambang in the mountains bordering

Thailand. The road via Treng runs through thick jungle. The pleasant climate made Pailin a popular holiday resort in the colonial period. Thai and Burmese minorities lived in parts of the town. **Wat Phnom Yat** and **Wat Rattanak Sophorn** are built in the Burmese style.

The area around Pailin is renowned for its jungle where herds of wild elephant roam and gibbons live in their hundreds. Now and again tigers used to come into the villages and the locals would mount hunting expeditions.

Pailin lies a good 650 ft (200 m) up in fertile red-earth country, which holds promise for rubber cultivation. In 1960 gem deposits were discovered, which were mostly mined by the Shan minority from the mountainous Myanmar (Burma) to the north, where gems are also found. Rubies, various kinds of sapphires, zircons and onyx have been found on the surface and down to a depth of 6 feet

Above: Evening return near Siem Reap.

(2 m). The whole area has been churned up, and diggings are packed close together. The red earth is washed to separate out the gravel which contains the gems. Many of the stones are too small or too pale in color to have any commercial value.

Families labor together from dawn to dusk, standing in the dust of the excavations, or knee-deep in water. At one time people looking for gems could dig anywhere they wanted. They had to pay the owner of the land from which they took the water to wash the stones. He received 25 per cent of the value of any stones found, while the dealer who sold the stones on the market took 50 per cent.

Today the gem deposits come under the control of the Khmer Rouge, who exchange them in Thailand for arms and other goods.

Sisophon lies 50 miles (80 km) from Battambang. The road passes though a sparsely populated and dusty plain, dotted with ponds which are the haunt of duck and other wild fowl.

PHNOM PENH
Arrival

Flights: To Phnom Penh: from Bangkok daily by Thai International, Kampuchea Airlines, Cambodia Airlines und Bangkok Airways. From Singapore by Silkair and Kampuchea Airlines. From Kuala Lumpur (Malaysia) by Malaysian Airlines. From Ho-Chi-Minh City (Vietnam) by Vietnam Airlines and Kampuchea Airlines. From Vientiane by Lao Aviation. From Hanoi by Kampuchea Airlines and Vietnam Airlines.

Pochentong airport is 4 1/2 miles/ 7km outside Phnom Penh. Take a taxi into town, but negotiate the fare (approx. US $5) before you start.

Airport tax: For outward flights abroad US $ 8, for flights to Siem Reap US $ 4.

By car: You can drive from Ho-Chi-Minh City (Saigon) to Phnom Penh (driving time excl. ferry is approx. 6 hours). The border-crossing must be entered in your visa.

Tours within Cambodia can be booked through: Diethelm Travel Cambodia Ltd., 8 Boulevard Saigon, Phnom Penh, Tel. 26648 or through Phnom Penh Tourism, 313 Quai Karl Marx, Phnom Penh, Tel. 24059.

Whether and when excursions into the country from Phnom Penh or boat trips on the Mekong are organized, depends on the political situation. You must ask about this at the travel agent.

Accommodation

Many big hotels are currently being converted, and the price structure is fluid.

FIRST CLASS: **Cambodiana Sofitel**, Quai Karl Marx near 240th St., Tel. 23-26288. 300 rooms from US $ 200 per night/person incl. breakfast. Swimming-pool, satellite TV, taxis, limousines, bar, restaurant with European and Chinese cuisine. **Floating Hotel**, on the river bank, Tel. 23-25231, 23-26585. 102 rooms from US $ 180 incl. breakfast. Pool, bar, satellite TV, restaurant with European and Asian cuisine. **Royal Phnom Penh,** Lenin St., Tel. 18.810 221. 40 rooms with IDD-Tel., satellite TV, bar, restaurant with west., Chin. and Thai menus, limousine service.

MID-PRICE: **Diamond Hotel**, 174-184 Achar Mean Blvd., Tel. 23-26635, 27221/2, 87 rooms with IDD-Tel., satellite TV, café. **Holiday International**, 84 St. opposite Calmette Hospital, Tel. 25085. currently 87 rooms with IDD and satellite TV, pool, internat. restaurant. **Pailin Hotel**, Achar Mean & Achar Hemcheay, Tel. 23-25231. 81 rooms with satellite TV, French/Chinese Restaurant.

BUDGET: **Asia Hotel**, Achar Mean, 120 rooms with satellite TV, restaurant. **La Paillote Hotel**, near the Central Market, 234/130 St., Tel. 23-22151. 24 rooms with satellite TV and IDD-Tel.

Good French restaurant. **Monorom Hotel** Achar Mean, near the Central Market, Tel. 23-26073. 65 rooms, restaurant. **What Phnom Hotel**, Tel. 26286, 25320. 47 rooms.

Restaurants

Most of the hotels have restaurants; apart from these there are always new restaurants, offering Asian and European food. In the evenings food stalls are put up by the riverside.

Entertainment

For the past three years, when there are enough tourists to make an audience, several dance groups perform classical Cambodian dances; the tradition had been carried on by the royal dance ensemble. In 1993, for the first time in many years, dances were performed with Angkor Wat as a backdrop. Information from travel agents.

Museums

National Museum, West side of 13th St. between 178th St and 184th St., Tel. 24369. Open Tu-Sun 8am-12.00 and 2pm-5pm. Photography forbidden. **Silver Pagoda**, Tu-Sun 7am-11am and 2pm-5pm. **Tuol Sleng Museum** (Prison-camp S 21), near the intersection of 113th St. and 350th St., daily 7-11.30am and 2pm-5pm.

Post, telephone, fax

Main post office: West side of 13th Street, between 98th St. and 102nd St. Tel. 24511, open daily 7am-6pm. Normal postal service, national and international telegraph and telephone links.

Post and telephone bureau: Opp. Hotel Monorom on Achan Mean Blvd. and 126th St.

The reception-desks of big hotels can handle airmail letters to Europe. The service-bueau in the Hotel Cambodia is quick and reliable.

Local transport / connections

Some hotels and travel agents rent cars with driver, for abt. US $ 20-30 per day. Always agree the price in advance.There is no shortage of taxis, nor of cyclos. There are overland buses, but they are hopelessly overcrowded.

Internal flights by Kampuchea Airlines, 206 A, Tou Samuth Blvd., Tel. 018-810300, 25105. Flights from Phnom Penh to Siem Reap, Battambang. Helicopter flights to Koh Kong und Sihanoukville.

Tourist information
Ministry of Tourism, Blvd. Monivong,

SIEM REAP
Accommodation
FIRST CLASS: **Taphrom Hotel**, New, 60 rms, minibar, satellite TV. Restaurant with west. and Asian cuisine. Reservations through: Mittaheap Hotel, 252 Achar Mean Blvd., Phnom Penh, Tel. 23454, 26492.

TEMPLES AND CITIES IN THE JUNGLE

THE TEMPLES OF ROLUOS

ANGKOR

Siem Reap, the capital of the province of the same name, was badly damaged by bombing and in fighting with the Khmer Rouge, and has suffered to such an extent that there are no longer any buildings of interest left standing. However, it is picturesquely located on both sides of the Siem Reap river, and has a lively market.

With the help of the USA, one of the great reservoir of the Angkor period, the Western Baray, was restored to use in 1957. Fed by the Siem Reap river, it has enlarged the rice-growing acreage of the province. To get an impression of the water systems on which the Angkor empire and its culture depended, it is worth visiting the reservoir, especially at dusk.

From 1979 the province was the scene of fighting between the Khmer Rouge and the Vietnamese army, whose place was taken, after 1989, by troops of the Phnom Penh government. Even after the arrival of the UN peacekeeping force, hostilities broke out time and again; the Khmer Rouge launched attacks on government troops and on the civilian population, especially the Vietnamese minority who live in fishing communities on the Great Lakes.

Previous pages: Aerial photo of Angkor Wat. Left: The temple of Banteay Srei in a jungle landscape.

However, to date tourists have never been under threat from the Khmer Rouge.

Sightseeing in Angkor

Nevertheless, visitors should never underestimate the dangers that can face them if they wander off the tracks or paths in the Angkor area. The Khmer Rouge have left anti-personnel mines everywhere, so that rambling is out of the question. Only the roads, tracks and paths in the neighborhood of the temples have been cleared of mines. Furthermore, inside the temple ruins a large number of the buildings have long been unsafe, and consequently routes within the site were marked out by the French as early as the beginning of this century. To make matters still worse, there are poisonous green vipers in the grass and undergrowth by the paths, which the local people call *hanuman* snakes. You should watch out for them on the paths and in the ruins as well, as they like to sun themselves on warm stones.

To visit all the buildings takes several days, and to study them thoroughly you should set aside a few weeks. The roads of hard-packed earth that were laid out by French archaeologists and restorers to make the monuments accessible, are

111

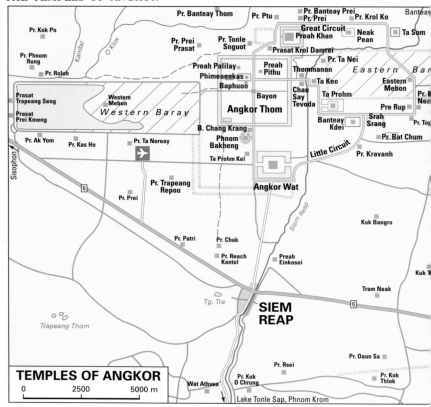

TEMPLES OF ANGKOR

0   2500   5000 m

called the Large and Small Cicuits and lead to the most important temples. However, many of the buildings do not lie directly on these roads, but are inside large walled compounds. They are reached by footpaths running for a mile or more through jungle and ruins, and some are even more remote, right in the midst of rice paddies.

The temples are known by popular names which they have acquired in recent times. Their original names are unknown today. Buildings of the same period on the whole resemble each other in architecture and decoration, so that after a while they seem to merge into a repetitive blur. For this reason it is best, on a short visit, to select just a few.

Visiting as many temples as possible in a short time leaves one dazed, whereas choosing a few things to look at in detail creates a much stronger impression.

To give a clearer overall view, the earliest temples of the Angkorian period, the temples of Roluos, are described here first. Then come the most important buildings, Angkor Wat and the city of Angkor Thom, with the Bayon, Baphuon and other buildings within the city walls. The remaining descriptions cover the temples on the Large and Small Circuits.

NOTE: *The buildings are marked with asterisks to give the following ratings:*

   *** must be seen on any visit

    ** for visits of 3-4 days

     * only for lengthy stays

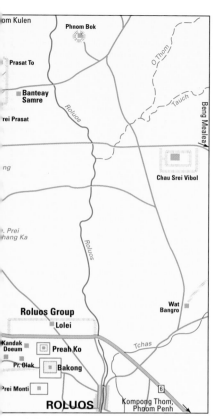

**THE TEMPLES OF ROLUOS

Angkorian period
Style of Preah Ko, c. 854-893
Built by: King Indravarman I, 877-889
and his son Yasovarman I, 889-900

The three temples of Preah Ko, Bakong and Lolei are called the Roluos group, after the village a 1/2-mile (1 km) away. Coming at the beginning of the sightseeing tours, they show the origins of the artificially constructed temple-hill which characterizes the later Khmer architecture, as well as the beginnings of relief sculpture.

About 15 miles (24 km) east of Siem Reap, on the National Highway 6, the temples lie on a north-south line, with Lolei in the north and Bakong in the south, scarcely a mile (1.6 km) apart.

Lolei, the most northerly of the three temples, was built by King Yasovarman I in 893 in the Preah Ko style. It was intended as a shrine in honor of his father, Indravarman I, and stood in the middle of a *baray*, or artificial lake, which has now dried up. The four brick towers with their tapering roof structures stand on a single two-tiered base. It is possible that six towers were originally planned.

The lintels and panels of the false portals are decorated with winding foliage, within which little figures play. Especially notable are the door frames made from a single block of sandstone and embellished with written characters, and the corners of the walls, with fearsome *dvarapalas* brandishing weapons, guardian figures or figures of women carrying flowers.

Preah Ko (Bako), built by King Indrvarman I in 880 in the style which is named after the temple, lies halfway between Lolei and Bakong.

The group consists of six brick towers (*prasats*) open to the east and arranged in two rows of three on a single base. They were built in memory of some royal ancestors, the front three towers for the male ancestors, and the three behind for the female. In front of them are two large buildings which open to the west.

Two sculptures representing the bull Nandi, the steed of the god Shiva, once stood here, explaining the name popularly given to the temple: *Preah ko* means "temple of the sacred ox."

The square site is surrounded by walls about 330 ft (100 m) long on each side. These are covered with stucco into which a little decoration has been carved; but this has crumbled away in many places. Some of the beautifully decorated sandstone lintels and panels of the false portals which were set into the walls, have remained intact.

Bakong, built in the Preah Ko style by King Indravarman I in the year 881, is the southernmost of the three temples. It is the first artificially constructed temple-hill to have been raised by a Khmer king in the plains.

The outer wall, half ruined and over-grown by jungle, measures a huge 2,310 ft by 2,970 ft (700 m by 900 m). A second protective wall was lined with small, richly decorated shrines, of which little now remains. Two approaches, between eroded and scarcely recognizable *naga* balustrades, lead over the moat, 200 ft (60 m) wide, separating the two walls of laterite stone which surround the inner area. The center is occupied by a 5-tiered temple pyramid, 200 ft (60 m) square at its base and tapering evenly upwards, with a *prasat*, a temple tower, on the highest terrace. It is a representation of the sacred mountain, the *meru*, of Indian

Above: Relief on the Bakong temple in the Roluos group. Right: Angkor Wat, seen from the west side.

mythology, the central point of the universe, upon which the 33 gods are en-throned. The five terraces, to which are added the level of the ground on which they stand and the tower-shrine which crowns them, make up the seven levels which the *meru*, the mountain of the gods, also possessed. Laterite stone was probably used to build up the temple-hill. It is faced with gigantic slabs of sand-stone. The corners of each platform are adorned with elephants carved from single pieces of stone.

On the top platform there now stands a small, dilapidated pagoda of more recent date. Of the buildings at the foot of the staircase only some on the west side have survived. Beside the pyramid there were originally eight towers, which were very fine examples of Khmer architecture but are now almost buried under rubble. The galleries near the entrance pavilions have also been destroyed. We now come to the free-standing sculptures. In a side sanc-tuary is a group representing the Hindu god Indra and his two consorts.

On the smooth sandstone surfaces there are not only figures shown standing next to each other, but, for the first time in Khmer art, bas-relief with a continuous sequence of scenes. On the fifth level, panels with scenes from mythology have been preserved. The ornamentation of the buildings at Bakong, the lintels and columns, panels and false portals, are the most beautiful of their epoch.

A fairly recent Buddhist monastery is situated in the temple precincts.

***ANGKOR WAT

Angkorian period
Style of Angkor Wat (c.1100-1175)
Built by: King Suriyavarman II
(1113-1150)
LOCATION: 3.75 miles (6 km) from Siem Reap, on the right of the road.

It is worth walking right round the temple in order to appreciate its massive size; also, in order to see it in different kinds of light, to watch it changing color and even, it seems, shape, as the light plays on it. This magnificent example of classical Khmer architecture combines Indian and Indochinese culture and the accumulated experience of centuries in one of the world's most beautiful monuments.

At the height of his power, Suriyavarman II, one of the most important of the Khmer kings, ordered the gigantic construction to be started from all four sides at once, so that, by a miracle of planning, it was completed in less than 40 years by numberless laborers, master builders and stonemasons. The king actually lived to see it finished.

Temple or mausoleum?

Historians do not agree as to why Angkor was built, although there is no disputing that its purpose was a sacred one. Even the god-kings of the Khmer built their palaces of wood and roofed them with straw or tiles. Stone was only used for buildings intended as places for worshipping the gods and deified rulers.

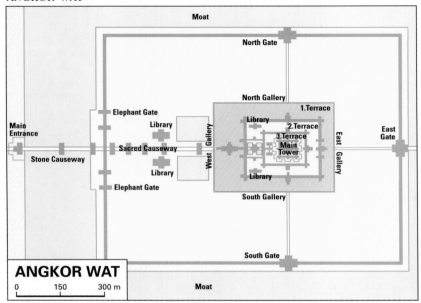

ANGKOR WAT

0   150   300 m

The main entrance of a typical Khmer temple, as in most oriental shrines, faces east to the rising sun. However, the entrance of Angkor Wat faces west, the same way as the temples of the dead.

There are known geographical reasons why exceptions are made when it comes to the eastward orientation. And such reasons can be found at Angkor – for instance the fact that it is bounded to the east by the Siem Reap river, or that it was located in the middle of what was then the capital city. But there are also clues that suggest it may have been intended as a mausoleum, a place where the king would have been venerated after his death. Angkor was dedicated to the god Vishnu, and Suriyavarman II was a devotee of Vishnu. No images of gods have been found in the temple; on the other hand, some scholars believe they have evidence that the king's ashes rested here. Moreover, the god-kings had been erecting mausoleums

Right: Visitors in the first courtyard of Angkor Wat

for their own posthumous veneration and that of their ancestors, since the 9th century. A further clue is a scene on a panel depicting a kind of "Last Judgement." A relief showing the king at the head of his troops also points to posthumous worship. Another piece of evidence that Angkor was built as a royal mausoleum, and one that is difficult to refute, is the fact that in order to understand the narrative sequence depicted in the reliefs, it is necessary to walk round the temple anti-clockwise, with the reliefs on one's left. This corresponds to the ritual of the dead, whereas, in the orient, temples to the gods must be walked round clockwise.

Architecture and symbolism

Masonry steps lead to the wide moat that surrounds the temple compound. It forms a rectangle, nearly a mile (1.5 km) long from east to west and over 3/4 mile (1.3 km) from north to south. The moat is linked to the Siem Reap river by a canal and was fed by it, as were the reservoirs

serving the town, palace and paddy-fields. The temple-hill within the moat is the Khmer interpretation of the *meru*, the Hindu mountain of the gods, surrounded by the world-ocean.

Between the moat and the laterite stone wall, 3,200 ft by 2,800 ft (1 km by 0.8 km), which surrounds the temple area, a broad footpath runs round the whole site.

Angkor is inaccessible from the north and south, as there is no way over the moat. To the east, however, it is crossed by an earth causeway which is passable in the dry season and may have been used for the delivery of building materials and supplies to the temple city. To the south, east and north, the laterite wall is punctuated by beautifully decorated entrance pavilions on a cruciform ground-plan, which were linked by paths to the main temple.

The single causeway from the west, 720 ft (220 m) long, is paved with large, irregular sandstone slabs, and leads to the turreted main entrance. Only remnants are left of the columns and the *naga* ba-

lustrade of the causeway. Stone steps lead to the turreted main and side portals with their large vestibules. The turrets are damaged, but one can visualize their former elegance, which gives a foretaste of the temple façade.

From the entrance, colonnades lead to the right and left, roofed with half-vaults which rest on square columns; many of these have fallen down. The colonnades end in small pavilions called elephant gates, which were the only entrances large enough for animals and carts.

The many-headed cobra, symbol of the *naga,* the serpent queen of pre-Hindu cults, appears thousands of times over in Khmer art as a decorative motif on the balustrades along approach paths, bridges, moats and pools. In Angkor Wat, on both sides of the entrance gates, snake bodies raise their seven heads, each with its hood outspread.

When one steps out of the darkness of the main portal into the bright light of the first courtyard, the breathtaking outline of the temple pyramid, still a long way off, comes into view. At first only three of the five towers are visible. (This "three-towered" Angkor is the emblem of the Khmer Rouge. The People's Republic used the five-towered Angkor as its emblem).

The temple-hill is not located in the center, as in most Khmer temples, but is set back towards the east and is reached by a processional way 1,140-ft-long and 30-ft-wide (350 m by 9.5 m), lined by serpents with their bodies erect, their heads raised and hoods outspread. The avenue widens in places to form lateral terraces ornamented with *nagas.*

By setting the temple-hill further back, the unknown architect of Angkor makes use of an effect that the Greeks also exploited. We cannot say whether this was something he had learnt, or had worked out for himself. But it is so designed that the temple is seen to best effect from a distance which is double the width of the building. In this instance the 1,140 ft (350 m) to the temple pyramid is twice the width of Angkor Wat's west façade.

Half way along the approach are two small buildings to the right and left. In front of them are ornamental pools, in which they are reflected. Their purpose is no more clear than the identity of their builder. It is conceivable that they were built by the monks who occupied Angkor for a considerable period from the end of the 15th century. They have recently lost much of their charm due to some rather unsuccessful restoration.

Step by step the visitor draws nearer to the three-tiered pyramid. The base of the first level measures 660 ft from east to west and 590 ft from north to south (200 m by 180 m) and is 13 ft (4 m) high; the second level is 380 ft by 330 ft (115 m by 100 m) at its base and is 20 ft (6 m) high; and the third is 200 ft (60 m) square and 43 ft (13 m) high. The main tower rises

from the third level, already at a height of 76 ft (23 m), by a further 138 ft (42 m), giving a total height of 214 ft (65 m). This makes it roughly the same height as the cathedral of Notre Dame in Paris, which was built at about the same time. The three tiers are surrounded by galleries, with towers at the corners and pavilions in the middle of the steps.

The main tower on the third level is linked to the pavilions by galleries, whose vaulted roofs rest on pillars. From one level to another, flights of roofed steps lead to the next pillared gallery. In place of outer walls to the colonnades and galleries, Angkor has either baluster windows, each comprising seven small spiral pillars, or else rows of pillars on which vaulted half-roofs rest. Enough light enters to illuminate the interior walls, which are decorated with reliefs, without allowing glaring sunlight and heat to penetrate. The elements of the building – towers, galleries and vestibules – are also found in earlier buildings, and in the temple of Baphuon they were used in a similar way; but at Angkor their abundance and variety are new, surprising, and carefully employed to give maximum effect.

The principal emphasis of Angkor is horizontal, but out of this the pyramid soars upwards. Its height is enhanced by the receding terracing of the lower structure, the wave-shaped roofing of the galleries and the jagged towers.

Techniques of the reliefs and of ornamentation

As well as the magnificent architecture, the ornamentation of the building and the reliefs also contribute to Angkor's unique quality. Pillars, skirtings, lintels, pediments, panels, capitals and cornices are covered with tendrils, winding foliage, decorative figures and other embellishment. A special magic emanates from the approximately two thou-

Right: Galleries at Angkor Wat.

sand goddesses (*devatas*) and semi-divine dancers (*apsaras*) who adorn the temple walls. Alone or in groups, facing strictly to the front and yet in harmonious, gliding movement, wearing high filigree crowns and sumptuous jewellery, no one of them is quite the same as any other. The enraptured, mysterious smile on their full lips is known as the smile of Angkor. Their beauty and grace, reaching its most consummate form at Angkor, is not achieved again in later buildings. The galleries of the first level, with an area of about half an acre (2,000 sq. m.), are covered with bas-reliefs over 6 ft (2 m) high, on which light and shade fall between the pillars and through the baluster windows. The execution of these reliefs is of extraordinary delicacy and perfection. The figures are chiselled into the huge, smooth sandstone blocks, just a few centimeters deep, and the decorative detail only millimeters, so that in the morning light they look like drawings, and in the soft afternoon light, more like paintings. According to some theories,

the figures were drawn first; then by shallower or deeper cutting, a range of tones was achieved. It is probable that the figures of important gods or kings were painted or gilded.

Giving a three-dimensional effect to people or motifs, by placing them on surfaces otherwise free of decoration, is a technique that was used in earlier buildings, but at Angkor, though evident, it is not as consistently applied as at Bakheng and Baphuon. Emphasis on the people or animals that are important in a particular scene is achieved by showing them larger than the others. The same protagonists are given different sizes in different scenes, according to their significance in a particular situation. Continuity is preserved by the presence of one key figure in every scene. Even unfamiliar themes become comprehensible thanks to the consistent iconography – the rigorously followed stylization of good and evil, of weak and strong characters, and the identifying features of victors and vanquished and of different social

groups. Important events are situated above unimportant ones, the winners of a battle stand taller and larger than the losers. Rulers and military leaders are seen above the mass of warriors, in chariots, on horseback or riding elephants.

The individual scenes are very large, but in the narrow galleries where you can only take a few steps back, they can be taken in visually. The total narrative stretches 160 ft (50 m) on the east and west sides and 330 ft (100 m) on the north and south sides.

Very few pieces of sculpture have survived wars and plunder, but those that have seem inferior in quality both to the architecture and the reliefs. Angkor's sacred objects, jewellery and furnishings are all in museum collections.

The temple was damaged by the Cham in 1177-81 and by the Siamese in the 14th and 15th centuries, and alterations

Above: Apsaras and devas, dancinggirls and goddesses adorn the walls. Right: Local people offer their modest wares for sale.

were made while it was being used as a monastery.

The reliefs of the first terrace

It is impossible to describe all the scenes in the reliefs, panels and lintels, and to look at them all takes a great deal of time. Just as with the buildings themselves, it is true that studying a few selected examples makes more impact than trying to see everything. The reliefs, which are the work of an unknown number of sculptors working in teams, vary noticeably in quality. The most beautiful are to be found in the west, south and east galleries and their pavilions.

West gallery: the southern section is reached by turning right from the main entrance. The reliefs, which are over 9 ft (2.85 m) high, above a 3 1/2 ft (1.1 m) plinth, depict scenes from the Mahabharata epic of Indian Vishnu mythology. The army of the Kauravas, advancing from the left, is meeting the Pandavas, marching from the right. The battle is in-

tended to restore the balance between good and evil. A final victory of good over evil is not conceivable in Indian philosophy. The world consists of positive and negative forces; keeping them in balance produces harmony. When this is disturbed, the gods come to the rescue. In the Mahabharata, Vishnu intervenes in his incarnation as the four-armed Krishna; as the charioteer, he shows the hesitating Arjuna, the leader of the Pandavas, the way to victory. This divine teaching, called the Bhagavad Gita, is a key part of the Hindu faith and is chanted in Indian temples.

The chieftains are represented as tall and magnificent. In one hand they hold a bow, in the other an arrow, and they maintain this pose in all the scenes.

In the upper part lies Bhima, pierced by arrows and mourned by his followers and family; as leader of the Kauravas, he represents the principle of evil. His appearance, with a coarse, round face and bulbous nose, is markedly different from that of Arjuna, who is slim, with a long,

straight nose. The warriors fighting alongside the heroes can also be distinguished by their physical appearance. Approximately in the center of the relief is depicted the most important scene: Arjuna in his war chariot with Krishna holding the reins.

The **pavilion at the end of the west gallery** has a cruciform ground plan. On the east wall of the northen arm of the cross is a depiction of Krishna (Vishnu) lifting a huge rock above his head. This well-known scene shows the god of herdsmen shielding them from the deluge sent down by the god Indra to drown them. On the upper west wall: a motif common in Angkor, taken from another Vishnu epic, the Ramayana, and showing gods and demons, helped by a snake, churning the Sea of Milk.

In the western wing, above the north corner, is another scene from the Ramayana: Ravana, an ugly, evil demon, cunningly abducts the beautiful Sita, wife of Rama (Vishnu), carries her off to the island of Sri Lanka with the intention of making her his bride. Rama and his brother Lakshmana, with the help of many others, among them Garuda, king of the birds, and the monkeys' leader, Hanuman, succeed in rescuing Sita. The giant Ravana is vanquished. In this epic, too, the underlying theme is the battle of good against evil. The scene on the panel shows Ravana changing himself into a chameleon in order to trick his way into Sita's chamber.

Southern wing, east corner, upper part: The dying monkey-king, Valin (also called Bali), pierced by an arrow, lies in the arms of his weeping consort, Tara. On the left are Rama, his brother Lakshmana, and between them a monkey named Sougriva.

West corner, upper part: Shiva is meditating on the mountainside in the Himalayas; beside him is his consort Parvati. At the foot of the mountain stands Kamadeva, the god of love, who tries to disturb Shiva's meditation by aiming at him with his bow and arrow. Shiva ignores him.

South gallery, west wing: The reliefs are divided into two unequal parts and show scenes from Khmer history. In the middle of the first picture sits King Parama Vishnouloka (Suriyavarman II), the founder of Angkor Wat, on a low throne, surrounded by a *naga* balustrade. He is giving his court staff instructions for the assembling of the troops. Illustrating an inscription, the next scene shows a procession on Mount Shivapada. On the left, at the bottom, princes march with their servants through the forest, with a background of hills. Above them can be seen armed warriors. Brahmans stand near the king, while the servants hold canopies over his head, to symbolize his authority. Under a tree, to the right of the throne, sits Srivarddha, turned towards the king in a gesture of devotion. The procession of princesses below the king's throne, and the warriors who are coming down from the mountains, lead on to a second picture.

This shows the king reviewing his army. The army commanders are mounted on elephants, and their rank can be seen from the number of canopies of honor which are accorded to them. Fifteen canopies are held above King Parama Vishnouloka, and his hair has been drawn up above his head into a conical shape, on which a diamond is prominently displayed. In his hand he carries a sword with a carved handle, of the kind that can still be seen in Cambodia today. The soldiers on the lower part of the panel wear headdresses that look like animals's heads, and are accompanied by riders. The last ranks of the column have to walk more quickly. Behind them come the officers on elephants.

In the final section we see Brahmans and priests with their hair coiled on their heads; they are ringing little bells and the chief priest is carrying his hammock with him, as priests still do today when they leave their monasteries. They carry the holy fire with them, in order to invoke the gods' blessing for the battle. In front of them are musicians, and just before the end of the panel a group of Siamese captives make their way, recognizable by their coarse clothes and their pikes.

South gallery, east wing: the scene, 217 ft (66 m) long, represents heaven and hell. The panel begins with the Day of Judgement, with its punishments and rewards, and shows a vision of life after death. Many details are reminiscent of medieval European depictions of tortures and torments. There are 37 heavens and 32 hells. In the middle of the panel is Yama, the many-armed god of hell, riding on a buffalo, accompanied by his two helpers, Dharma and Shitragupta. He is surrounded by the dead, who are waiting for judgement to be pronounced.

Right: Baluster windows with seven turned columns.

Punishments for lesser transgressions are scarcely less severe than for serious crimes. If people have stolen flowers, they are tied to a tree and nails are hammered into their heads. Above these places of damnation live the good, in magnificent palaces.

East gallery, south wing: The scene, which is 164 ft (50 m) long, shows one of the best-loved episodes from the epic of the Ramayana, and one which is frequently represented in Angkor, the churning of the Sea of Milk, from which both gods (*devas*) and demons (*asuras*) want to extract *amrita*, the elixir of immortality. They have obtained the help of the snake Vasouki and have wound it round Mount Mandara, which rests on the back of a turtle. On the left-hand side the *asuras* hold the head of the snake, on the right-hand side the *devas* hold the tail. The *asuras* have round, staring eyes and surly faces, and wear crest-like helmets. The *devas*, on the other hand, have almond-shaped eyes and hair piled up on their heads. A monkey holds the end of

the snake's tale. The gods and demons have already been churning the sea for a thousand years. Because of this a great turmoil has been caused among the sea creatures; gigantic fish and sea monsters rise to the surface.

The *apsaras* gradually appear, the beautiful dancers who are depicted on a panel above the relief and on all the walls of Angkor. Next comes Lakshmi, the goddess of beauty; and last of all the elixir of life will be created. In the middle, between gods and demons, Vishnu is enthroned on Mount Mandara and observes events as a judge. A second snake beneath the relief is interpreted as Vasuki resting at the bottom of the sea. At each end of the panel stand guards and servants.

East gallery, north wing: In the central vestibule in front of the gallery is an inscription from the 18th century. In it, a governor announces the consecration of a burial stupa for his family. The ruins of the stupa stand on the path which leads round the temple, near the inscription.

The reliefs in this gallery have no unifying theme, but represent individual people and events. From the execution of the reliefs it is clear that the sculptors here did not possess the same mastery as those responsible for other parts of the temple.

North gallery, east and west wings: The scenes from the Vishnu-Krishna legend, again, do not attain the perfection of those described earlier.

Pavilion at the northwest corner: The reliefs in this pavilion are among the most beautiful in Angkor Wat, even though badly damaged in places.

Western arm of the cross, south wall: Vishnu (Krishna) returns from a successful campaign, mounted on his steed, the divine bird Garuda, and accompanied by his warriors and servants who carry the spoils. Garuda has brought a boulder, which was the reason for the expedition,

Above: Occasionally devout Buddhists come to pray. Right: The third tier of the pyramid with its five principal towers.

and which can be seen in the background. To the right of Garuda, Krishna's wife can be seen.

North corner, upper part: Vishnu (the upper part of whose body is missing) rests upon a snake, which lies stretched out in the water (its head is also missing). Vishnu's consort sits at his feet. Lotus blossoms grow from Vishnu's body and *apsaras* carrying flowers glide around him. In the lower part, nine gods pay homage to him: Suriya on the sun's chariot, with the sun behind him; Kuber, the god of prosperity, son of Shiva, rides on a yak; the god Brahma on a goose, *hamsa*; Skanda rides a peacock; an unknown god is on horseback; Indra rides an elephant; Yama, the god of death, a buffalo; Shiva is mounted on the bull, Nandi; the last god on the right has not been identified.

Northern wing, west corner, upper part: When Rama, the seventh incarnation of Vishnu, doubts Sita's fidelity on her return from Sri Lanka, she submits herself to trial by fire, climbs on the pyre and leaves it again, unharmed. (This panel is badly damaged).

Western wing, over the north corner: the scene shows Rama's triumphal progress through Ayodhya. He sits enthroned on a richly decorated chariot. This huge vehicle was born of the goose, *hamsa*, Brahma's steed. In the lower part of the scene, monkeys accompany the chariot.

South corner, upper part: Sita meets Hanuman, leader of the monkeys, in the forest of Ashoka during her imprisonment in Sri Lanka. Next to her is a maidservant with her hair worn in a strange style. Below are Sita's guards, many with animal heads.

Southern wing, east wall: A scene at the court of King Janaka. Rama returns as victor, and to his right sit King Janaka and a Brahman with coiled hair. In front of Rama, Sita can be seen dressed in fine clothes, with her hair in three braids forming a coronet on her head. She is sur-

rounded by her entourage. The center of the scene is dominated by an archer who is shooting arrows through a wheel, while it turns on a pole.

Southern gateway: A monster whose body is simply a gigantic head and two arms, is faced by two men with swords, presumably Rama and Lakshmana.

Eastern gateway: Rama with his bow and Lakshmana with his sword try to win the support of the monkey Sougriya.

Northern gateway: A giant named Rakshasa has captured Sita and is challenged by two archers, who we take to be Rama and Lakshmana.

Western gateway: Monkeys in a forest; a giant is fleeing, but this one is Vibhishana, brother of Ravana.

The second terrace

Between the gallery of the first and the base of the second terrace lies a grassy courtyard. Two buildings, described as libraries, stand on raised footings. From the northwest and southwest corners of the courtyard one has a wonderful view of the central temple. The high base of the second tier of the temple is elaborately decorated.

Not all the stairways in the temple area are usable, but some have been made safe. A flight of steps in the west of the first gallery leads up to a terrace in the shape of a cross, formed from three intersecting galleries, halfway up between the first and second terraces of the pyramid. The covered galleries make four courtyards, whose pillars, columns, flights of stairs and dainty baluster windows give them an intimacy which distracts one's attention from the monumental nature of the building as a whole. Its clean, severe lines dissolve into curves and flourishes, and the spiral columns resemble delicate woodcarvings.

Sunk into the four courtyards are bowl-shaped depressions lined with stone, which may once have been filled with water – but why? So far, no one has been able to prove that they contained water, although there is no evidence pointing to any other use. The idea that they provided a kind of stage for dances is also quite a fascinating one.

Here, as in no other part of the temple, one is struck by the realization that the walls and panels, the carved pillars, the architecture that exudes a sense of eternity, and of being an end in itself – that all this was just the backdrop for transient, colorful daily life; it is hard to recall that lotus flowers and roses were carved in the wood that lined the ceilings, that the galleries and courtyards were furnished with bright carpets and fabrics, with vivid pictures and golden statues, and that crowds of people breathed life into the whole scene.

A wealth of panels display beautiful bas-reliefs with well-known subjects, the churning of the Sea of Milk, and Vishnu resting on the snake. On the lower parts of the columns, partly destroyed by damp, ascetics sit praying under a canopy of flowers. In the northwest corner one can see a stele, which was found near the temple. It dates from later than the building of the temple, and is inscribed with a eulogy to five priests who served under several kings.

The second terrace is reached by the stairs in the north gallery, which have been made safe. The galleries are narrow, and light only enters them from the inner courtyard which surrounds the central part.

Perhaps the priests came here for their meditation, and the towers at the corners of the galleries were small shrines.

The third gallery

The last tier of the pyramid is surrounded by a narrow inner courtyard. Rising up from it with exhilarating steepness is the high, square platform of the third terrace, with its majestic central tower surrounded by four corner towers. Again and again one's gaze is drawn to the soaring, apparently infinite height of the main tower, and it is not easy to take in the whole scene at once. As you walk round it, the light falling on the temple-hill constantly changes, making it shimmer in a variety of colors.

On all four sides, steep stairways with high, narrow steps lead up to the main shrine. One of them has been made safe, with its steps cemented, and a rope to hold on to at one side. It leads up to an entrance with a vestibule. The open-sided outer galleries are very narrow. Passages lead through the shrine to the gateways on the four sides of the tower, forming four small courtyards. At one's feet the colossal temple site is spread out, with the jungle pressing in on all sides; it seems to be kept at bay only by the moat. From this bird's eye viewpoint one can trace the route one has taken up through the courtyards and galleries.

To the northwest lies the temple-hill of Bakheng, covered in jungle; to the right of it, hidden beneath high trees, is Angkor Thom. To the northeast one can make out Phnom Bok, and behind it the mountain ranges of Phnom Kulen.

In the main tower, Buddhist monks who lived here closed up the open sides with walls, in which they carved standing Buddhas. Even in this highest tower French archaeologists in 1908 were disappointed to find that treasure hunters had long since stolen everything that could be moved.

*The temple-hill of Bakheng

Angkorian period
Bakheng style (893-925 AD)
Built by: King Yasovarman I, 889-900
Date: 893, built as a shrine to Shiva
LOCATION: 3/4 mile (1.2 km) from Angkor Wat, 1,000 ft (300 m) from the south door of Angkor Thom, on a hill.

Right: The staircases to the upper galleries are steep. Far right: Entrance to the West Gallery.

Yasovarman I built his capital, Yasodhapura around a natural hill, 213 ft (65 m) high, on which he constructed his temple. Three narrow footpaths lead to the platform on which the temple is built and the large terrace in front of it. The most direct and steepest way up, which has few steps still intact, is guarded by two stone lions. It begins on the road to Angkor Thom. The other two paths are longer and more tortuous, and were used by horses and elephants.

The temple of Bakheng is in a very ruined state, and the tall trees that have grown up around it obscure the view of Angkor Wat to the southeast, which must once have been breathtaking, especially at dusk. To the west lies the Western Baray (reservoir) and in the distance Phnom Krom and the Great Lakes. Vast forests stretch away to the east and north, from which the city of Takeo and the temple of Bayon rise up. A few Buddhist relics date from the beginning of this century, when monks ran a theological college here.

On the hill, cut into the rock, rose the five-tiered pyramid on its square terraces. If one includes the ground level and the buildings at the top, this had seven levels in all. It is now scarcely possible to make out the wall around the shrine. The bottom terrace measures 236 ft (72 m) on each side of its base, and the top tier, 131 ft (40 m). From the top platform rose five towers (*prasat*), which for the first time in Khmer architecture were not built of brick but of sandstone. In line with them, flights of stairs led up to the shrine. The temple-hill was constructed according to the rules of cosmology. It is both a stone calendar and a representation of the *meru*, the mountain of the gods in Indian mythology.

A total of 108 small shrines surround the central *prasat*. The Indian calendar with its four phases, each of 27 moonrises gives the number 108. On the seven terraces of the *meru* sat 33 gods. The observer standing directly in front of the pyramid saw instead of 108, only 33 shrines – the others were hidden.

*Baksei Chang Kran*g
Angkorian period
Style of Bakheng 893-925 AD
Built by: King Harshavarman I, 900-922, date of construction: 921
LOCATION: near the hill of Bakheng, 660 ft (200 m) from the beginning of the balustrade of Angkor Thom, standing some way back from the road in the forest, on the left side.

King Harshavarman I left few buildings that we know of. The small, square based pyramid with four terraces is one of the last buildings in Angkor to be constructed of brick. The bottom tier has sides 88 ft (27 m) long, while the fourth tier measures 49 ft (15 m) along each side. Its platform is 39 ft (12 m) high. The outer wall has disappeared, except for the remains of a gateway which can still be seen on the east side.

Above: The south gate of Angkor Thom with its giant faces. Right: The Street of Giants – gods and demons churning the Sea of Milk.

The narrow, badly damaged terraces are most easily climbed on the north and south sides. The shrine is built facing the east. The richly decorated false portals and panels of sandstone have been obliterated by damp, and only the motif on the main portal is still recognizable; typical of its period, it shows a figure with an elephant's head rearing its trunk.

The brick walls were once covered in stucco, but nothing remains of this now, and so the ornamentation has also disappeared. There is an inscription in Sanskrit dating from 948, above a door frame on the north side; it dates from the reign of Rajendravarman, and names Hindu gods and the founders of the Kambu empire, Pera and Kambu Svayambhuva. It also reports that the king had *lingams* erected in various places.

The floor of the small inner room lies below the level of the terrace outside, a characteristic feature that can be observed in many Khmer temples. On the altar there is a reclining Buddha from a later period.

Prasat Bei, comprising three semi-ruined brick shrines, arranged in a north-south alignment, stands near the moat which surrounds Angkor Thom.

*** THE CITY OF ANGKOR THOM

Angkorian period
Style of Baphuon 1010-1080
Built by: King Udayadityavarman II
1050-1066. Renovated in the post-Ang-korian period, after 1181, by King Jaya-varman VII, 1181-1219.
LOCATION: The southern gate is c. 1 mile (1.5 km) from Angkor Wat

The present day town of Angkor Thom – the name means Great City – has been built directly on top of the capital of King Udayadityavarman II. However, most of the buildings, the town wall and its gates date from the reign of Jayavarman VII. An inscription reads: "The city, adorned by a palace built of precious stones, was taken as a bride by this king, in order to beget the universe."

The Buddhist Jayavarman VII built his city as a symbol of the cosmos as it is conceived in the Ramayana, the Indian epic of Vishnu. Surrounded by the ocean, which is symbolized by the large or-namental pools, stands the *meru*, or mountain of the gods, represented by the Bayon temple in the very center of the city. The temple also recalls an episode of the Ramayana, the churning of the Sea of Milk, which is portrayed in many of Angkor's buildings. Not only the temple but the whole city is incorporated in this symbolism: outside the city gates, with their backs to the city, sit 27 demons on the right, and 27 gods on the left-hand side, who hold the gigantic serpent across their knees. The body of the snake, wrapped around the Bayon, is held, at its tail, by a stone giant standing at the north gate. There are similar giants at the east and west gates. Their violent heaving is supposed to set the Bayon spinning. If you are coming from Angkor Wat, you reach the "Street of Giants" outside the south gate. The same view is gained from

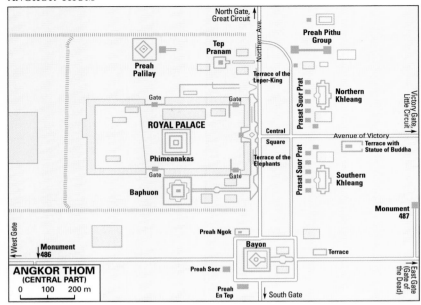

North Gate, Great Circuit

Northern Ave.

Preah Pithu Group

Tep Pranam

Preah Palilay

Terrace of the Leper-King

Gate · Gate

Prasat Suor Prat

Northern Khleang

Victory Gate, Little Circuit

ROYAL PALACE

Central

Square

Avenue of Victory

Terrace with Statue of Buddha

Phimeanakas

Terrace of the Elephants

Prasat Suor Prat

Gate · Gate

Southern Khleang

Baphuon

Monument 487

West Gate

Monument 486

Preah Ngok

Bayon

Terrace

ANGKOR THOM (CENTRAL PART)
0   100   200 m

Preah Seor

East Gate (Gate of the Dead)

Preah En Tep

South Gate

other directions, except that the other gates are not all in such a good state of repair.

Angkor Thom has five gateways: there is one in the middle of each side, while the fifth, the Victory Gate, stands 1,650 ft (500 m) north of the east gate, the Gate of the Dead. Causeways take the Streets of the Giants across the wide moat surrounding the city on all sides. At the end of the streets stand the 66-ft-high (20 m) gates with sculpted faces 10 ft (3 m) high facing the four points of the compass. These giant faces are a "trademark" of Jayavarman VII and can be found on many of his gates and shrines, as well as on the Bayon. The king saw himself as the incarnation of the Bodhisattva Avalokiteshvara (in Khmer: Lokiteshvara).

The face of the Bodhisattva has the features of the king as we know them from statues. Is he gazing out in all directions across his land?

Right: Relief on the Bayon temple, Angkor Thom.

130

Between the stone faces one can see small female figures, and the god Indra on his three-headed elephant, which is picking lotus flowers with its trunk.

As you walk through the mighty gates, you can see how hurriedly they were thrown up by piling stones on top of each other. On both sides niches have been erected for the gods of the city or for watchmen. From timbers that still remain in the roughhewn stone ceiling, one can tell that it was once lined entirely in wood.

Whoever enters Angkor Thom is followed by the gaze of the Boddhisattva or the king. The gateways lead through the wall of laterite stone, 26 ft (8 m) high in places, with which Jayavarman VII hoped to protect his city against attack by the Cham. An earth rampart was banked up against its inner side; along the top of the wall a foot- and bridlepath for the sentries runs for 7 1/2 miles (12 km) right round the city.

If one includes the 330-ft-wide (100 m) moat, Angkor Thom covers an area of three-and-a-half square miles (9 sq. km). A large part of it today is overgrown with jungle and scrub. Among the the 82 different species of trees there are a number which have died out in the rest of Cambodia. The only area that is kept clear is that around the temples and the ruins of the palace, which all lie to the north of the Bayon. It is difficult, standing here, to visualize a city with 100,000 inhabitants, living in thatched or tiled houses, such as the Chinese travellers described. It was surrounded by rice fields which provided them with food, and with reservoirs which irrigated the rice paddies and supplied the city with drinking water.

*** The Bayon Temple

Post-Angkorian period
Style of Bayon 1177-1230
Built by: King Jayavarman VII, 1181-1219.
LOCATION: In the geographical center of the city of Angkor Thom.

Looking at the Bayon, it is easy to see that the themes and conception of its design were altered several times during its construction. It is possible that it was built on the foundations of an earlier temple. Even before its completion, the two upper terraces were enlarged, making it necessary to widen the lower levels as well. This must be one of the reasons why some parts of the terraces collapsed. At the time when the Bayon was being built, Shivaitic Hinduism, the idea of the god-king, had lost its meaning. Jayavarman VII sought to re-establish the endangered authority of the throne with the help of Mahayana Buddhism. The Bayon represents a new concept of apotheosis and is an attempt to give it expression. It was to become a "manifestation of the meaning of God."

The temple-hill is a three-tiered pyramid with its entrance facing east. The lowest, outer gallery serves at the same time as an enclosing wall. From the inner

courtyard rises the pyramid. At its base it measures 525 ft by 460 ft (160 m by 140 m), while the topmost platform, on which the 75 ft (23 m) high central shrine stands, measures 230 ft by 262 ft (70 m by 80 m). In total the pyramid reaches a height of 141 ft (43 m) but the effect is massive rather than tall. It lacks the clear lines of the Angkorian temples and appears simply monumental.

Originally the ground plan was in the shape of a Greek cross, whose outer corner-angles were later closed off by transverse galleries so that, as the building rose up, the plan became an almost perfect square. Above it was built the round central shrine, and radiating out from it, twelve lesser shrines, in a design that was unusual for Angkor. The central structure, and the outer towers and pavilions, are crowned by more gigantic faces. Originally there were 54 of these, of which 37 have been preserved. From every tower these faces, each 10-15 ft (3-4.5 m) high, gaze out to the north, south, east and west. They are all a little differ-

ent from one another, yet each is the same face, that of Lokiteshvara with the features of Jayavarman VII.

In the central shrine was a *naga*-Buddha, an image of the Buddha often found in Angkorian Buddhism. The Enlightened One sits sunk in deep meditation on the coiled body of a snake, which spreads its hood protectively over him. The image is drawn from a legend in which the Buddha did not notice that a storm had broken and the river had risen over its banks. The snake-king carried him safely over the water.

The walls, pillars and lintels of the upper terrace are richly decorated with *apsaras*, *devas*, tendrils and ornaments. They do not attain the delicacy of the reliefs at Angkor Wat, and in any case it is difficult to concentrate on them because of the great stone faces all around. These are oppressive and rather alarming,

Above: The face of the Bodhisattva or of the king? Right: The Bayon temple.

though there is also something reassuring in their smiles, which seem to come from a deep knowledge and wisdom of the ages. If Angkor Wat is an introduction to the art of the Khmer, then the Bayon is a dialogue with their greatest king.

If you are approaching from the southern gate, the mighty south front of the Bayon is the first thing you see. The entrance to the temple leads in from the east side up to the steps, across a terrace of great paving stones. resting on pillars. The depressions in the ground on either side are believed to have held water. The remains of a laterite stone wall date from a later epoch; unlike all other Khmer temples, the Bayon originally had no wall around it. It is obligatory to walk round the temple in a clockwise direction.

The walls of the lower, double gallery are richly decorated with bas-reliefs, which were not completed during the king's lifetime. In their artistic value they are very inferior to the reliefs of Angkor Wat and other temples; nevertheless they are of great historical significance.

At the Bayon, as elsewhere, the king and his campaigns take pride of place in the scenes depicted on the reliefs. But here the artists seem to have been allowed more freedom. On the fringes of the victory parades and palace scenes they show the colorful daily life of the Khmer: market and hunting scenes, contests, games and riverside activities. The ordinary people, their clothing and hair styles, weapons and equipment, wagons and houses, are all shown as if in a picture book about the Khmer in the 12th and 13th centuries.

Following the east gallery to the left is a portrayal of prisoners shown beneath the victory procession – they are almost certainly Cham. After this come scenes at the palace; birds perch on the roofs and cooks are busy indoors.

Particular care has gone into the carving of the reliefs depicting *apsaras* and gods, on the walls and lintels of the pavi-

lions interspersed between the galleries. A long relief shows scenes on the river bank. All kinds of water creatures and fish are hanging in the branches of trees – a sight which can still be seen beside the Great Lakes each year, after the floods have receded. The scenes are humorous and animated, and depict intimate situations such as that of a woman about to give birth. Men discuss the proceedings at a cockfight, traders argue with customers at a market. Fishermen go about their work and a Chinese junk can be seen. A bear-hunt and wrestlers, artists and farmers alternate with palace scenes. Every so often openings in the wall give a view of the central shrine.

Climbing up and down between the galleries is not advisable except on the stairways that have been made safe. From the middle of the south gallery and through the inner courtyard, one reaches a steep flight of stairs to the second terrace. In its dark inner galleries a *naga-*Buddha sits in a little pavilion. A ladder has been installed for climbing to the third terrace. It is best to come down on the north side; the steps on the east and west sides are not safe to use.

***The Baphuon Temple

Angkorian period
Style of Baphuon 1010-1080
Built by: King Udayadityavarman II,
1050-1066. Constructed: 1060.
LOCATION: North of Bayon, at the beginning of the Great Square in front of the Royal Palace. From the road a staircase leads to the left (west).

The Baphuon, whose name means "copper tower," stood at the center of the capital city of Udayadityavarman II. The beauty of the architecture, ornamentation and reliefs of this great, three-tiered pyramid would, if it had better weathered the centuries, be comparable only to Angkor Wat. The outer walls enclosed a rectangular area of more than 13 acres (5.2 ha).

The Baphuon was, however, the most poorly constructed of all the temples in

Angkor. This is not helped by the practice, common in the 11th century, of inserting supporting timbers into the masonry. Some of these can still be seen. The gilded copper sheeting weighed heavily on the roof of the main tower, which was probably built, not of sandstone, but of some lighter material, so that soon after completion the upper level collapsed and the lower ones began to crack. Penetration by damp completed the work of destruction. The temple was repaired a number of times but never fully rebuilt. In 1958 restoration work was resumed, but was halted prematurely because of the difficult political situation at that time. What remains today is essentially the result of those efforts. At the end of the 1980s the area was cleared of trees and undergrowth.

From the ruins it is possible to tell how imposing the dimensions must have

been. The temple-hill must have been more than 164 ft (50 m) high; even today the ruin is still 80 ft (24 m) high. The main entrance in the east is reached by steps from the street that runs north and south. Behind the gateway is a path 660 ft (200 m) long leading to the temple-hill. Some way along the path is a building on a cruciform ground plan, but all that is left of it are the remains of walls.

The first tier of the pyramid, 13 ft (4 m) high and measuring 394 ft by 328 ft (120 m by 100 m) at its base, once supported a gallery, of which nothing now remains except the entrance pavilions. The gates and pavilions of the Baphuon have large vestibules.

In more recent times monks attempted to use the stones of the gallery to make a large reclining Buddha on the west side of the second storey, but only hints of this remain.

The second tier has two ledges, each 14 ft (4.3 m) high, and can be climbed from all four sides. On the south side the height of the steps has been halved by the

Above: The Baphuon temple in Angkor Thom. Right: A Buddhist nun.

addition of intermediate concrete steps. The second storey is surrounded by a narrow gallery, which is punctuated by towers at its corners and mid-points.

The temple was dedicated to Shiva, since Udayadityavarman II was a devout Shivaist. But in its reliefs many motifs from the Vishnu epics can be seen. The reliefs are set like pictures in rectangular frames, placed next to and above each other, with decorative geometric or botanical borders. The themes are taken from the Ramayana and Mahabharata epics and Buddhist legends, and show either single persons or little scenes. They display sharp observation and a sense of humor, and make a lively and earthy impression. The individual subjects, set off against a plain background, are of great beauty. Typical of these are the framed animal heads, some of which have been preserved at the entrance to the first terrace. The ornamentation is without doubt the most perfect in Khmer art.

The Royal City

LOCATION: The north-south road through Angkor Thom, Jayavarman VII's processional route, leads across the Great Square, the central point of the city which was the capital of Rajendravarman II, 944-968, Udayadityavarman II, 1050-1080, and of Jayavarman VII, 1181-1219.

The Great Square is bounded in the east by the 12 towers of Prasat Suor Sat and the North and South Khleangs behind them.

To the west of the Great Square lie the Royal terraces, and behind them the Royal Palace. It is encircled by a double rampart of laterite, which stretches 1,980 ft (600 m) from east to west and 990 ft (300 m) from north to south. In many descriptions it is referred to as Phimeanakas, but this is in fact the name of the small temple pyramid in the middle of the palace. The outer rampart is badly damaged, and its eastern part has been replaced by the royal terraces. The inner, well-preserved rampart is as much as 20 ft (6 m) high in places. Between the ramparts are the remains of water channels.

The palace grounds

There are two gates each on the north and south sides leading into the palace grounds. Between the two northern gates there is a further small entrance. The northern gates connect the first and second courtyards of the palace with the Terrace of the Leper-King and the temples of Tep Pranam and Preah Palilay. The southern gates lead from the courtyards into the grounds of the Baphuon temple. The main entrance to the east has two side gates and is on the same level as the Terrace of the Elephants. Above the outer central gate of the vestibule there are fine decorated lintels. The inscriptions on its walls contain the oaths sworn by the court officials, servants and vassals of King Suriyavarman II.

The date 933 *caka* corresponds to the year 1011 AD by western reckoning. This oath, or one very similar, was sworn right up to the present century.

In the five great courtyards, all that remains of the palace buildings is their foundation walls. The upper parts of all secular buildings, including the Royal Palace, were constructed of wood and have disappeared without trace. All buildings of stone, brick or laterite had religious functions.

In the first courtyard, which is 230 ft (20m) long with three gateways, stands one of the buildings described as libraries. The palace must have stood in the second and largest courtyard, which has a length of 300 yds (280 m). It was certainly not, as is often claimed, situated on one of the terraces beside the Great Square. The temple pyramid known as Phimeanakas, which will be described

Above: Terrace of the Elephants in Angkor Thom. Right: Terrace of the Leper-King.

136

later, occupies the center of the courtyard. A terrace on the southwest side could have been the site of the king's audience pavilion. From here a path leads to the south exit, where there are four small rectangular buildings of brick, laterite and stone, with vestibules facing west; their purpose is not known.

The third courtyard, 500 ft (150 m) long, is divided into two, so that there are actually five courtyards in total. In these last two courtyards were the working quarters of the royal household, and also the rooms where the royal family lived, and the quarters of the queen and and the king's other wives; these have pools with steps leading down to them.

The final courtyard has no separate exit. On a small terrace, panels decorated with elephants have been preserved.

*** Terrace of the Elephants

Built by: King Jayavarman VII, at the end of his reign, early 13th century.
LOCATION: West of the north-south street, on the Great Square.

To the east the palace grounds are bounded, not by an outer rampart, but by a terrace 1,140 ft by 45 ft (350 m by 14 m). Here, according to descriptions by 13th-century Chinese travellers, stood pavilions built from a material that has not survived. From this vantage point, the royal family could watch processions, parades and games on the Great Square. An audience or council chamber is also described, with mirrors and gilt window frames.

The terrace has three platforms of different heights, to which five flights of steps lead up; the northern one was probably built later than the others. The terrace takes its name from the outstanding depiction of elephants and of an elephant hunt, which takes up the major part of the frieze.

Alternating with the elephants, however, *garudas* and lions can be seen. The five-headed horse, Balacha, an incarnation of the Bodhisattva Lokitesvara, is represented on the north frontage, as are gladiators, artists and polo players.

***Terrace of the Leper-King
Built by: King Jayavarman VII at the end of his reign, early 13th century.
LOCATION: On the Great Square, north of the Terrace of the Elephants.

There is no path connecting the two terraces. This one owes its name to a sculpture which used to stand here. It was of King Yasovarman, 899-910, who originally founded Angkor and was popularly known as the "Leper-King" because he died of leprosy. This statue is now in the National Museum in Phnom Penh, and in fact does not represent a king in his regalia, but, very unusually in Khmer art, a seated, naked ascetic, perhaps an incarnation of Shiva.

This terrace, like the other one, served as the foundation for a lightly constructed pavilion. The suggestion that it was where high-ranking officials were cremated is not correct; this would not have been done in such a prominent place.

The bas-reliefs, in six or seven tiers, show kings, sword in hand, surrounded

by their retainers. The lower tiers are decorated with *nagas* and fish. The terrace appears to have ended at a lake which was a continuation of the Great Square, but which was filled in by Jayavarman VII in order to build the processional avenue. The palace scenes and shoals of fish on the friezes are similar to those on the reliefs at the Bayon and are among the most beautiful works of Khmer art.

**Phimeanakas

Angkorian, post-Angkorian periods.
Style of Khleang 978-1010 and style of Baphuon 1010-1080.
Dates: Begun by Jayavarman V, 968-1001, completed by Udayadityavarman II, 1050-1066.
LOCATION:In the center of the second courtyard of the royal palace. Can be reached through the east gate of the palace.

Above: Phimeanakas temple in the grounds of the royal palace in Angkor Thom.

The base of the three-terraced pyramid measures 115 ft by 92 ft (35m by 28m). The height of the three tiers decreases: the lowest is 15 ft (4.6m) high, the second 13 ft (4m) and the top one 11 ft (3.4m).

On the top tier there once stood a small building with a cruciform ground plan, and four entrances facing the points of the compass, but none of it has survived. However, it explains the name of the temple, which means "celestial palace." It is said that the tower had a golden roof.

The total height of the pyramid, without this added building is only 40 ft (12 m), but the stairways going steeply up each side make it look much higher. The corners of each terrace are decorated with lions and elephants. The final tier is surrounded by a gallery only 3 ft (1 m) wide, built of sandstone, with baluster windows and small corner towers, which give it great elegance.

According to legend, here the king met the snake-queen in the form of a beautiful woman. Their union created wisdom, which assured the prosperity of the land.

*Tep Pranam

Angkorian period.
Built by: King Yasovarman I, late 9th century.
LOCATION: Through the north exit of the first or second courtyard of the royal palace or beyond the Terrace of the Leper-King beside a narrow path going west.

On the terrace, which measures 270ft by 110 ft (82 m by 34 m) there is a 13-ft-high (4m) seated Buddha. An inscription states that a monastery was once here. A wooden pagoda also stood on the site. Around the terrace remains of burial stupas can still be seen, and a standing Buddha has been reassembled from fragments; only the face is missing.

A little further to the west is a dried-up lake whose northern bank was lined with sandstone blocks.

*Preah Palilay

Angkorian period.
Built in the mid-12th century.
Renovated by Jayavarman VII.
LOCATION: East of Tep Pranam.

A path leads west from Tep Pranam to a laterite rampart enclosing Palilay, in an area 55 yds square (50 m by 50 m). In front of the tower shrine are two adjacent terraces of different heights. Stone sentries and lions guard the east stairway. The main attraction of the site is the *naga* balustrade, one of the few that remain in good condition.

The small pavilion through which the shrine is reached has three passageways. The shrine has unusual decoration and its odd outline resembles a chimney.

The lintels over the east and west doors are very beautifully decorated. The figurative ornamentation is drawn from Hindu and Buddhist iconography. As one enters the shrine one can still see some large wooden beams that were used as door hinges.

THE TEMPLES ON THE EAST SIDE OF THE GREAT SQUARE

*The Prasat Suor Prat

Probably built by Jayavarman VII at the beginning of the 13th century.

Twelve small towers built of laterite stand facing the the Terrace of the Elephants, at the edge of the jungle on the east side of the Great Square. They are often described as pavilions for the dancers who entertained the king and his household. To the local people, however, they were known as Prasat Suor Sat, "the towers of the tightrope-walkers," because the performers stretched their high wires between them. However, a Chinese traveller stated that they were places where justice was dispensed.

They stand on a north-south line, equidistant from each other. They are two storeys high, each with two gables but no staircases. Altars and images of gods suggest a religious purpose. They are open to the west so that they can look on to the Great Square. They appear not to have been completed inside or outside, since not all the sandstone walls have been dressed; a number of the stones appear to have been put to some previous use.

North and South Khleang

Angkorian period.
Khleang style (965-1010), built under Jayavarman V and Suryavarman II.
LOCATION: To the east of the Great Square, hidden in the jungle behind Prasat Suor Prat. From the road facing the Terrace of the Elephants, which leads to the east gate, narrow paths go to the left and right into the jungle.

The present name, Khleang, means no more than "storehouse," but there is no doubt that these are sacred buildings, which were surrounded by courtyards and smaller buildings. They faced west, towards the Great Square and the royal palace, and they once had terraces in front of them, though these are no longer recognizable. Terraces and courtyards, with buildings and galleries, also lay to the east of the Khleangs. In the courtyard to the east of the North Khleang a small shrine has been preserved, with its lower walls decorated and friezes embellished with figures. Of the buildings of the South Khleang there are only ruins to be seen. Altars with a *linga* and figures were found in both the Khleangs. The Buddhist relics date from a later period.

The North Khleang is better preserved. Both Khleangs have porches built on the east and west fronts and galleries at the side. Laterite and sandstone were used in their construction. The stones have been carefully laid on top of each other, and the interior is paved with sandstone.

The side galleries were roofed in wood. The façades are richly decorated without being overly ornate. A similarity can be noticed between the entrance pavilions and those at the temple pyramid of Ta Keo.

From the North Khlenag a narrow footpath brings you to Preah Pithu.

*Preah Pithu

Angkorian period.
Style of Angkor Wat
Built by: A successor of Suriyavarman II
LOCATION: On the high ground where Tep Pranam and Preah Palilay are sited, but east of the north-south road; or reached by the footpath from the North Khleang.

The five small shrines are scattered in a random fashion over rough terrain and are badly damaged. If they were still intact, all five shrines of the Pithu group would be real gems of Khmer art.

Beyond the North Khleang and to the right is a small shrine surrounded by a

Right: Dancers from the Academy of Arts performing at Angkor Wat.

rampart of sandstone; there are two entrance pavilions on the east and west sides. There is a terrace on two levels with a beautiful *naga*-balustrade, comparable to the one at Preah Palilay. The decoration on the pyramid-shaped base of the shrine is especially remarkable. The churning of the Sea of Milk is shown several times, and *devatas (tevodas)* embellish the corners of the walls.

To the east of the first shrine is a smaller, badly damaged one on a single-tiered base. Surrounded by a rampart, it has richly decorated walls. Two stone sentries have fallen from their pedestals by the western entrance. On the west wall are several depictions of the four-armed Shiva dancing. Each temple is surrounded by a small artificial pond.

To the east a path leads between the ponds to a third shrine on a simple 12-ft-high (3.6 m) platform, with a surface area of 13,000 sq. ft (1,225 sq. m). The interior resembles a monk's cell and is decorated with Buddhas. To the east of the temple on a raised laterite embankment, is a terrace which is reached by a flight of sandstone steps, flanked by stone sentries and *nagas*.

Only traces of a temple are still recognizable here. Certain characteristics of the statues of Buddha seem to suggest to the trained eye, that the building must have been restored during the Siamese occupation. About 60 ft from the steps are two small stone elephants, 5 ft (1.5 m) high.

The fourth shrine lies to the north on a two-tiered base with ornate friezes. The building itself is simple, and the entrance porches were added at a later date. From a few lintels that were left unfinished it is possible to observe the working methods of the Khmer sculptors. A surrounding wall stretches almost as far as the Great Circuit.

The fifth shrine is situated further north and differs from the other four, being more like the buildings which are

described as the lodgings provided by Jayavarman for pilgrims, such as those found on the sites of his great monasteries. They are square, tower-like buildings, each with a long room built on to the front. In this case, the two parts are linked by a narrow passageway. The beautiful bas-reliefs on the building show religious scenes.

Monument 487
Date of construction: 1296
LOCATION: From the road to the east gate, which starts opposite the Bayon Temple, follow a path to the left, parallel to the Great Square, for about 990 ft (300 m).

This isolated and unnamed building is simply listed in the catalogue as No. 487. It faces east, and consists of a monastic cell on a cruciform ground plan. From the outside it looks like a square windowless tower. Inside it houses a statue of the Brahman Manggalartha, on a double plinth.

On the lintels are illustrations of the legends of Vishnu/Krishna: the churning of the Sea of Milk, Krishna holding the mountain aloft, the three steps of Vishnu with which he strides across the world, and the four-armed dancing Shiva.

Monument 486
Date of construction: Late 13th century.
LOCATION: Halfway along the road to the west gate, on the left. Really not worth visiting.

This was the site in the 10th century of a shrine to Vishnu built of laterite and sandstone. In the 14th century a pagoda stood here; it was 50 ft (15 m) long and contained a statue of the Buddha, of which only the plinth now remains. Behind it were three small buildings in a row on a single base; the middle one, the largest, had a cruciform ground plan and was raised higher than the others. The lintels over the doors resembled those of Banteay Srei. These dated from the end of the 10th century. The motifs are drawn

141

from Hindu mythology, while those on the walls are of Buddhist origin.

THE BUILDINGS ON THE LITTLE CIRCUIT

**Thommanon and Chay Say Tevoda
Angkorian period
Style of Angkor Wat 1100-1175
Built by: King Suriyavarman II, 1113-1150
LOCATION: The Little Circuit begins at the triumphal gate of Angkor Thom. After about 1 1/4 miles (2 km) Thommanon is found on the left, and Chau Say Tevoda opposite on the right hand side of the road.

It is thought that both shrines were built at the same time, and that the architect tried to create or to try out different effects by means of small variations in

Above: The Ta Keo temple in Angkor. Unlike the other Khmer buildings, this five-tiered pyramid has no relief decoration.

the design and decoration of the main shrine.

Thommanon, the shrine to Vishnu, is surrounded by a rampart of which the east and west gateways still survive. It consists of a tower shrine with three false doors and large porticoes. The fourth portal leads from the east side through a portico into the large interior. The width of the building from east to west is 72 ft (22 m) The tower, with plain pilasters at its corners, contrasts with the side wings which are decorated with continuous friezes all the way round. In Chau Say this concept is modified. The lintels, friezes and pilasters are richly decorated with scenes from the Vishnu epics, especially the Ramayana.

Opposite is **Chau Say**, set some 100 ft (30 m) back from the road, and said to date from 1160. The main shrine with its four wings and central space, stands on a large plinth and faces east. It differs from Thommanon in that the temple tower is linked as single entity, with the wide wings, by ledges running round it which

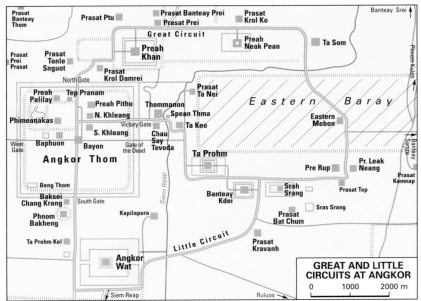

GREAT AND LITTLE
CIRCUITS AT ANGKOR

0   1000   2000 m

have the same decorative motifs. In this it resembles the towers of Angkor Wat. The side wings have baluster windows, and the decoration gives the impression that the building has several storeys. However, the upper part of the tower was never completed.

The porch running from east to west has four doors and four false windows. The eastern end connects it with the main tower, whose walls also have balustered false windows.

The main buildings, surrounded by two libraries and gates, are linked by terraces with *naga*-balustrades.

Chau Say is a shrine to Shiva in which *lingas* and sculptures of Nandi have been found. The ornamentation is, however, taken mainly from the Vishnu legends.

Spean Thma. About 2,300 ft (700 m) east of the triumphal gate, close to the road, there is one bridge of sandstone still standing: all the others being built of laterite. It is decorated with a *naga*-balustrade.

**Ta Keo

Angkorian period
Begun by Jayavarman in the style of Khleang, in 965-1010. Construction continued in the reign of Suriyavarman, in the the style of Angkor Wat, yet still seems to have been left unfinished.
LOCATION: On the Little Circuit, about half a mile (1km) beyond the Thommanon.

It may have been the great size of this impressive building, or the materials used in its construction, which prevented work on it ever being completed. The five-tiered pyramid has a unique place among Khmer buildings since it has nothing to show in the way of decorative reliefs or sculptures. That has given rise to the mistaken belief that it was stripped of its decoration by the Cham, or even that it was used for human sacrifice.

The enormous blocks of very hard sandstone that were used in Ta Keo were difficult to work. The outline of the temple looks plain, even bald. There is

143

nothing to distract the eye from the clear lines of the architecture, or from the effect of its impressive proportions. The structure, when completed, was to have reached a height of about 165 ft (50m).

Five tiers serve as the base for the central shrine, which was surrounded by four smaller towers.

The first terrace, 7 ft (2.2 m) high, has a base measuring 328 ft (100 m) from east to west and 400 ft (120 m) from north to south. Pavilions aligned on these axes lead to the inner courtyard, from which further terraces rise.

On the east side of the courtyard stand two small, ruined buildings which are generally considered to have been libraries, treasure chambers, or possibly lodgings for pilgrims.

The second terrace, on a plinth 18 ft (5.5 m) high, and measuring 262 ft by 246 ft (80 m by 70 m) at its base, is surrounded by a gallery which is punctuated

Above: Huge trees threaten the temples of Angkor.

by pavilions along its length. The third platform, 154 ft (47 m) square and surrounded at its foot by four pavilions, has three bases with heights of 19 ft, 15 ft and 12 ft (5.8 m, 4.5 m and 3.6 m). These bring the total height, including the towers, to 72 ft (22 m).

There are examples of lovely ornamentation 40 ft (12 m) up on the east façade, which were sculpted from the top downwards, and on the friezes around the second tier. Inscriptions tell us that Ta Keo was built as a temple to Shiva, and there have been finds of *lingas* and statue of Nandi. As in other temples, the statues of the Buddha date from a later period, when monks lived in Angkor. One inscription gives details of a hospital which was located near the temple.

From the topmost terrace the hills of Phnom Kulen can be seen far way to the northeast.

*Prasat Ta Nei
Post-Angkorian period
Style of Bayon 1177-1230
Built by: Jayavarman VII at the beginning of the 12th century.
LOCATION: 3,000 ft (900 m) east of Ta Keo, reached by a footpath.
The rampart and gates are in a ruined condition.

The method of construction using a mixture of materials, laterite and sandstone, is typical. The main Buddhist shrine lies some way to the west in a courtyard measuring 118 ft by 115 ft (36 m by 35 m). The gateway behind it leads to the galleries which surround the temple. About 270 ft (80 m) further on is the east gate, with a representation of the Bodhisattva Lokiteshvara.

***Ta Prohm
Post-Angkorian period
Style of Bayon 1177-1230
Built by: King Jayavarman VII, 1181-1219. Date of construction: 1186

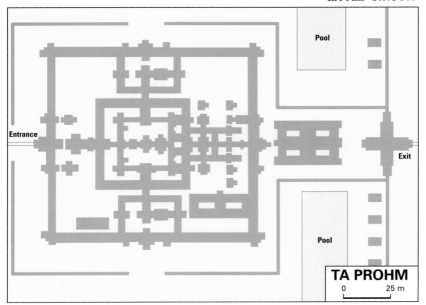

TA PROHM

0   25 m

LOCATION: On the Little Circuit, entrance through the west gate by the 4th kilometer stone; exit through the east gate.

There is hardly a temple anywhere else that shows so clearly the destructive power of the luxuriant tropical vegetation. When French archaeologists first discovered the site of the temple, they left the giant trees standing, even though their huge roots were coiling themselves like enormous snakes around the temple, penetrating its stonework and breaking it up. But now some of these giants will have to be felled in order to save the temple.

Jayavarman VII had the monastery built as a residence for his mother, who had been deified as Prajnaparamita. Ta Prohm looks rather like a smaller version of Angor Thom.

The laterite rampart encloses a large space with an area of 175 acres (73 ha). At the west gateway there is a towering stone face, like those to be seen at the gates of Angkor Thom and at the Bayon, in an excellent state of preserva-tion. The *dvarapala*, guardian figures, the *garuda* and *naga* balustrade, on the other hand, are badly damaged. A path paved with sandstone leads across the outer moat to the second rampart and its entrance pavilion which is not well preserved. The main shrine is in the center, surrounded by dense green jungle, into which light filters through the branches of tall trees.

A 12th century inscription carved in a stone post tells of the king's victories over the Cham and describes life in Ta Prohm. It appears that the monastery and the queen mother's household comprised 18 chief bonzes and 2740 monks, as well as 2232 other residents, including 615 dancers. Altogether 66,625 men and women from the surrounding villages worked in the service of the monastery.

You have to walk about 1/4 mile (400 m) into the jungle on a marked path, to reach the balustrade around the inner moat and the laterite rampart behind it, which encloses the inner temple area.

145

The entrance building consists of a large hall with three cloisters, and nearby there is another with square columns. Beside the rampart there are about 100 monks' cells with porticos of laterite. The path leads into a large courtyard whose walls are decorated with false gates.

The temple, which measures 476 ft by 410 ft (145 m by 125 m), is a labyrinth of passages, galleries and halls, made even more confusing by the jungle vegetation forcing its way in from all sides. The path is marked to help one avoid places where the building is crumbling.

After making one's way through small courtyards and galleries one reaches the main shrine, which rises out of a courtyard 80 ft (24 m) square. It is in a very ruined state. The tower has no decoration, but might once have been covered in metal sheathing.

Above: A soldier detailed to protect the temple of Banteay Srei. Right: View across the artificial lake of Srah Srang.

The older parts of Ta Prohm display careful workmanship and a variety of ornamentation; dancing *apsaras* are almost as common as at Angkor Wat. The later parts are carelessly executed in the manner typical of the end of Jayavarman's reign. They show the haste with which he urged the completion of his numerous building projects.

Ta Prohm was built as a monastery for a large number of people, not as a place for worshipping the gods or god-kings, as were the temples of the Angkor period.

This explains the completely different design. Around the main building there are many small pavilions, cells and shrines, as well as houses for accommodating pilgrims. The marked footpath leads on to the east gate, which has lost its giant stone face.

**Banteay Kdei

Post-Angkorian period
Style of Bayon 1177-1230
Built by: Jayavarman VII, 1181-1219
Date of construction: 1181
LOCATION: From the east gate of Ta Prohm return to the Little Circuit. Cross this and you come to the west gate of Banteay Kdei.

Banteay Kdei is similar to Ta Prohm in its overall conception, so that it could be given a miss if time is short; but it does have the advantage of being less confusing and also there is a greater unity in the way the sculptures are executed. Most importantly, it has largely been cleared of vegetation.

Jayavarman VII had it built for his tutors, as the first of three great monastic sites in Angkor. The outer of the two ramparts measures 2,300 ft by 1,650 ft (700 m by 500 m), and the the entrance gateways are flanked by giant stone faces. A short path brings you to the inner temple complex, which is 1,050 ft by 990 ft (320 m by 300 m). The main temple is 207 ft by 164 ft (63 m by 50 m).

In two small buildings in the northeast and southeast courtyards there are some statues of a kind rarely found in Angkor: carefully sculpted female deities. One leaves Banteay Kdei by its east gate, where there is a well-preserved *garuda*.

*Srah Srang

LOCATION: Opposite the east gate of Banteay Kdei.

The small artificial lake was probably created at the same time as Banteay Kdei. Brick steps lead down to the the water, which covers 80 acres (32 ha). To the west it must have been linked to Banteay Kdei by a terrace, on which stood pavilions built of some impermanent material. In the middle of the lake, a heap of stones is all that remains of a former building.

The lake is locally known as the King's Bath or Monk's Bath. In its setting of green, it presents a delightful panorama, especially in the soft light of the evening sun.

**Prasat Kravanh

Angkorian period
Style of Koh Ker, 921-944
Built by a court official around 921.
LOCATION: Between the 7th and 8th kilometer stones on the Little Circuit. It is inaccessible during the rainy season.

Prasat Kravanh, a shrine to Vishnu, is one of the last large brick buildings in Angkor and still belongs to the artistic trend that began in the reign of Indravarman. It has reliefs carved directly into the walls, and signs of having been completely painted inside. It consists of five large, windowless tower-shrines standing side by side. The sandstone door frames are decorated with foliage and small figures of riders.

Tower shrines of the Indravarman period are not usually decorated inside, but Kravanh is an exception as its central tower has reliefs carved directly on to the interior stonework. These can be seen at their best when the evening sun slants into the inner rooms.

147

Prasat Bat Chum

Angkorian period
Style of Koh Ker, 921-944
Approximate date: Mid-10th century.
LOCATION: About 1/2 mile (1 km)
northeast of Prasat Kravanh, and 1/4
mile (400 m) south of Srah Srang.

The small three-towered shrine made of brick has fine sandstone lintels.

THE TEMPLES ON THE GREAT CIRCUIT

**Preah Khan

Post-Angkorian period
Style of Bayon, 1177-1230
Built by: Jayavarman VII, 1181-1219
Date of construction: 1191
LOCATION: The Great Circuit begins at
the north gate of Angkor Thom. The outer
moat of the Temple of Preah Khan is
about 900 ft (250 m) north of the moat

Above: The Preah Khan temple on the Great Circuit.

round Angkor Thom. From the north entrance of the temple a footpath leads along beside the temple to the east entrance.

The third of Jayavarman's monasteries was built for his father and is called Preah Khan, "Holy Sword," after the protective symbol of Cambodia. The site is one of the largest temple compounds in Angkor and is defended by four concentric walls. To the south and east the site is bounded by the now dry Eastern Baray, a reservoir, in the middle of which stands the temple of Preah Neak Pean. The design of the building is similar to that of Ta Prohm and Banteay Kdei. However, the entrances do not have those great stone faces. From the east and west, roads flanked by stone pillars lead to the temple. The first rampart has outer dimensions of 2,700 ft by 2,295 ft (800 m by 700 m) and is surrounded by a wide moat, once guarded by *garudas*, 23ft (7 m) high. On all four sides, a "Street of Giants," as in Angkor Thom, leads across the moat.

The entrance pavilion in the outer rampart has three passages, each with a tapering tower decorated with a double crest of lotus leaves. The middle entrance was for elephants. Only the two side entrances have porticoes and vestibules, in which idols might once have stood. Within the walls a path leads through the jungle to a terrace decorated with snakes and lions, in front of the inner temple. The rampart around the central shrine is 570 ft (175 m) wide and 660 ft (200 m) long. On each side there are entrance pavilions with ornate porticoes.

However, the second, higher rampart of laterite is entered through plain doors. It is 270ft long and 320 ft long (83 m by 90 m) and was once surmounted by a gallery, but this has not survived. The main shrine and its adjoining buildings are richly decorated. The lintels, bas-reliefs, pediments, friezes and panels are all adorned with Buddhist motifs and scenes from the Hindu epics with goddesses, dancers and a wealth of other detail.

The paths are littered with blocks of stone from the ruined monuments, and with the dense undergrowth the going can be difficult. It is advisable to return to the east entrance.

Prasat Banteay Prei
Post-Angkorian period
Style of Bayon 1177-1230
Built by: Jayavarman VII, 1181-1219
LOCATION: 1/4 mile (400 m) north of the northeast corner of Preah Khan.

Near the entrance pavilion of the rampart, which measures 243 ft by 177 ft (74 m by 54 m), there is a gallery 100 ft by 80 ft (30 m by 24 m) enclosing a very small shrine. This has no noteworthy features.

Prasat Prei
Post-Angkorian period
Style of Bayon 1177-1230
LOCATION: In the jungle, a little way south of Banteay Prei.

The small, ruined shrine has large false doors and a library built of sandstone and laterite.

Prasat Ptu

The building north-west of Preah Khan is reached by a footpath, and is about 2 miles (3 km) away. It is built of laterite and may have been used as a lodging for pilgrims.

**Neak Pean
Post-Angkorian period
Style of Bayon, 117-1230
Built by: King Jayavarman VII, 1181-1219
LOCATION: Near the 6th kilometer stone on the Great Circuit, the road crosses the dyke of the Eastern Baray and turns southward.

Standing in the middle of the Eastern Baray is a square platform, measuring 1,140 ft (350 m) on each side, with flights of steps up each side. Only one of the sandstone elephants guarding them, on the northwest corner, still survives. On two sides the Great Circuit runs along the top of the dykes. Inside the walls of the shrine there were once several artificial lakes. Only one remains, surrounded by four pools 80 ft (25 m) wide, to which brick steps descend.

The four outer pools were linked to the middle one by small pavilions built up from the bottom of the pools. Their vaulted roofs were at the same level as a paved footpath running round the central pool, which is 230 ft (70 m) square. It served as a walkway around the shrine, which was consecrated to the Bodhisattva Lokiteshvara.

In the middle of the central pool stands a small sandstone temple on a round platform 46 ft (14 m) in diameter, to which steps lead up.

Writhing around the base of the platform are two coiled *nagas*, whose heads and torsos rear up towards the east en-

trance while their tails curl vertically towards the west entrance. The name Neak Pean means "coiled snakes."

The temple symbolized Lake Anavatapta in the Himalayas, in which the four great rivers which give the world the sacred and lifegiving benison of water, are said to have their source.

Neak Pean has lost its *prasat*, which rose up from a lotus-shaped base. Trees and plants have invaded the site. The reliefs are difficult to make out and the pools are only filled with water at the end of the rainy season. Nevertheless, it has retained much of its charm.

Prasta Krol Ko

A small shrine, 115 ft by 82 ft (35 m by 25 m), displays the same decoration as Neak Pean and also dates from the reign of Jayavarman VII.

Above and right: The temple of Banteay Srei, built by a Brahman, is a jewel of architecture and sculpture.

**Ta Som
Post-Angkorian period
Bayon style, 1177-1230
Built by: Jayavarman VII, 1181-1219
LOCATION: Near the 8th kilometer stone on the Great Circuit.

Above the west entrance gate is a giant stone face. The outer wall is 660 ft by 780 ft (200 m by 240 m). The architecture and reliefs are similar to those of Banteay Kdei and Ta Prohm. The trees and bushes on the temple site have been left largely undisturbed.

Under the Khmer Rouge regime, there was an army field hospital in Ta Som.

**Eastern Mebon
Angkorian period
Style of Pre Rup, 947-965
Built by: Rajendravarman II, 944-968
Date of construction: 945
LOCATION: On the Great Circuit, between the 10th and 11th kilometer stones, in the dried-up Eastern Baray. Inaccessible during the rainy season.

The temple stands on what was once an island in the Eastern Baray, and was built by Rajendrvarman II as a shrine to his ancestors.

The square platform has sides of 425 ft (130 m) and is 11 ft (3.4 m) high. At its four corners stand elephants, delicately carved in sandstone, with bells round their necks. Other well-preserved stone elephants can be found on the east side.

In general style, the temple belongs to the Indravarman epoch which began with the Bakong temple at Roluos. In the entrance pavilion of the outer wall there is an inscription, which praises King Rajendravarman II and states that he had eight *lingas* put up, as well as statues of Vishnu and Brahma.

In the courtyard lie the ruins of small laterite shrines, which had porches. Pavilions provide access through the inner wall, and the terrace is surrounded by small brick buildings. The elephants at each corner are not so well preserved. The top platform is 105 ft (32 m) square and supports the central shrine. The

upper structure resembles the pyramid of Ta Keo, the central tower being surrounded by four smaller ones. However, the reddish brick gives a greater effect of warmth, and the sandstone settings are very carefully worked. Holes in the brickwork are a clue that the walls were once decorated with stucco.

**Pre Rup

Angkorian period
Style of Pre Rup, 947-965
Built by: Rajendravarman II, 944-968
Date of construction: 961
LOCATION: Near the 12th kilometer stone on the Great Circuit. Inaccessible during the rainy season.

This is a three-tiered temple-hill surmounted by a principal shrine around which four *prasats* are arranged symmetrically. It faces west and was built by King Rajendravarman II as his mausoleum, and a shrine where he would be worshipped after his death. The temple pyramid is similar to the nearby Eastern

Mebon, though its function as a mausoleum gives it some unusual features.

The pyramid is 164 ft (50 m) square at its base, and its top terrace is 115 ft (35 m) square. The five tower-shrines are built of brick. Stone lions guard the stairways, and small shrines stand on the two terraces. Around the lower terrace, the stone gallery with wooden beams and a tiled roof, is a new addition. It is intended to look like the wooden gallery that was there before.

The stone sarcophagus of the king is on the second terrace, and in front of it stands a *lingam*. A stele on the left tells the history of the building of the temple. The small building in the southwest corner of the terrace is where the bones of the king were kept; his ashes were contained in a golden urn in the main tower.

Prasat Lak Neang

Style of Pre Rup, 947-965
LOCATION: At the northeast corner of Pre Rup, on the far side of the road.

This small shrine dates from 960. A sandstone lintel shows Indra on his three-headed elephant.

*Banteay Samre

Angkorian period
Style of Angkor Wat, 1100-1175
Built by: Suriyavarman II
LOCATION: At the southeastern corner of the Eastern Baray. At the 11th kilometer stone on the Great Circuit, take the road to Phnom Kulen. After about 1,200 ft (350 m) you come to a path leading into the jungle.

The central part of this temple, built on level ground, is well preserved. Its overall plan and architecture are easy to grasp, and its friezes and reliefs are carefully executed.

The first rampart consists of a gallery which is only open on the inward side. Its timber roof has not survived. At the southeast corner of the gallery a gap in the wall provides access through the second rampart into the central part of the temple. The east pavilion of the inner gallery measures 120 ft by 115 ft (37m by 35 m) and is in good repair. The reliefs show scenes from the Vishnu/Krishna legends. With the exception of the tower, the main shrine is also well preserved. The building is considered to be the most beautiful ground-level temple built in the Angkor Wat style.

***Banteay Srei

Angkorian period
Style of Banteay Srei 965-1000
Built by: the Brahman Vajnavaraha, of royal descent, tutor of kings Rajendravarman II and Jayavarman V.
Date of construction: 967
LOCATION: 12 miles (20 km) northeast of Angkor Thom

Banteay Srei is a traditional local name and means "Citadel of Women." This temple to Shiva used to be called Tribhuvana Mahesvara, and stood in Isvarapura, the city of Shiva. Like all non-royal temples Banteay Srei is a small shrine and was built by the Brahman on property which had been granted to him by the king.

To the east and west, moats were dug in front of the double rampart around the temple. A gatehouse gives a foretaste of the perfection that awaits the visitor: the harmonious design and the beauty and richness of the decoration.

In the center of the inner courtyard three tower-shrines with porches stand upon a single plinth. They are built of glowing pink sandstone and the effect of this color contributes to the enchanting impression that the temple makes. Two libraries and several long halls fit into the relatively confined space.

Lavish decoration covers walls and lintels, pediments and friezes, though no motif is ever repeated. The stairways are

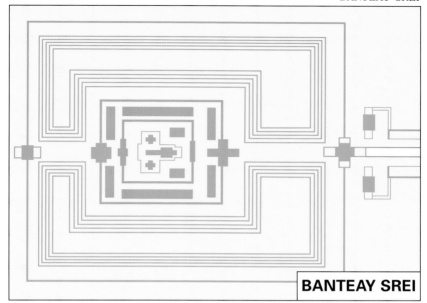

BANTEAY SREI

flanked by guardian figures with animal heads, which appear to be those of lions and monkeys.

Features that are especially beautiful are the triangular pediments, which have been adopted from the Koh Ker style, and the tympanums filled with foliage. The lintels over the doors are among the most beautiful in Khmer art. One can see the successful combination of older styles with new ideas, appearing here for the first time.

It is easy to overlook the elegant simplicity of the ground plan and design, so absorbed is one by the wealth of detail. Shiva is frequently represented, and there are many variations on themes from the Krishna and Vishnu legends. It is difficult to describe the countless graceful goddesses and dancing girls who adorn the walls.

Banteay Srei with its interplay of form and color cannot be compared with the monuments of the classical Khmer period but it is the supreme achievement of a charming artistic imagination.

EXPEDITIONS FROM ANGKOR

In the Angkor area there are very many small, out-of-the-way buildings, which take a long time to find, let alone visit. It is essential to have a guide with local knowledge, because due to the war and the civil war many of the paths are mined as well as overgrown.

Buildings to be seen include:
– **Prasat Prei** near Prasat Banteay Prei
– **Prasat Ptu** to the NW of Preah Khan
– **Prasat Banteay Thom** and **Prasat**
– **Krol Damrei** by the north gate of Angkor Thom
– **Prasat Tonle Snguot** and **Prasat**
– **Trapeang Repou**, 2 miles (3 km) from Phnom Bakheng.

Expeditions to the Great Lakes and to the **Phnom Krom** have recently become possible once again.

It would also be worth paying a visit to **Phnom Kulen**, but only when the political situation has been stabilized and after the roads have been cleared of mines.

WHEN A RIVER REVERSES
ITS CURRENT

When the moon begins to wax, in the month of *kattik*, or November in our calendar, the villages on the four rivers become restive and seized by an unusual amount af activity. Phnom Penh, Cambodia's present-day capital, stands where the Tonle Sap flows into the Mekong and this river immediately divides again into the Bassac and the Lower Mekong. When it was founded in 1434 its name was Chattumuk – Four Rivers. This is where the water festival has a special significance.

All over the country statues of the Buddha are washed in their pagodas, processions take place, and neighbors and strangers alike sprinkle each with with beneficent water. The festival is joyfully celebrated with boa traces, music, singing and games.

Above: Fishingboats near Phnom Penh.
Right: Ferries bring visitors to the festival.

Many days before the festival the long, narrow boats are hauled out of their sheds in monasteries and villages, and carried down to the water. Then the crews begin their training. Forty or more oarsmen sit close behind one another in the boats that are as much as 100 ft (30 m) long. The helmsman sets the rhythm for their powerful strokes and the boat seems scarcely to touch the surface as it shoots forward.

When the festival day is imminent, the boats are varnished and golden eyes are painted on to the bow. They carry with them rice and fruit as sacrificial gifts to the gods of earth and water. Many boats are accompanied by monks or by village dignitaries, as they make their way to the capital. They are followed by orchestras with bronze gongs and drums with stretched snakeskin heads.

From every direction come not only racing boats but hundreds of fishing craft, ferries, canoes and sampans, all heading for the riverside city. Meanwhile spectators are arriving on bikes, motorbikes, rickshaws, trucks and buses.

In the terrible years of the war and the tyranny of the Khmer Rouge many traditions seemed to have been lost. But when Prince Sihanouk returned to Phnom Penh for the water festival in 1991, all the old memories were reawakened, and ancient rituals were revived, which only the oldest of the people could still remember. The younger generation listened to them in amazement; the thronging crowds and the jubilation were unimaginable. The water festival lasted three days; even the nights were turned into day with illuminations, fireworks, music, song and unbridled merriment.

The traditional proceedings begin with the arrival of the boats and the festival guests. Not far from the royal palace, near the bank of the Tonle Sap, a miniature replica of a floating palace lies at anchor. It was from here that the king and queen ruled for the three days and took part in the ceremonies. This tradition was maintained by Prince Sihanouk and his consort, during the 40 years that he ruled the country.

The boat races take place in the afternoons. The oarsmen, spurred on by rhythmic singing, drumrolls and shouts of encouragement, seem to gain in strength the nearer they come to the finishing-line. At night, fantastically decorated dragon boats cruise up and down, fireworks soar into the skies and are reflected in the river. Music can be heard coming from the boats.

By tradition each boat has three candles on board. They represent the district from which the boat comes, and the two neighboring districts. As the candle-wax melts and drops on to banana leaves, it forms patterns, which give a prediction of the rainfall and therefore of the harvest in the coming year.

When the full moon is reflected in the water, the festival reaches its climax, but is also approaching its finale: in a solemn ceremony the king commands the Tonle Sap, together with the Bassac and Mekong, to flow to the sea. And within a short time the river does indeed obey this command.

Its waters first come to a standstill, and then, as the Cambodians believe, the river is set free from evil spirits and flows in its natural direction towards the sea.

During the six months from May to November, the melting snows in the mountains of Tibet raise the level of the Mekong, and its tributaries, swollen by the monsoon rains, add their waters to the flood. By the end of May the water level can have risen by as much as 40 ft (12 m). This means that, like most rivers in Asia, it would normally have to overflow its banks and flood large areas of land. However, the river Tonle Sap, which has practically no incline and connects the Great Lakes, also called Tonle Sap, with the Mekong, takes off a huge volume of water from the Mekong and carries it back *upstream* to to the Great Lakes. This is a huge low-lying area filled with fertile mud, which is only 5 ft (1.5 m) deep in

Above: Fishingboats at Sihanoukville. Right: Fish is an important element in the Cambodian diet.

the middle. It begins 80 miles (130 km) northwest of the confluence of the Tonle Sap with the Mekong.

The water then causes a flood of vast extent. The lakes take up the water which would otherwise submerge the entire Cambodian plain. The people who live beside the lakes have not only adjusted to this annual inundation, they make a living from it. The surface area of the lakes increases from about 1,160 square miles (3,000 sq. km) to 4,247 square miles (11,000 sq. km), and its depth increases to 46 ft (14 m).

The forest region that stretches from Kompong Thom in the east to Sisophon in the west, lies under water, with only the tops of the trees visible. Boats are the only means of transport between the houses built on piles, whose floors are just above the level of the water.

The livestock will have been driven in good time up to the higher ground, but carts and farm equipment are left in the water, beneath the houses. Fortunately this regular flooding is predictable; the water never rises above a certain level and so no catastrophe ever occurs. On the contrary, it provided the basis for the advanced civilization of Angkor. Thanks to their outstanding hydraulic technology, this body of water was exploited for the irrigation of the rice fields, and to this day it provides a livelihood for the densely populated areas around the Great Lakes, where three-quarters of the inhabitants of Cambodia live.

When the glaciers in Tibet are once more frozen solid and the flow of water abates in the tributaries of the Mekong, the waters of the Mekong itself drop to their lowest level of the year. This is the moment when the Tonle Sap – in obedience to the king's command – reverses the direction of its flow and carries the water from the Great Lakes into the Mekong and onward down to the sea. The people who live on the lakes anxiously await this phenomenon.

THE SEASON OF THE GREAT FISH HARVEST

While the floodwaters turn the Great Lakes into an inland sea, huge quantities of fish are able to feed on algae, plankton and plants and insects from the submerged forests. The inland waters of Cambodia are probably richer in fish than any in the world. No official figures have yet been given for the catches – but they are said to exceed 100,000 tons per year. There is no knowing what quantity of fish the population consumes, either fresh or in the form of *prahoc*, a spicy fish sauce. And in addition there has always been a lot of smuggling of fish from Cambodia to neighboring countries.

When the water recedes, the flooded areas are laid bare and the lakes return to their normal size, the fish are prevented from escaping with nets, traps and various kinds of barriers made of woven bamboo. Men, women and children all take part in the fish gathering, the like of which can be seen nowhere else in the world. They wade through the layer of mud which gets deeper with every flood. The fish are "harvested" by hand, either taken down from the branches of trees in which they have been caught, or else picked out of the mud.

The people work tirelessly, and the great fish harvest does not end until every last fish has been collected. During this time, the fishermen and their families live in temporary huts which can easily be dismantled and transported, so that the familes can move forward and follow the water as it recedes. Only when the harvest is completely finished do they return to their villages.

As the floodwater retreats, a layer of fertile mud remains on the flooded ricefields. Small dykes are quickly built to hold the water back just as long as is necessary for the young rice shoots to appear and grow in the water

The basins, which the ancient Khmer so cleverly built to catch the water, the *baray* of the empire of Angkor, have almost entirely disappeared.

LAOS: THE LAND
AND ITS PEOPLE

Laos, or to cite its full title, Sathalamalid Pasathu'paait Pasasim Lao, (the Laotian Democratic People's Republic), lies on the peninsula of Indochina and is part of the subcontinent of South-East Asia. The country suffers not only from geographical disadvantages, particularly in regard to water, but also ethnic, economic and political problems; and despite its wealth in hard- and softwood, waterpower and minerals, it is one of the poorest nations in South-East Asia.

Mountains, hill country and high plateaus occupy more than 70 per cent of the land area. Laos possesses a little alluvial lowland in the Mekong valley, and some fairly large bowls around Vientiane, Paksan-Pakdang, Sebangfai, Sebanghiang-Sedone and Champasak. Between the mountain ranges there are plateaus of mesozoic sandstone or basalt, which permit intensive cultivation and a relatively dense population. The mountain chains lying parallel and close to one another, are a spur of the Himalayas. Composed of crystalline slate, gneiss and granite, with soaring pillars of karst, they run from northwest to southeast, with narrow, steep-sided valleys cutting deeply between them.

On the subcontinent of South-East Asia, which consists of more water than land, Laos is the only country that is landlocked. The shallow seas between the mainland and the islands of South-East Asia, which once formed a landbridge, have always provided better communications than the land routes across the difficult mountain terrain.

Previous pages: Landscape in northern Laos. Woodcarving is a craft which has a long tradition in Laos. Left: A cheerful little Laotian girl in Luang Prabang.

Laos has no railway. Its road network consists currently of 2,100 miles (3,387 km) of national highways, of which 975 miles (1,571 km) are asphalted all-weather roads and 655 miles (1,055 km) have a gravel surface. In addition there are 3500 miles (5,640 km) of provincial roads and 2,500 miles (4,000 km) of local roads. There are about 800 miles (1,300 km) of Routes Coloniales, built by the French, which include what is today the National Highway 13 from Luang Prabang through Vientiane and Savannakhet as far as the Cambodian frontier, with spurs numbered 6, 7 and 9 over high mountain passes to the Vietnamese ports of Haiphong, Dong Hai and Da Nang. In order to provide Laos with economic links to the world, these roads were repaired by Vietnam with the aid of 65 new bridges delivered from Sweden. Near Dong Hai the coastal plain of Vietnam reaches its narrowest point: the mountains of Laos are only 32 miles (52 km) from the coast.

Due to the ravages of war, the Trans-Laotian Highway 13 is also in bad condition over much of its length. Roughly half the road bridges in Laos need to be replaced. About 50 per cent of the rural population have no direct access to cross-country highways

For this isolated country, the natural connection with the outside world begins beyond the Mekong in Thailand but after 1975, when Laos was incorporated into communist Indochina, this link was severed. Since 1991, however, six border crossings between Laos and Thailand have been reopened. From the Thai border there are good fast roads and rail lines across the Korat plateau or through northern Thailand to Bangkok with its international port. The financing and construction (at a cost of US $30 million) of the "Friendship Bridge" over the Mekong, from Nong Khai in northeast Thailand to Tha Nalang, 6 miles (10 km) south of Vientiane, was undertaken by Australia in November 1991.

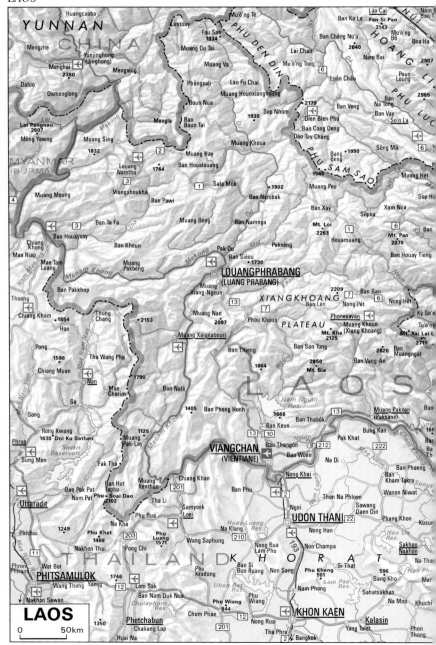

YUNNAN

CHINA

Huangcaoba

Mengzhe

Menghai
2380

Yunjinghong
(Jinghong)

Mengxing

Daluo

Damenglong

Loi Pangmao
2607

Mông Yawng

MYANMAR
(BURMA)

Muang Sing
1832

Louang
Namtha
3

Mengla

Ban
Boun Tai

Mu'ô'ng Tê

Lantouy

Fou San
1934

Muang Ou Tai

Muang Va

Phôngsali

Lao Fu Chai

Boun Nua

Muang Hounxianghoung

Boun Tai

1930

Sop Nhom

Ban Ko La

Na

Fan Si Pan
3143

Ban Chêng Nu'o'

Lai Châu

2640

Mu'o'ng Tong

6

Luân Châu

2179

Dien Bien Phu

Ban Cong Deng

Dèo Tay Chang

2907

Nam Bai

Poun
Loung

Ban Veng

Na Tong

Ban Vay

So'n La

2985

Mu'o'ng
Bô

Boa Ha

Lào Cai

Nam
Ban T

HOANG LI

PHU LUC

6

Muang Khoua

Bang
Bèng

1990

PHU SAM SAO

1540

Muang Peu

Muong Het

Sông Mã

6

Muang Meung

4

Viangphoukha

Ban Pawi

Sala Môk

1

1902

Ban Nambak

Ban Xay

Sôpka

Ban Namnga

Xam Nua

Sop H

Muang Bèng

Ban Ta Fa

3

Ban Houayxay

Ban Kheun

Muang
Pakbeng

Pak Ou

Ban Siêou

1730

Pakxeng

Mt. Loi
2263

Houamuang

1

Mt. Pan
2079

6

Ban

Ban Houay Tieng

Chiang
Khong

Mae Riap

Mae Tam
Luang

Ban Pakkhop

LOUANGPHRABANG
(LUANG PRABANG)

Muang
Xiang-Ngeun

XIANGKHOANG

2209

Nong Pêt

7

Ban Ban

6

Nong Hèt

Kỳ So'

Thoeng

Chiang Kham
1854

Hae

Thung
Chang

2153

13

7

Muang Nan

2097

Phou Khoun

PLATEAU

Ban Lèn

Phonesavan

Muang Khoun
(Xiang Khoang)

Mt. Khe
2125

Tu'o'n

Mt. Xai Lai L
2711

Pong

1586

Tha Wang Pha

Muang Xaignabouri

Ban Thieng

1864

Ban San Tong

2850
Mt. Bia

2620

Ban
Vang-An

Ban
Muangngat

Chiang Muan

Nan

1790

Mae
Charim

Ban Nalè

1405

Ban Phong Honh

L A O S

Nam Ngum
Res.

Sa

Song

Rong Kwang
1630 Doi Ku Sathan

1125

Muang
Pak-Lay

1666

Ban Keun

Ban Thabôk

13

Muang Pakkan
(Paksane)

Ban

15

Phrae

Sung Men

Fak Tha

13

10

Ban Thangon

Ban Woen

Pak Khat

Bung Kan

212

222

Ba
Th

Uttaradit

Ban Pak Pat

Nam Pat

Ban Hut
Taphu
Phu Soai Dao
2102

Muang
Kenthao

Chiang Khan

VIANGCHAN
(VIENTIANE)

Na Di

Nong Khai

2

Ban Phaeng

Ban
Kham Takra

Songk

1249

Tha Li

Samyoek
Loei

Ban Phu

Thon Na Phloen

Wanon Niwat

Phichai

Phu Khat
1468

203

Na Kha

Phu Rua

Phu
Luang
1571

Ngoi

Na Klang

UDON THANI

22

Sawang
Daen Din

Phang Khon

Kusur

11

Nakhon Thai

Pong Chi

Wang Saphung

210

Nong Han

Non Champa

Nan Nu
Res.

Sakhon
Nakhon

Na Tho

Phrom
Phiram

Wat Bot

1746

12

THAILAND KHORAT

Phu
Kradung

Ban Si
Bun Ruang

Non Sang

Nong Bua
Lam Phu

193

Phu Kheng
501

Si That

596

Sang Kho

Nan Ph

Mar

PHITSAMULOK

Wang Thong

Yaeng

Lom Sak

Ban Nam Duk Nua

Chulaphon
Res.

Ubon Rat
Res.

Phu
Wiang

Nam Phong

Lam Pao
Res.

Sahatsakhan

Na Mon

Khuchi

Nakhon Sawan

1350

Phetchabun

Chaliang Lap

Huai Na

Chum Phae

Phu Wiang
844

12

Nong Rua

Tha Phra

KHON KAEN

Yang Talat

Kalasin

Phon

2 Bangkok

LAOS

0   50km

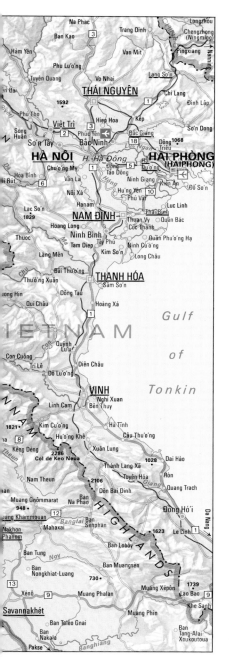

The 3,850-ft-long (1.17 km) road bridge will have two carriageways and two footways. It is intended to bind Laos more closely to the west and will be the first bridge to span the Mekong in its 2,800-mile (4,500 km) length. Australia's economic aid illustrates the commitment and interest which that country has shown towards the former Indochina.

Under agreements in 1962, 1963 and 1974, China has built about 600 miles (1,000 km) of economically and strategically important highways from its southern province of Yunnan into the north and northwest of Laos, connecting with Highway 1. In 1978, after the outbreak of the Third Indochinese War, the intervention of Vietnam brought all construction work, aid programmes and foreign relations to a halt. However, in 1991, in the wake of a new Laotian policy, which made the country no longer entirely dependent on Vietnam, these were started up once again.

Size and shape

With an area of 91,500 square miles (237,000 sq. km) Laos is about 30 per cent larger than Cambodia. It stretches nearly 600 miles (1,000 km) from northwest to southeast and lies between latitudes 22° and 14° north, and longitudes 100° and 108° east. The mountainous north between the Mekong and Red rivers comprises a roughly circular area with many indentations. The northern mountains rise from 5,000 to nearly 10,000 ft (1,600-3,000 m) with ridges of about 6,500 ft (2,00 m). The highest mountains, topped by the 9,350-ft Phu Bia (2,850 m), lie on the southern edge of the Xieng Khouang or Tranh Ninh Plateau, which includes the Plain of Jars (4,250 ft/1,200 m). A narrow strip of land with a spine of mountains runs southeastwards between the Mekong and neighboring Vietnam, as far as the Cambodian border. The country's narrowest point, a

mere 75 miles (120 km), is near Paksane. Near Savannakhet, on the west side of the range of mountains, begins the plain which continues beyond the Mekong, through Thailand as far as the Menam river. East of Pakse the basalt-covered Boloven plateau rises to 5,000 ft (1500 m).

To the north, Laos borders with China, to the east with Vietnam and to the south with Cambodia. In the northwest, the Mekong forms a 120-mile (200 km) border between Myanmar (Burma) and Laos. For long stretches it is also the border with Thailand.

The Mekong

Laos is one of six countries through which the 2,800-mile (4,500 km) long Mekong flows: the others are China (including Tibet and Yunnan) Myanmar,

Above: Elephants work in the teak forests.
Right: By the Nam Ngum reservoir near Vientiane.

Thailand, Cambodia and Vietnam. For a third of its length, 930 miles (1500 km) it flows through Upper, Central and Lower Laos. Together with its 15 major tributaries, it drains Laos with nearly 1500 miles (2,400 km) of waterways. However, only some 530 miles (850 km) are navigable all year round, and some parts only for six months of the year and then only with flat-bottomed boats. Many stretches are merely of local importance. The upper reaches of the Mekong are barred by rocks. Until recent times, the territory of tribal chieftains only extended from one rapids to the next.

When the snow melts in the Himalayas and the rainy season starts, bringing erosion from the mountains, the river carries great quantities of fertile sediment down to the plains. In the dry season, when the water level is low, alluvial banks and islands are exposed, where vegetables can be temporarily cultivated. In many places, panning for gold in the river sand repays the tedious work involved.

The river valley widens at the point where a tributary, the Nam Kane (Nam Khan) flows in from the east. The two rivers form a peninsula on which stands the royal city of Luang Prabang (Louang Phrabang). Downstream, as far as Vientiane, rapids such as the Keng Lang, "King of the Whirlpools," obstruct passenger and freight traffic. To avoid this a 3-mile (5 km) stretch of narrow-gauge railway was built in the colonial period – the only railroad in Laos. Not until one reaches the 435-mile (700 km) stretch between Vientiane and Savannakhet is the Mekong navigable all year round and therefore economically important. Because of this the development of river traffic on the Mekong and its tributaries is to be speeded up.

High water levels and flooding along the Mekong have always been predictable and catastrophes have been rare. The last devastating flood in Vientiane was in 1966. After that the dyke was raised.

However, the catastrophic and repeated flooding of the rice fields, since 1991, in the provinces of Pakse and Savannakhet and in northern Laos, are an alarming sign of a disturbance to the balance of the hydrology, caused by irresponsible forest clearance in the Laotian mountains. In Savannakhet Province, forest covered 72 per cent of the land in 1971. Today the figure is 48 per cent. Similar reports come from other provinces.

Flooding and plagues of rats, with droughts elsewhere, are causing crop failures and food shortages, so that grain has had to be imported.

At Vientiane the Mekong is already a mile and a quarter (2 km) wide, but its bed is only 1,300 ft (400 m) above sea-level, and it has another 1,000 miles (1,600 km) to flow before it reaches the sea. It therefore flows gently and is easy to cross, especially in the dry season when large islands appear. Thailand lies on the opposite bank.

In 1967 an international committee was set up, with the task of obtaining more benefit from the middle and lower reaches of the Mekong, by building dams, hydroelectric power stations, drainage and irrigation canals, correcting the course of the river for flood control, reclaiming agricultural land and putting up navigation marks for shipping. One long-term goal is to make the river navigable all the way from its mouth to Laos. The work of the Mekong Committee was hindered by political disputes between the riparian states, by two Indochinese wars and by financial problems. However, it has been resumed, and even if no spectacular results have been achieved, some notable successes can be demonstrated on certain sections of the river.

Flora and Fauna

All the countries of South-East Asia possess similar flora and fauna, as these are dictated by the monsoon climate, and only minor variations result from local climatic conditions, temperature, humidity, altitude and soil composition. In the Laotian mountains the climate is temperate. Tropical rain forest grows on the windward side of the mountains, where the annual rainfall ranges from 47 to 118 inches (1,200-3,000 mm), and up to 158 inches (4,000 mm) in exposed places. Sheltered mountainsides are covered with deciduous forest and at greater heights there is monsoon hardwood forest. In the north there are mixed forests, with evergreen oak and subtropical pine. On the leeward side of the mountains, grass savannah appears. On the lower slopes there is slash-and-burn clearance, the gound is cultivated with the hoe, and crops include mountain rice, maize, taro, cassava, coffee, tea and medicinal herbs. In the valleys and plains there is intensive cultivation of irrigated rice, sugar cane, millet, maize, vegetables, fruit, cotton, and rubber. In this subsistence economy, the people can grow or make tools, weapons, household utensils, houses, clothing, ornaments and cultic objects, as well as food, from plants which they find outside their front door.

Rare species of animal live in the mountains of Laos, while elephants, as in all South-east Asian countries, are caught and domesticated. They are indispensible for dragging huge tree trunks from the mountain forests down to the rivers or roads. Like the water buffalo, they are sensitive to the heat and can only work in the mornings. Right up to the present century elephants were used in war, for personal transport and for carrying freight. Even in the Indochinese wars they were still used by the Vietnamese, the French and the Americans, for hauling supplies. Water buffalo and zebu, the Indian hump-backed cattle, are used in the plains as beasts of burden, and to pull ploughs and carts. Unlike the Chinese, the Laotians do not carry loads slung on bamboo poles, but always put them on to

Right: Young Meo men from the mountain villages, in Luang Prabang.

animals – only the women carry water-jars on their heads, as they do in India. The aggressiveness of the heavy water buffalo when confronted by foreigners, whose smell seems to irritate them, has even been used as a weapon in wars. In the colonial period, French soldiers from Africa introduced the mule.

Hunting is very important to the tribal minorities in the mountains. Up to now pigs and chickens have only been kept by the peasants as sacrifices to the gods of nature and their ancestors.

Population

In June 1985 Radio Vientiane announced that the population of Laos was 3,584,803. At the end of the civil war and Indochinese war, which lasted from 1980 to 1987, the rate of growth was 2.9 per cent, and infant mortality was 12.3 per cent. Even today life expectancy is only somewhere between 40 and 50 years. By December 1991 the population had grown to 4.24 million, and in 1995 it is expected to reach 4.71 million. With 44 inhabitants per square mile (17 per sq. km) the population density of Laos is low but unevenly spread. Two-thirds of the population live in the fertile plains, which produce 70 per cent of the rice harvest.

A large proportion, nearly one-fifth, of the people live in towns. And it is here, particularly, that unemployment and underemployment are noticeable, although the new constitution guarantees everyone the right to work. There is inadequate provision of health care and education, though these are also promised by the constitution.

For thousands of years South-East Asia has been a melting-pot of races, cultures and religions. The migrations from north to south followed the river valleys, and only a few hill-tribes crossed the mountain ranges. There is no such race as the Laotians. One of the country's greatest problems is its ethnic diversity and lack

of an integrated population. The Lao account for just on half the inhabitants, and the rest is made up of 68 minorities from five major language-groups, who occupy more than 80% of the land. Laos has more minorities than any of its neighbors. (Vietnam has 53, accounting for barely 10% of its population, while Cambodia has only ten minorities). The hill peoples straddle the borders with other countries of South-East Asia and with China.

Three principal population groups can be distinguished by the altitude at which they have settled, by the time in history when they arrived in Laos and by the ethnic characteristics of their culture and customs. These groups and sub-groups seldom mix with each other.

The Lao-Lum (Lao-Loum) live in the lowlands, and with as much as 55 per cent of the population, are the national race. They live from rice growing, in paddy fields, on land up to 300 ft (100 m) above sea-level. They belong to the large group of Thai peoples, as do the the Lao-Thai sub-group, whose different tribes are known as the White, Red and Black Thai, according to the color of the clothes worn by their women. The Lao-Thai live on both sides of the border in somewhat higher valleys where they grow paddy rice and mountain rice. In Laos, the only true hill-people in the Lao-Thai group are the Lao-Dam, or Black Thai. However, there are many Lao tribes living in northern Thailand.

Ninety per cent of the Lao-Lum are followers of Hinayana Buddhism, but also worship *phi*, the gods and spirits of nature. There are also some animists among the Lao-Thai.

There are some 46,000 Protestants and 35,000 Catholics who live predominantly in the towns.

The language of the Lao-Lum is one of the Chinese-influenced Thai languages and is made up of one-syllable words, which can have a wide variety of meanings, depending on which of the six different tones or pitches they are pronounced with. The Lao language has 33 consonants and 28 vowels, but a very

169

simple grammar. There are numerous dialects. The dialect spoken in Vientiane is understood by most Laotians and has the status of official language. In common with other Thai peoples, the Lao-Lum did not develop a script of their own, and only when they had settled in their present homeland did they adopt from the Khmer an ancient Indian alphabet, to which they added signs to indicate the tones.

There is such a close relationship between Laotian and certain Thai languages, especially Esan, which is spoken in northeast Thailand, that their speakers can make themselves mutually understood. The main foreign language spoken is French, but increasingly English as well. Many young Lao have studied in Moscow and speak Russian.

The Lao-Lum are racially mixed; many have round, full faces, wide, flat noses, stiff, black hair and brown eyes,

Above: Family scene outside a house in 13th Street, Luang Prabang.

often with Mongoloid folds over the lids, but one also sees narrow faces with fine long noses. Their nature is characterized by a friendly reticence, equanimity, individuality and a readiness to compromise. A Laotian proverb says: "Let the dog bark, let the caravan pass by." The Lao-Lum live in family groups in scattered settlements, hamlets and villages, with no strict organization or work-sharing. On the other hand, neighbors arrange to help each other as the occasion arises. In 1975, the attempt to collectivize agriculture failed, since there was no village organization on which to base it.

The Lao-Lum's clothing and their houses built on piles resemble those of the Cambodians. The women wear a wrap-around skirt called a *sinh* (*phasin* in Thai) and blouses of cotton or silk, or nowadays also from imported fabrics. The men wear long trousers and an open shirt. The silver belt is the pride of every Laotian woman and is now imitated in Thailand. The Lao-Lum wear no hats or other headgear. On the other hand you will often see women and girls wearing the flattering traditional hairstyle, a bun at the side of the head, decorated with pearls or flowers.Western clothes are enjoying growing popularity, especially among the young.

Laotian food is similar to Indian, but is very varied, thanks to the influence of Chinese cuisine. Rice is the staple ingredient, eaten with fish more often than meat, and with vegetables, salad and fish-sauce.

The Chinese minority (3-4 per cent of the population) live mainly in the towns, as owners of restaurants and workshops, or as wholesalers or retailers. The Vietnam-ese minority (about 1per cent) earn their living in a similar way, but in the country or in border regions. This figure does not include the advisers, party executives, officials and other recent incomers from Vietnam. The Vietnamese build their houses directly up from the ground. In the 17th century this led to one of the few instances in South-East Asia of a frontier being drawn according to ethnic criteria: villages where the majority of houses were built on piles with entrances facing east, were assigned to Laos. On the other hand, if the houses were built on the ground, facing south, the village was allotted to Vietnam.

There is a growing number of Thais who have come to Laos for business reasons, some Indian and Bangladeshi shopkeepers and tradesmen, as well as a Khmer minority, about 4.6 per cent, mostly living in the south of the country, and a few hundred Europeans, Americans and Australians, who usually only work in Laos for a limited period.

The second largest group are the **Lao Theung** (Lao Theng), a mountain people, who represent 27% of the population. They tend to settle up to about 3,000 ft (1,000 m) on mountainsides and high plateaus, principally in the north and east of the country. To designate them as Lao, is ethnologically misleading, as it is also

for the third largest group, the Lao-Soung, and only refers to their nationality. The Lao-Theung are Austro-Indonesian tribes, and are therefore also called the Indonesian Group. They are very early settlers, with a megalithic culture, who were driven into the mountains by the Lao tribes and known by them as *Kha* (slaves). Tribes related to the Lao-Theung are living in the Indonesian archipelago. The urns found on the Plain of Jars were created by their ancestors. Culturally they are not as advanced as the Lao-Lum and Lao-Soung. Members of the La, Lamet and Kamu tribes acted as servants to the princes, and today are still often found doing poorly paid manual work.

A number of the Lao-Theung tribes adopted the Laotian language and the Buddhist faith, others remained animists. They live from hunting and from slash-and-burn cultivation, but many have settled on the land and grow rice, tobacco, cotton, tea and coffee, using simple implements. They also breed livestock. The villages and tribes which have a chieftain are more strictly organized. Very often the Lao-Theung live as extended familes in long houses built on piles, with each family unit around its own hearth. The settlements include storehouses and houses for bachelors, meetings, spirits and burials. The buildings are constructed with care and skill, to last a long time. They are made from timber, bamboo and woven cane, and have high, steep roofs. Originally they were built without recourse to glue, saws, nails or any other metal equipment, since these were unknown. In the villages they keep pigs, chicken and water buffalo.

The **Lao-Soung** (Lao-Xung), or mountain Lao, are the third major group, with a 15 per cent share of the population. They have settled around the mountain peaks, above 3,000 ft (1,000 m). If they are cultivating fields lower down the slopes, they return to their mountain villages at night. They live in the northern and north-

eastern parts of the country and in the the province of Xieng Khouang. Ethnically the Lao-Soung are the most clearly differentiated. To this group belong the Yao, Mien, Ho, Lolo, Man and the Meo or Hmong, called Miao in China, who were driven southwards from Tibet.

The Lao-Soung were the last migrants to come across the mountains from South China into Laos and are therefore known as the Chinese Group. From their previous homeland they brought agricultural methods, utensils, axes and manual skills, and many of the tribes produce textiles and silver ornaments. Alongside nomadic tribes, whose way of life is based on slash-and-burn and temporary cultivation, there are settled farming communities, who grow mountain rice, sugarcane, maize, tapioca, yams, lettuce and poppies, from which they make opium. They also breed dogs, chickens,

Above: At the barber on the street corner.
Right: The young riceplants are thinned and planted out.

water buffalo, cattle, and even horses. For many of them, opium-dealing is the only source of income, but this activity has caused many problems for the Laotian government and it is now being officially combatted.

Methods of building houses vary from tribe to tribe. Many of the stilt houses rest on massive wooden pillars, the walls are made of wood or woven cane; the nomadic tribes build less solidly, but have better clothes and ornaments. The women usually wear skirts, loose jackets, headbands or caps, cloth leggings to protect them against thorns, and opulent silver ornaments. They formerly made their own fabrics from fibre, but nowadays they use cotton and imported textiles. Many tribes pierce their ear lobes, but tooth-filing is rare. However, tattooing is common, though not decorative scarring of the face. The Lao-Soung are animists who worship their ancestors. Every activity and each daily event is considered from its religious aspects, and there is a corresponding variety of cults. Their

priests are at once magicians, sooth-sayers, astrologers, healers and exorcists. The life of these tribes is simple but hard, and up to now the government has done virtually nothing to assist their development and education.

Among the Lao-Soung, the Meo, or Hmong, occupy a very special place. In Indochina they live north of the 21st parallel. During the colonial period the French played them off against the lowlanders, and in the Second Indochinese War they fought for the USA against the Pathet Lao, though they were also to be found in the rebel ranks.

Among all the minorities, who are being brought into contact with the outside world through modern communications and transport, one can observe a rapid change in their way of life.

Economy

Laos is one of the countries which is "starving on a treasure." The land has rich resources: softwood and hardwood timber, hydroelectric energy and minerals. It is thinly populated and should therefore be capable of feeding all its inhabitants.

From 1955 to 1973 the USA poured more aid into Laos than any other country. Regrettably, the money was swallowed up by corruption, war and civil strife, so that the economic breakthrough never came; nor did it when the East Bloc states later stepped in with their own aid program.

Laos continues to have large foreign debts, but currently receives aid from various countries, which goes toward balancing its deficit. Between 1975 and 1985 relations between the USA and Laos were largely frozen, but not broken off. Once Laos agreed to start combatting the drug-traffic and said it was willing to cooperate in the search for missing American servicemen, diplomatic relations were resumed in 1991.

In 1992 Laos signed ASEAN's Treaty of Amity and Cooperation, as a first step towards full membership.

Since 1991 China has once again been providing economic aid, chiefly through road building, but also in the sphere of education and training, and in building up Laotian industry. In 1992 a treaty between Myanmar, Laos and China settled disputed frontiers, especially in the mountains. These are now to be surveyed and marked out with border posts.

The considerable reserves of hardwood in the mountain forests have brought in substantial revenues. But forestry and reforestation cannot keep up with the rate of timber felling and shipping, which is mainly being carried on by Thai companies.

Every year more than 1,100 square miles (3,000 sq.km) of mountain forest are being lost to timber-felling and clearance by minority tribes. The soil in the mountain is not very fertile, and even when fertilized with the ashes from the burnt forest, it will only produce one or

Above and right: Water and timber are valuable resources in Laos.

two crops, then the local inhabitants move on.

The bare mountain slopes are subject to erosion and desertification. The water is no longer retained by the forests but rushes down into the valleys and floods the rice fields. At other times it produces catastrophic droughts. Decisions and decrees by government and the National Forest Conferences of 1988 and 1991 attempted to prevent the wholesale stripping of the forests; but these were cleverly circumvented by the timber-merchants, and the minorities saw their existence threatened, so that the government provisionally had to settle for a quota system, and has called for international assistance for its forestry program.

Only a tiny proportion of the vast potential for hydroelectric power is being exploited. Between 1972 and 1975, in the wake of an international Mekong project, the Nam Ngum dam and power station were built, 56 miles (90 km) from Vientiane. Most of the current it produces is exported across the Mekong to neighboring Thailand, because that way it earns the country much-need hard currency. But even this valuable export has been severely impaired by the felling of the mountain forests. The huge volumes of water which rush down to the valley in the rainy season, cannot be trapped by the dam, and afterwards the water level is too low. In 1991 the amount of electricity generated by the Nam Ngum dam dropped by 16.6 per cent. That meant a loss of revenue of 17.7 million US dollars from exports to Thailand.

A power station on the Nam Dong river supplies Luang Prabang, another at Xeset Dam on the Boloven Plateau provides current for the south of the country. Other major projects have so far failed to reach fruition because the problems of transport add so much to the construction costs.

Very little of the mineral wealth of Laos is being extracted at present. De-

posits of iron ore, coal, copper, lead, manganese, gold and even oil, are waiting to be opened up, and some have still not been located. The remoteness of the deposits and therefore once again the heavy transport costs make mining an unprofitable venture for foreign investors.

Only seven per cent of the potentially arable land is exploited in this thinly populated country. Rice is grown on two-thirds of the agricultural land. Even in the plains there is a lack of irrigation, so that often only one crop, the "monsoon rice," can be harvested in a year. Rice production is largely in the hands of small family farms; cooperatives and producer groups hardly come into the picture.

The natural disasters of recent years have made it necessary to import rice. Livestock breeding is to become more intensive in the highlands. Modern farming methods, intensive irrigation, fertilizers and better agricultural machinery could produce higher yields. However, it is difficult to persuade the population to accept innovations, and in any case, Laos does not have the technically trained people to teach them these skills.

Laotian industry does not extend beyond some 250 state-owned companies and small businesses run by families. Not until 1992 was a start made on expanding the private sector through the sale of some state-owned companies.

So far there are manufacturers operating in the fields of textiles, leather, paper, food processing, sawmills, glass, metal products, chemicals and pharmaceuticals, as well as small workshops for carpentry and handcrafts.

Vietnam has been ousted from its controlling position. Thailand has now, in spite of the political debacle, become Laos' most important trading partner and investor.

But Australia and Japan are also heavily involved, and China has once again become active. Relations with the USA were soured by the persistent drugs problem, but in 1992 a senior US delegation visited Vientiane and a full embassy may again be established there soon.

175

THE HISTORY

OF LAOS

Traces of early human history have been found in Laos going back some 10,000 years, to the end of the last Ice Age, when there began an unceasing migration of tribes and peoples from north to south. In the entire migratory zone of the Indochinese peninsula, no race has retained its purity. For thousands of years cultures and have met and mingled even if maintaining their own identity.

The Lao belong to the large Thai group of peoples. They originated in southern Siberia and are related to the Yueh, the ancestors of the Vietnamese. In the 7th century, Thai and Lolo tribes founded the empire of Nan Chao in the south Chinese region of Yunnan, during their southward migration. They made an alliance with the then powerful Tibet, and the T'ang dynasty of China was forced, after some painful defeats, to recognize the empire of Nan Chao in 728 AD.

Some historians believe that the Thai tribes only played a subordinate role in Nan Chao and see the Tibeto-Burman peoples as founders and guardians of the state. Nevertheless it can be proved that in the 13th century, after the fall of the Nan Chao empire, Thai tribes migrated in large groups from southern China into the regions they now inhabit, and founded kingdoms whose successor nations exist to this day. The Thai are one of the peoples on the edge of the Chinese empire who were influenced by it. Small groups and tribes came under pressure from the southward movement of the Han Chinese and settled on the Upper Mekong, but here they were absorbed by the Mon and the Khmer, who were then at the height of their power.

Left: The emblem of the Laotian People's Democratic Party.

It was in 1253 that the Nan Chao empire was conquered and destroyed by the Mongol leader Kublai Khan, a grandson of Jinghis Khan, who founded the Yuan dynasty in China. In doing so he set in motion another migration of peoples into South-East Asia. The Thai retreated into Hainan, Vietnam and Assam, while the Shan, or Chan, settled in Burma, now called Myanmar. The early power-centers of the Thai were formed in the north of the Mon empire of Dvaravati, around Lampun. Lao tribes headed for the upper and middle reaches of the Mekong, where they either drove the resident Khmer southwards or mingled with them.

The forging of alliances between Thai principalities, called *muong,* in the region around present-day Luang Prabang, Bhamo, Chiang Sen and Chiang Mai, gave birth to the first great Thai empire, Sukothai. The later empires of the Thai were called Siam, and their inhabitants, Siamese. The modern nation did not adopt the name Thai, which means "free," until it had succeeded in escaping the shackles of colonialism.

The Thai peoples brought a feudal system with them from China, as did the Shan in Burma and the Muong in northern Vietnam. They probably also brought iron ploughs, knowledge of rice growing in irrigated paddy fields and various manual skills including the production of glazed pottery. It is also probable that they came into contact with Buddhism through their connection with Tibet and Vietnam. They had no script of their own. Many scholars even claim they were uncivilized tribesmen, who first learned rice growing and handcrafts from the Mon and the Khmer.

The three kingdoms

Legends of the Lao tell of the deified chieftain Khuon Borom, who divided his realm among his seven sons. Hundreds of

years passed, from the destruction of the empire and the founding of a Lao kingdom on the upper Mekong. From the many small, local fiefs or *muong*, governed by chieftains, called *chao*, three emerged, from which the modern Laos has developed: these are Muong Swa (Luang Prabang), Muong Phu Eun and Viang Chan (Vientiane).

In Muong Swa as many as 33 rulers, all known to us by name, had reigned before the middle of the 14th century, when a deposed prince, Phi Fa, and his son Fa Ngum, sought help from the Khmer court in Angkor. Fa Ngum married a Khmer princess, and in 1353, with the support of the Khmer, he succeeded in reconquering his principality of Muong Swa. By this time the Hinduism of the god-kings in Angkor had been replaced by Theravada Buddhism; only the court ceremonial of the Hindu Brahmans had survived.

Above: Waterbuffalo are happy to be looked after by children. Right: Statues of the Buddha in Luang Prabang.

Fa Ngum adopted Therevada Buddhism, Indian culture, script, literature and art, as well as the Brahman court ceremonial. The Khmer princess brought with her a number of priests and a small golden Buddha, the Pha Bang, after which both the kingdom and its capital were named Louang Phabang, which is now Luang Prabang.

Although the Lao nominally adopted Buddhism, they clung to their nature- and fertility-gods. The *phi*, earth spirits and the *naga*, water spirits, even today play an important part in the lives of the Lao.

In 1353, with Fa Ngum, begins the history of the three kingdoms, which were not given the name Laos until the French formed them into a protectorate at the end of the 19th century.

Since the founding of the three kingdoms, the same difficulty has remained apparent, right up to the present: the inaccessible geography of the country, which can only be ruled along the watercourses, "from one rapids to the next," and the ethnic diversity and fragmentation of the

population, have hindered the emergence of a nation. Externally, the country, divided into small fiefs, was unable to ward off the influence and incursions of its neighbors, China, Siam, Burma, Dai Viet (Vietnam) and the Khmer. The Laotian kingdoms needed allies, but then soon became dependent on them. And since these neighbors were enemies of each other, every alliance with one meant the hostility of another. Attempts to preserve neutrality failed. Laos eventually became a bone of contention between countries with divergent interests and was ground between the wheels of world politics.

Back in 1353 Fa Ngum succeeded in uniting Muong Swa with the principality of Muong Chan (Viang Chan) and named his kingdom Lan Xang (Lan Chang), land of "a million elephants." Lan Xang, with its capital at Muang Swa, stretched from northern Cambodia up to the southern border of Chinese Yunnan, and from the border with Siam in the west across to the kingdom of Dai Viet. Fa Ngum was

forced to wage continual frontier campaigns and was finally deposed by his war-weary officials.

He was succeeded by his son who, according to the nation's first census in 1376, ruled over 300,000 men of Thai stock. He consolidated his empire and its army and married a Thai princess from Ayuthia, thereby enabling Siam to gain influence over Lan Xang. This cast a cloud over the previously good relations with the neighboring Dai Viet, which lasted for several decades beginning in 1428. The king had offered help to the Vietnamese in their war against the Ming dynasty of China, but his soldiers deserted to the larger Chinese army. However, the Vietnamese first defeated the Ming forces, then, in 1471, the Champa empire, which threatened their southern border, before taking their belated revenge, in 1478, on their Laotian neighbors, when they captured Louang Phabang and banished the king. Under his successors, peace reigned for many years between Lan Xang and Dai Viet.

King Vixun Harath married a princess from Chiang Mai. His son, Pothisarat (1521-1547), temporarily moved his capital to Viang Chan. The name means "Citadel of the Moon," and was only changed to Vientiane by the French. In 1545 a dispute arose in Chiang Mai over the succession to the throne, and Pothisarat, who had a claim to the crown on his mother's side, intervened. His eldest son, Setthathirat, was crowned king in Chiang Mai in 1548. In the same year his father died, and when he went to claim his inheritance in Louang Phabang, the Burmese took advantage of his absence from Chiang Mai. They conquered the kingdom in 1556. In 1560 Settathirat was forced to accept their sovereignty and made an alliance with the kingdom of Ayuthia. He transferred his capital to Viang Chan. He had brought with him from Chiang Mai a famous Buddha, the

Above: Indra on Erewan, the 3-headed elephant. Right: Erewan, symbol of the three kingdoms, on the palace, Luang Prabang.

Phra Keo (in Laotian, Pha Kaeo), the Emerald Buddha. This was a 2-ft-high (60 cm) statue of green chrysoprase or jade, for which he built a temple in Viang Chan.

From 1654 to 1712, under King Soligna Vongsa, Louang Phabang enjoyed another period of prosperity and expansion. When the king died, he left no immediate successor, but his nephew was able, under Vietnamese suzerainty, to extend his kingdom as far as Viang Chan, and to add the northern and northeastern provinces to it. In 1707, as a result of further dynastic disputes, the kingdoms of Viang Chan and Louang Phabang split up.

During the long years of war between the Burmese kingdom of Pagan and the Siamese kingdom of Ayuthia, the two Laotian kingdoms fell under the domination of whichever had the upper hand. In 1767 the Burmese destroyed Ayuthia. No sooner had Siam recovered than it attacked Viang Chan, in 1779, for having supported the Burmese. The Siamese invaders took the Phra Keo Buddha back with them, and when the Chakri dynasty, Thailand's present royal house, founded the kingdom of Bangkok in 1782, they built a temple for the Phra Keo in the royal palace, where the statue is venerated to this day.

In 1826 Viang Chan attacked the Siamese, but they retaliated in 1828 and destroyed the city. With this defeat the kingdom of Viang Chan also came to an end, and the honor of kingship fell to Louang Phabang. Until the end of the monarchy in 1975, the king of Louang Phabang assumed a superior place among the three Laotian kings. (In 1866 a French expeditionary force discovered the ruins of Viang Chan in the jungle.)

In 1752 Louang Phabang fell under Burmese and in 1778 under Siamese overlordship, and in 1792 it was conquered by the Siamese, and badly damaged, but rebuilt again. With the help of Viet-

180

nam, Louang Phabang was able to expand its territory as far as Viang Chan.

Around 1800 three kingdoms were created from the territories of quarrelling princes: Louang Phabang, Viang Chan and, in the south, Champasak, which had belonged to Cambodia. China and Vietnam both briefly held sway over them. Bands of Chinese marauders, known as the Yellow, Red and Black Banners, terrorized the north of the country, and Louang Phabang, in the 19th century. However, by the beginning of the colonial era all three kingdoms had fallen under Siamese suzerainty.

The Protectorate of Laos

Around the middle of the 19th century Europe began looking in Asia for sources of raw materials and markets for the products of their expanding industries. They thought they could find these in the populous Chinese empire. While Britain took the sea-route, capturing the southern Chinese port of Canton and staging the

Opium War (1840-1842), France tried to penetrate the markets of South China by way of the Mekong and later the Red River. Their expeditions came to a halt at the rapids on the Mekong. They were equally unsuccesful in developing trade with China along the Red River. But Vietnam, Cambodia and the Laotian kingdoms possessed raw materials, were suitable for planting cotton and rubber, and offered France some compensation for the loss of their Indian colonies to the British.

Having occupied Vietnam and Cambodia, the French wanted to round off their colonial conquests with the empire of Lan Xang. This involved lengthy negotiations with Britain and Siam, and waging a minor war in Upper Laos against the Siamese and the Chinese raiders.

Backed by a show of force with French warships off Bangkok and the – temporary – cession of the right bank of the Mekong to Siam, France succeeded in 1893 in uniting the three Laotian kingdoms to form the Protectorate of Laos with its capital in Luang Prabang. France signed

181

Above: Signing the Treaty of Independence between Laos and France. Right: Laotian state visit to France.

the treaty of protectoracy with Siam, but not with the king of Laos.

Laos was now part of the French colonial empire in Indochina, which was ruled by a French Governor-General in Saigon, and consisted of the colony of Cochin China (the Mekong delta), and protectorates of Tonkin (North Vietnam), Annam (Central Vietnam) and Cambodia. A Resident was appointed to Laos.

The three kingdoms remained in existence and chieftains and tribal princes, who collaborated with the French, were able to increase their power. The colonial government fanned the flames of discord among the kings, the tribal chiefs and the minorities, and played one off against another. The junior posts in the civil service were filled by Vietnamese. During the colonial period, administration, education and health-care scarcely progressed at all.

High taxation and the arrogant behavior of tax collectors and officials were the most frequent causes of uprisings and rebellion. In the lowlands, unrest among the Lao-Lum was quickly stamped out by the superior weaponry of the French.

The revolts of the well-organized Lao-Theung lasted longer. In the highlands of Boloven and Xieng Khouang the French had difficulty in deploying their heavy armaments. On the hilltops the Lao-Soung could only be temporarily pacified by a blockade of their supplies or a remission of taxes. However, the Laotians were unable to overcome their geographical and ethnic divisions, and failed to organize any nationwide campaign of resistance.

In 1941 the Japanese occupied the rest of Indochina but did not enter Laos until April 1945, when they took control of government and interned the French. However, the hope of the peoples of Asia that they would be liberated by the Japanese, was not realized. The Japanese regime proved to be even more intoler-

able than that of the French. In August 1945 resistance against the Japanese broke out in Laos, first in Vientiane, then in other provincial capitals.

At this time the king ruling from Luang Prabang was Sisavang Vong, who had studied in France and had been installed by the colonial government in 1904. Subordinate to him were his nephews, the regents, Prince Phetsarath in Vientiane and Prince Boum Oun in Champasak. For three centuries – with only brief interruptions – the king of Louang Phabang had represented the whole nation. However, with the arrival of the French colonists his authority was curtailed.

Following the Japanese surrender in August 1945, the king in Luang Prabang and Prince Phetsarath in Vientiane declared their country independent. The prince founded the Lao Issara, the Laotian Liberation Front, as an umbrella-organization for all resistance forces. It was the first of many attempts to subordinate the many different ambitions and

ideologies to the common goal of liberating their nation. The prince had graduated in technical studies in Paris. Only two of his twenty brothers and half-brothers followed his example. The others underwent military training in France, then joined the army. Prince Souvanna Phouma obtained an engineering degree in Paris, and Prince Souvannouvong (Souvanna Phong), the youngest of the brothers, studied in Hanoi and Paris and also became an engineer. He was preoccupied with the ideology of the French Revolution and met the revolutionary Ho Chi Minh in Vietnam. In 1945, when the French returned to Indochina, he began to build up a revolutionary resistance movement in Laos, modelled on the Viet Minh. He worked alongside Kaysone Phomvihan, who was later Secretary General of the Laotian Communist Party.

In 1945 opinion was divided, both among the royal princes and in the country as a whole. Prince Phetsarath and Prince Souvanna Phouma were initially prepared to see Laos become an inde-

pendent state within the French Union. But some voices called for a union with Thailand, while others demanded complete neutrality and independence.

Prince Souvannouvong wanted to tie the country more closely to Vietnam. When France set about re-occupying Laos, the Lao Issara, led by Prince Phetsarath, established an alternative government. Throughout the country, especially in the north and northeast, in the provinces of Xieng Khouang (Xiang Khoang), Sam Neua (Phan Houa) and Phang Saly, resistance groups were formed, led by tribal chiefs and village headmen, which began to wage war against the French, as was already happening in neighboring Vietnam. Prince Souvannouvong set up his headquarters in the mountains of northeast Laos. The resistance fighters suffered bloody losses in the battle for the town of Thakhet on

Above: Volunteers fighting rebels (1967).
Right: Prince Souvannouvong, the "Red Prince," and Prince Souvanna Phouma.

the Mekong. Prince Souvannouvong was seriously wounded, but was able to escape to Thailand with a small number of his troops.

Within five months the French were in control of the most important towns. Prince Phetsarath, Prince Souvanna Phouma and their provisional government fled from Vientiane to Thailand, from where they continued to function. Meanwhile, King Sisavang Vong, residing in Luang Prabang, was appointed king of the whole of Laos by the French. When Prince Souvannouvong had recovered from his injuries he was the only member of the Provisional Government to return to Laos, where he went underground and began to reorganize the resistance movement, supported by the ethnic minorities in the north. The Lao Soung in Xieng Khouang province provided one of the best-known leaders of the resistance, the village elder, Faydang, who later became a minister.

In 1947 Laos became a democracy under a constitutional monarchy, and in

1949 France offered the country independence within the French Union. Souvanna Phouma and other members of the government returned to Vientiane and the Provisional Government in Bangkok was dissolved. Only Prince Phetsarath remained in Bangkok. He did not fully share the Marxist convictions of his half-brother Souvannouvong, but neither was he willing to cooperate with the French.

In 1950 a conference was called in Vientiane, which once again demonstrated a desire for national unity. Everyone who had played a leading part in politics and the resistance attended the sessions. In this, as in later efforts to unify the country, the princes had a decisive role, even though their political convictions were increasingly divergent.

The future of Laos depended on the outcome of the First Indochinese War. In 1953 the country achieved full independence from France. In the following year Vietnam's struggle for independence entered its final phase. The Viet Minh army captured the mountain fortress of Dien Bien Phu, which had been built near the Laotian border to control Laos, China and North Vietnam, and was believed to be impregnable. The French expeditionary force lost the flower of its men and France had to abandon its colonial empire in Indochina.

The Second Indochinese War

The Geneva Peace Conference, held in July 1954, was intended to end the Indochinese War and to prevent Laos, Cambodia and South Vietnam from being integrated into the Communist bloc. Laos, which people had scarcely heard of until then, became one of the world's political hot-spots. The chairmanship of the Geneva Conference was shared by Britain and the USSR. North and South Vietnam, China and France were represented as participating states, and the USA sent observers. The most important points in the agreement that was reached were the setting up of an international commission to guarantee the independence of the countries of Indochina and the holding of free elections. All foreign troops were to be withdrawn and none of the countries were to be allowed to enter into any military alliances, nor to undertake or permit any military activity within their borders. They were only to receive such military aid and advisors as were essential for their national defense.

France declared its readiness to withdraw its troops, and all the signatories guaranteed the independence and sovereignty of the three states of Indochina.

The politics of the following decades, a consequence of the Second World War, have gone down in history as the Cold War. The west was obsessed by the domino theory: if one piece in the game falls – that is to say, a country goes Communist – the neighboring countries will automatically follow. America saw itself as being called upon to replace France in a Holy War, and took up the struggle

against the Vietnamese communists, their allies and sympathizers. It was the age of the proxy war, in which small countries fought each other on behalf of the Great Powers. In Indochina there was a conflict between the divergent interests of the USA, the USSR and China. Global politics were played out in the little bar of the Lan Xang Hotel in Vientiane. Laos became a happy hunting ground for secret servicemen and journalists. But for years it was also the only place where any kind of dialogue between East and West could take place.

Even after 1954 the king in Luang Prabang continued to represent the whole country, but the head of government, based in Vientiane, was the neutralist Prince Souvanna Phouma. In Pakse, Prince Boun Oum of Champasak formed the right wing, leaning towards Thailand, and later the USA. Prince Souvannou-

Above: Laotian soldiers wait for their orders.
Right: US tanks and infantry see action in Laos.

vong remained leader of the left-wing resistance, which emerged under the new banner of Pathet Lao, Land of the Lao.

In 1955 the first political party in Laos was formed, the LPRP (Laotian People's Revolutionary Party). This followed the dissolution of the CPI, the Communist Party of Indochina, which had been led by Ho Chi Minh. The LPRP remains to this day the governing organ of the country. As a result of the common struggle for freedom it also retained close ties with Vietnam until the beginning of the 1990s.

Despite all their ideological differences, a new coalition government was formed, led by the three princes. None of the signatories of the Geneva Agreement of 1954 abided by the provisions of the agreement. Elections were only held in Cambodia under Prince Sihanouk. In 1955 the USA began supporting and financing the right-wing forces in Laos; while the left drew their support from Vietnam, the USSR and the People's Republic of China.

In 1959, on the death of his father, Savang Vathana succeeded to the throne in Luang Prabang. He was the last king of Laos. In 1960 there was a coup led by the left-wing, but non-communist paratroop commander, Kong Le. He was followed by the right-wing general Phoumi Nosavan, who promoted American interests, until he was dropped by the USA. Adventurers and army commanders got involved in politics. Events followed in quick succession. Laos was in the grip of civil war. Members of the Hmong (Meo) minority fought under their general Vang Pao on behalf of the Americans, in the ranks of the CIA and in the forces of the Luang Prabang government, but were also to be found in units of the Pathet Lao.

A change of government and another coup led to a crisis in 1961. The neutralists joined forces with the Pathet Lao to oppose the supporters of the USA and of Thailand, who had sent troops to help them. The Pathet Lao controlled three-fifths of the country. At the same time Kennedy and Khrushchov met in Vienna and agreed that the USA and the USSR should adopt a policy of neutrality and non-involvement and favored non-alignment for Laos.

In 1962 a second conference was held in Geneva, at which 14 nations guaranteed Laotian neutrality. However, an end to the war was still not in sight. Again, under the leadership of the three princes, a troika government was formed, while each prince continued to control his own part of the country.

In 1964, in the wake of events in Vietnam, the fighting in Laos escalated, first with the arrival American military advisors, then with B52 bomber attacks later in the same year. These aircraft took off from northeast Thailand near the town of Korat, on the "Friendship Road," of which sections had already been built by the USA as a runway. They dropped more bombs on the northern Laotian

provinces of Xieng Khouang, Sam Neua and Phong Saly, than had fallen on Europe in the whole of the Second World War. Officially these bombardments were aimed at the Ho Chi Minh trail, along which the North Vietnamese communists sent material to help the Vietcong in the south. This supply line had to be rerouted partially through Laotian territory, once the Americans had set up an impenetrable electronic barrier, the MacNamara Line, in central Vietnam, 55 miles (90 km) north of Hué. But the bombs were also dropped on the villages and towns held by the Resistance; they destroyed homes and temples, and transformed rice fields into a lunar landscape of craters.

Once again opinions in Laos were sharply divided. Prince Souvanna Phouma wanted peace and neutrality, Prince Boun Oum of Champasak thought that peace could best be assured by linking up with Thailand, and Prince Souvannouvong sought it through an alliance with Vietnam.

Laos since 1975

The years 1972 and 1973 brought a cease-fire in Laos, the withdrawl of American and Thai troops, as well as negotiations with the Pathet Lao and the LPRP, which led to a compromise, and meant that nothing would change: each part of the country would remain under the control of its existing government. The Pathet Lao controlled all the provinces with the exception of Luang Prabang, Vientiane and Pakse. In 1974 a third coalition cabinet was put together, but in the following year fighting broke out again and continued until the final victory of the Laotian communists.

On 2nd December 1975 the monarchy in Laos came to an end after 622 years. The king was sent to one of the "seminaries" in the north of the country, in which the LPRP tried to convert people

Above: Troops of the Pathet Lao. Right: The late Kaysone Phomvihan, state president, and chairman of the LPRP.

to their philosphy. He died there. The LPRP, which had grown to 20,000 members took over the government of the Democratic People's Republic of Laos. But until the end of the 1980s it was effectively controlled by Vietnam. China also sought to gain influence in Laos and to push the Vietnamese and the Russians aside.

After 1975, in place of the western advisors, eastern specialist appeared on the scene; the USSR and China pursued their differing policies through their satellites, in Indochina as elsewhere. China supported the Khmer Rouge in Cambodia, and at the end of 1978 Vietnam entered the Third Indochinese War against Pol Pot. This put an end to Chinese influence in Laos. Only since 1991 have relations between Laos and China improved.

From 1977 onwards, Cambodia and Laos were closely allied with Vietnam and the Soviet Union through treaties and pacts of friendship and assistance, which even provided for a Vietnamese military presence. This drew them into the conflict between Vietnam and China, which had lasted almost two thousand years.

Another long-standing conflict, whose roots lie in the mentality and geography of the countries of Indochina, broke out once again in 1975: two sparsely populated countries, Laos and Cambodia, whose self-sufficient inhabitants tend towards contemplative calm and Buddhist passivity, possess large areas of undeveloped land and unexploited resources. They are surrounded by active and energetic neighbors: China, Thailand and Vietnam, all three of whom seek to gain supremacy over Indochina.

Since 1975 Laos has been a People's Democracy, which owes its existence to the LPRP, the Laotian People's Revolutionary Party, whose dominant role was once again confirmed in the 1991 constitution. In 1979 the Laotian Front for National Construction (LFNC) was

founded, with Prince Souvannouvong as president. It brought together all mass organizations such as trade unions and youth and women's associations.

The prince was also state president from 1975 until 1983. When he retired, he was succeeded by Kaysone Phomvihan, who had held the post of Secretary General of the LPRP for 35 years. The princes Phetsarath and Souvannah Phouma are now both dead. Kaysone Phomvihan died on 21st November 1992 and with his death came the end of an era in Laos. The funeral ceremony for the Secretary General was conducted according to Buddhist ritual by 22 monks from various monasteries across the country. His offices were divided among two successors. The post of state president was taken by Nouhak Phoumsavan, who up to now had been prime minister and number two in the hierarchy. Five years older than Kaysone, he can also look back on a lifetime of party activity and resistance.

The new Secretary General of the LPRP, hitherto the third man in the hier-archy, is Kamthay Siphandone, who likewise has a long political and military career behind him. Neither are so closely tied to Vietnam as Kaysone, whose father was Vietnamese and who studied in Vietnam. But both were members of the CPI, the Communist Party of Indochina, and so were closely connected with Ho Chi Minh. When they were sworn in they did not expressly declare allegiance to Marxism-Leninism, but said they would follow the example of Kaysone Phomvihan.

Elections at district and provincial level took place in 1988. Laos is made up of 16 provinces (*khouang*) and the independent prefecture (*kamhaeng nakhon*) of Vientiane. The provinces are divided up into regions (*muang*), districts (*tasseng*) and villages (*ban*). There are 13 ministries headed by 45 ministers and deputy ministers. Since the beginning of the 1990s a certain relaxation of policies has been noticeable in Laos, in tune with the changes in Russia and Eastern Europe. Something similar has been happening, though more hesitantly, in Vietnam.

After the People's Republic of Laos had been in existence for 16 years, a constitution was introduced for the first time on 15th August 1991. It comprises ten sections and 80 articles, and in its preamble it refers to the polyethnic people, the kingdom that lasted over six centuries, and the leading role played formerly by the Communist Party of Indochina and now by the Laotian People's Revolutionary Party. In the Democratic People's Republic of Laos all power is in the hands of the people. All minorities have equal rights.

The National Assembly, previously known as the People's Assembly, is the organ of popular representation, elected by a universal, equal, direct and secret ballot. Its decisions are founded on the principles of democratic centralism. In Section 4 of the constitution the National Assembly is designated as the legislative body and at the same time the body which controls both the executive and the judiciary.

The constitution also enumerates virtually all the rights of a citizen in a democracy: the right to vote, civil freedoms, the freedom to choose one's residence, the right to education and employment, assistance in old age and incapacity for work, equality of rights for men and women, for all classes of society and for minorities, the inviolability of the person and of property, freedom of speech and of publication, freedom of assembly and of demonstration.

But rights and duties are modified at the end of almost every article by the following remark: in as far is this does not contravene the law, or: according to the provisions of the law; or: except in the cases specified by the law. There are other clever formulations, such as: the economy will operate under the mechanism of market forces, subject to regula-

tion by the state. And Article 30 guarantees Laotians the right to practice or not to practice a religion. To sum up, for every right enshrined in the constitution, there is a law which limits it, invalidates it or even contradicts it, like the feared small print on an insurance policy. Who knows all these laws? More than half the population of Laos are illiterate and a similarly high proportion certainly knows nothing about the constitution and the rights which it grants them, let alone the laws which take them away again.

On various occasions the government has informed official foreign visitors that it intends to adopt a "Laotian" approach to human rights, press freedom, equality for women and other democratic rights.

On 20th December 1992 nationwide elections to the National Assembly were held by "universal, equal, direct and secret" ballot. The election committee consisted of 15 trusted party members. There is no multi-party system, just one party to vote for.

The fact that the final election results were only announced on 25th January 1993 can be explained by the difficult terrain and lack of communications. But on 31st December 1992 a document had been presented to the election committee.When one is told that 99.3 per cent of all those over the age of 18 and entitled to vote, had in fact voted, and that only 0.16 per cent of voting papers were invalid, it is amazing that one can nevertheless extract some interesting details from this election. Incidentally, it took place shortly after the death of Kaysone Phomvihan.

From a field of 154 candidates 85 were elected to the National Assembly. Their composition is revealing and even more revealing is to see which of the 154 were elected. The figures in brackets refer to the elected candidates:

34 (30) candidates came from the central administration and 120 (55) from local administration, among whom there

Right: Propaganda poster in Vientiane.

were 16 (8) women. Ethnically 108 (52) were Lao-Lum, 29 (16) were Lao-Theung and 17 (17) Lao-Soung.

Looking at their educational background, 63 (45) came from the intellectual class, and 7 (3) were business people. Examining their qualifications in more detail: of those elected 3 only had elementary education, 33 had secondary education, 28 had some form of further education and 21 had attended a university or similar establishment.

Finally, a look at the age of those elected, bearing in mind that in Asia the old still command a certain precedence: the youngest candidate to be elected was 31, the oldest 79, and the average age was 50. Seven candidates were under 40 years old, 38 between 40 and 49 years old, 28 between 50 and 59 years old and 21 between 60 and 79 years old.

What these figures do not, however, reveal, is the part played by a dozen leading families, who have for years held important positions in the party or its mass-organizations.

Among the problems facing the Laotian government, apart from those already touched on, are the rescue of the forests, the support of agriculture, the development of industry, and the control of unemployment and underemployment. These can partly be tackled by reducing illiteracy and the shortage of teachers, which in turn is caused by the inadequate training facilities and poor pay for the teaching profession. The target of introducing compulsory education for all by the year 2000 does not at present seem achievable. The appalling conditions in the health service also give cause for great concern. Epidemics occur frequently, malaria and other diseases are reported to be on the increase, and there is an acute shortage of doctors, medically trained staff, hospitals and mobile health-centers. This particularly affects the rural districts and mountain regions.

The Meo (Hmong) are a rebel element who not only create a security problem along the Thailand-Laos border and thus strain relations with Laos' neighbor; they

have also always been a permanent cause of unrest in the country, going back to before 1975. They have a justifiable grievance about the inadequate educational facilities and medical provision, but it is more the ban on slash-and-burn cultivation and the campaign against drug production driven by Thailand and the USA, which has incited the Meo to active resistance. When the government, following the example of Thailand, attempted to resettle the unruly tribes in lower, more easily controllable areas, the Hmong saw their freedom being encroached on, and also their health threatened by the unfamiliar climate of the lowlands.

Dating from the struggle for or against the Pathet Lao prior to 1975, the government still finds support among the partisans of Faydang Lobliayao, who died in 1986, whereas it is bitterly opposed by the supporters of General Vang Pao, who

fled to the USA. Also opposed to the government are the *Chao Fa*, or Soldiers of the Clouds, who split away from Vang Pao's forces and belong to the Ethnic Liberation Organization of Laos. Their objectives are not so much political as the preservation of the cultural heritage and social structure of the Hmong.

They accuse the government of having attacked the Chao Fa with chemical weapons, the so-called "Yellow Rain," in the late 1970s and early 1980s, a charge which is denied in Vientiane.

Since 1975, about 360,000 Laotians, mainly Hmong, but also including members of the intelligentsia from all ethnic groups, have taken refuge in Thailand. Some 200,000 Hmong emigrated from there to the USA and other western countries. Official figures from Thailand state that in 1992 there were still 53,736 Laotians living in Thai refugee camps. Of these 6,378 are inhabitants of the lowlands, and 47,378 are mountain people, mainly Hmong, who are incapable of being integrated anywhere else.

Above: On the hill of Phou Si in Luang Prabang. Right: A market in Vientiane.

Laos made the justifiable accusation that there were at least 8000 rebels living in camps near the border, who were "right-wing former allies of Thailand and the USA," some of whom possess American passports. Since this is a problem which Thailand is partially responsible for, the Laotians claim, it is up to Thailand to disarm them. In 1992 the governments of Thailand and Laos agreed to to take joint action against the Hmong rebels.

These operate from Thailand territory against Laos. They attack Laotian villages as well as Thai villages close to the border, where Laotian settlers are living. There have been several artillery battles on the border in which inhabitants on both sides have been killed or wounded. For decades the Hmong rebels have been causing a severe strain in relations between Thailand and Laos. At first Thailand made an attempt to move the 30,000 inhabitants of the Thai camps near the border further into the interior and to close down the camps. Many Hmong es-

caped from this resettlement and from repatriation. Thailand then tried to make clear its position with regard to Laos through a series of spectacular arrests of rebel leaders.

Many Hmong emigrants have proved to be able and hard-working in their new homelands, and have done well for themselves. They support their relatives, and the rebels as well, in Thailand. This counteracts all efforts to get the refugees to return to Laos in the near future.

In February 1992 a treaty of friendship and cooperation was concluded between Laos and Thailand, which stressed the shared history and ethnic affinity of the two nations. In order to safeguard this treaty and foster economic relations, the refugee problem is to be resolved by a repatriation program under which Thailand is insisting on a guarantee that the returnees should not be punished, that their livelihood be assured and that any property they left behind should be restored to them. However, these efforts have so far had little success.

THE ART AND CULTURE
OF LAOS

The culture of Asia is rooted in a religious tradition; Asiatic art is religious art. Its works were usually created from impermanent materials that were exposed to a pernicious climate and the ravages of continuous wars.

The art and culture of Laos evolved from the 14th century onwards in the kindoms of Louang Phabang and Viang Chan. Laos is part of the Indian cultural sphere, though unlike Cambodia, it never had any direct contact with India. When the Lao first encountered the empire of the Khmer, the Hinduism of the god-kings of Angkor was already in decline. Buddhism had swept through Indochina and had become a mass religion, which was also adopted by the kings. With the exception of Vietnam, which adhered to Mahayana Buddhism, Indochina adopted the Theravada form, which was based on Hinayana,the earliest form of Buddhist teaching. Theravada, the Teaching of the Ancients, originated in Sri Lanka and is set down in the *Tripitaka*, a collection of writings in three parts, also called the Pali canon. The north Indian Pali, the language of Theravada Buddhism, replaced the Sanskrit of Hinduism in Indochina.

People responded readily to the Buddhist message of salvation, which promised the faithful a better life hereafter, if they earned it by good deeds in this life. Theravada Buddhism tolerated the cults of nature, fertility and ancestor-worship which had survived from the pre-Hindu period, and also adopted the figures of the Hindu pantheon.

Laotian art and culture was therefore able to draw on three religious sources:

Left: The tall, slender That is typical of Laotian architecture.

the pre-Buddhist animistic and ancestor cults, Hinduism and Hinayana Buddhism. The last of these provided the strongest motivation and most pronounced characteristics. It corresponded to the peace-loving and self-sufficient mentality of the Lao and directed their thoughts towards a world to come and *nibhana* (in Sanskrit, *nirvana*), the culmination of a series of rebirths.

The three pillars of Theravada Buddhism are: *Buddha;* his teaching, *dharma;* and *sangha,* the community of monks. For every man, whether he be king or peasant, is commended to spend a year of his life, or the three months of the rainy season each year, in a monastery. Nowadays, most Buddhists limit themselves to a few weeks of monastic life. Children are taken to a monastery for instruction or attend monastic schools.

While the monks are already on the road to Nirvana, the laiety, and especially women, can only earn merit by worshipping Buddha, living according to his teachings, respecting the monks, donating food and clothing to them, and endowing temples and statues of the Buddha. The donor is grateful to the monks for accepting his gifts, since this enables him to increase his store of credit in a future life. To endow a thousand statues of Buddha means earning merit a thousandfold.

Not all these pious objects are works of art. Far from it. The striving for beauty, based on a European concept of aesthetics, is something foreign to the Asiatic mind. The religious efficacy of a sacred work of art is solely dependent on the closeness with which it adheres to traditional iconography.This leads to elaborate symbolism and stylization. Only within the iconographical framework does the artist have any freedom to develop his own design. Therefore many works are simply devotional objects; admittedly created with loving skill and craftsmanship, but scarcely art.

The earliest surviving evidence of the architecture and sculpture of the Lao dates from the 16th century. Their capitals at Viang Chan and Louang Phabang were captured and destroyed again and again, so little that is original has been preserved. However, there are reconstructions which closely follow the traditonal styles and recreate early works.

Laotian art has produced no great original achievements to compare with the high culture of the Khmer and the Cham. It does not go directly back to Indian models for its inspiration, but received its impulses from the Indianized kingdoms of Mon and Dvaravati, from the Burmans and the Khmer. The closest affinity is with the art of Thailand, but neither is that an independent source in its own right, since it drew on the same sources. Works on the history of oriental art only devote a few lines to Laotian art, if they

Above: A Vihara in the style of Vientiane.
Right: A Vihara in the Luang Prabang style.

196

mention it at all. It is usually treat-ed as a regional variant of Thai art.

In the 17th century, works were created in Laos which had assimilated the various different influences and fused them into an autonomous local style, which can be described as typically Laotian. The French architect Henri Parmentier studied the ancient buildings and sculptures of Laos between 1922 and 1927, and wrote a history of Laotian art. Its publication also introduced people for the first time to pagodas and statues which at that time had already been destroyed or only existed as ruins.

Architecture

At first, Laotian temples were built of wood and other impermanent materials. The use of brick and stucco can be traced to the influence of the Siamese architecture of Ayuthia. The sandstone building methods of the Khmer were not adopted by the Laotians. The use of gold and silver is traditional, but the multicolored mosaics are of more recent date.

Part of a temple complex is the *vihara*, a Pali word which is pronounced *vihan* by the Laotians, who also call it *sim* in their own language. This protects the image of the Buddha and is considered the holiest of buildings. The *vihara* consists of a single nave, usually surrounded by a gallery or an open colonnade. From a support of brick columns, a series of three-, five- or seven-tiered roofs soar elegantly upward – odd numbers are considered lucky in Asia. The weight is distributed through crossbeams in the timberwork of the roof. The edges of the roofs are curved upwards in *chao fa* ("princes of heaven"), on which evil spirits are supposed to get caught. The gables are richly decorated with carved wooden panels or stucco. Particular attention should be paid to the wooden doors carved with decorative foliage and figures, which fill the surfaces with har-

monious compositions. Excellent carving can even be found in more recent work and on the doors and gables of reconstructed temples. However, the frescoes and wall-paintings seldom possess anything more than iconographic value. Decorative elements on the outside and inside of the buildings, altars, lamps and ritual objects are often elaborately worked and are examples of sophisticated craftsmanship.

The *sim (vihara)* can be divided into three types according to their ground plan and structure. They are named after the cultural center in which they most frequently occur.

The **Style of Vientiane** is strongly influenced by the Thai styles of Ayuthia and Bangkok. The relatively tall *vihan* has four sidewalls of equal height. It is surmounted by a single or tiered saddle-roof, more rarely there are narrow, single-hipped roofs on all four sides. The columns of the porch are square.

The **Style of Luang Prabang** is recognizable by the low long sides and higher fronts of the *sim*. Two- or multiply-tiered roofs follow the ground plan. The pillars are round. This style shows influences from the Thai temples of Chiang Mai (Lan Na).

The **Style of Xieng Khouang** also has low side walls. The high saddle roof drops down steeply at the sides and is very imposing. The pillars are round. There is a noticeable influence of the art of Chiang Mai. The finest examples of this style were in the highlands of Xieng Khouang but these fell victim to US bombing in the Second Indochinese War.

Libraries (*hao trai*) are small, windowless buildings, which are modelled on those of northern Thailand. They are built of wood on stone or brick plinths, and are decorated with stucco or woodcarvings.

Several of these structures date from the 16th and 17th centuries, the age of Burmese domination, and show elements of Burmese style. Originally the *hao trai* served for the safe keeping of the sacred books of the Pali canon, the *tripitaka*.

197

Today they are often adorned with a picture of the Buddha. They bear little resemblance to the libraries of the Khmer, but to describe them as chapels is equally misleading.

The **That** – the Laotian name for a stupa – is typical of Laotian architecture. They stand on high plinths, and can be straight-sided, bell-shaped or more or less hemispherical, and are crowned by a slender, spire-shaped superstructure.

The construction of the *that* is based on the style of Sukothai in northern Thailand. However, the That mak Mo, in Luang Prabang, with its distinctive hemispherical shape, is possibly influenced by Sri Lanka. Originally *thats* were built to contain relics, but also serve to hold the ashes of the departed. Erecting a *that* is considered a meritorious act.

Kouty are buildings for the monks. Their construction is usually simple.

Above and right: Guardian-figures at the temples are there to frighten off evil spirits.

However, they can also be examples of very beautiful architecture.

The **sculptures** to be seen in Vientiane show some Khmer influence but more from the Thais of Sukothai; in Luang Prabang the predominant influence is that of Chiang Mai.

The Phra Bang Buddha has served as a model for many other statues. Laotian Buddhas are often stylized to an exaggerated degree, are lacking in life and often look stiff. The stylization stifles the artist's freedom of expression.

Typical forms are standing, sitting or walking Buddhas made from wood or bronze. They are similar to the Buddhas of Sukothai, but appear more rounded and have more sharply defined, aristocratic profiles with curved noses. The shape of the face is harmonious, less angular than that of the Thai Buddhas. Particularly noticeable are the large, stylized, snail-shaped ears and the sharply delineated eyebrows. The clothing falls in several folds from the neck and is held by a belt with a buckle.

Walking Buddhas wear garments that cling closely to the thighs in order to stress the forward movement. At the side they are pulled up and billow out from the shoulder.

Most Laotian Buddhas seem to be confined by their clothes, and some have overlong arms hanging stiffly at their sides down to below the knee. This posture is never seen in other South-East-Asian cultures and may be connected with a rain-making ritual.

Really well executed works of art are rare, but can be found with local variations. The *mudra*, or positions of the hands, correspond to the symbolic language of Buddhism. Many of the statues are difficult to attribute to a historical period. So far no systematic study of Laotian sculture has been undertaken.

Sculptures of animals, often serving as guardian figures, are also heavily stylized and seldom look lifelike.

CITADEL
OF THE MOON

VIENTIANE
THE AREA AROUND VIENTIANE

Vientiane, formerly called Viang Chan, has been the country's capital since 1975. It has 120,000 inhabitants, while its prefecture has 160,000 and the surrounding province 267,000. It gives the impression of a spacious provincial town with wide streets and houses built in the French colonial style. Compared with the cities of Bangkok, Saigon and Hanoi, it really is no more than a town. No amount of garish neon signs, bars, clattering motorcycles and increasing motor traffic can erase this impression. The town's public transport is augmented by bicycles and *samlor,* cycle-rickshaws, trishaws or three-wheelers and *tuck-tuck,* which are motorized rickshaws imported from Thailand.

Before the Lao took possession of this land in the 14th century and founded a *muong,* or principality, along the Mekong, the influence of the Khmer extended into this region. In 1563 King Setthathirat (1548-1571) transferred the capital of his kingdom of Lan Xang, from Louang Prabang on the Upper Mekong to the middle reaches of the Mekong, and surrounded the town with a double rampart reinforced with bastions.

Previous pages: Bathing in the Mekong. Left: That Luang in Vientiane, the national shrine.

Legend tells of city called Djanthabuli Si Satthanak Maha Nakhorn, the Moon City of the Great Serpent King. It seems that King Setthathirat wanted to build a settlement on the other side of the river, but the seven-headed Serpent-King showed him the site for his city and then took it under his protection as its guardian spirit. Other legends attribute the choice of the site to Buddhist sages. Djanthabuli lay on the eastern edge of the present town, where there is still a suburb called Si Satthanak. The name Viang Chan means "Citadel of the Moon."

In 1828 Viang Chan was destroyed by the Siamese. In 1866 the French found ruins overgrown by the jungle and beside them a fishing village, which, because its position was favorable for communications, rapidly expanded. However, until 1938 there were no cars in Vientiane.

Between 1911 and 1927 the French scholar Henri Parmentier described 42 temples and monasteries which he found in ruins or in a reconstructed form.

The Mekong, which the Laotians call Mae Khong or Me Nam Khong, traces a wide curve for two miles (3 km) beside Vientiane. In the dry season, a large island called Don Chanh appears out of the river, which is a mile and a half (2 km) wide at this point. Then, between the island and the mainland, the Mekong

seems like little more than a narrow
ditch. A wider arm flows on the far side
of the island by the Thailand shore. At
this time of the year it is hard to imagine
the broad current which in the rainy season fills the riverbed right up to the path
along the bank. In the evening the sun
sets on the far side of the Mekong, and in
the rainy season it is reflected in the
waters of the river; by night the lights of
the Thai city of Nonh Khai shimmer on
the opposite bank.

At about six o'clock, by the first light
of dawn, the monks, wrapped in two yellow or orange cloths, set out with measured step from their monastery, carrying
their begging-bowls. Anything from 10
to 50 monks live in a *wat* and they take
the same route each day. Even before
they have turned the first corner the faithful, mostly women, have come out of
their houses, removed their shoes and
wait, kneeling in small groups along the
road. Each monk receives a handful of
rice in his begging-bowl from the
women's laden dishes. Then the donors
pray, bowing low to the ground, and give
thanks that their gifts have been accepted.
The monks continue on to the next group
without speaking a word, their express-
ionless faces gazing into the distance, one
behind the other. When the sun has fully
risen they return to their monastery,
where they may only eat what has been
given to them. The monastery bell sum-
mons them to their one meal at eleven
o'clock; the afternoon is spent in prayer
and study.

In 1975 the population were forbidden
to feed the monks and no Buddhist instruction could be given. The monks
were made to cultivate fields to provide
their own food and were to restore their
temples themselves. However, this con-
travened the precepts of monasticism,
and it meant that the laiety could no
longer earn their rewards in the next life.
Dissatisfaction was so great that the ban
was lifted at the end of 1976, and further-

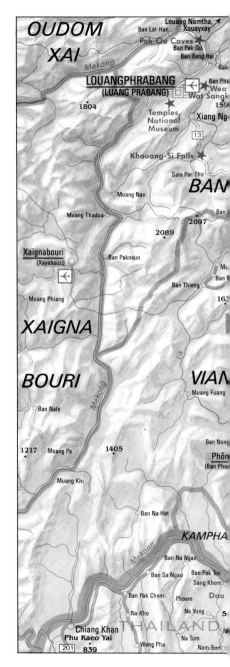

204

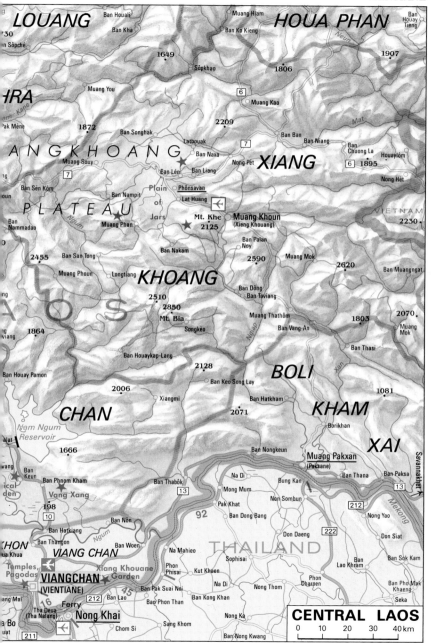

LOUANG

HOUA PHAN

Ban Houay Tieng

'30

n Sôpché

Ban Houali

Ban Kha

Muang Hiam

Ban Ko Kieng

1649

1806

1907

Sôpkhao

Muang You

6

Muang Kao

Mat

ak Mène

1872

2209

IRA

Ban Songhak

Ban Ban

am Kane

ANGKHOANG

Latbouak

7

Ban Naxa

Ban Niang

Ban Chuong La

Houaylôm

Muang Souy

7

Ban Lên

Ban Liang

Nong Pét

XIANG

6

1895

ng

Ban Sèn Kôm

Plain

Phônsavan

Nong Hét

oun

Ban Nampit

of

Lat Huang

Ban Nammadao

PLATEAU

Jars

Mt. Khe
2125

Muang Khoun
(Xieng Khouang)

VIETNAM

2230

Ngum

Muang Phan

Ban Palan Noy

2455

Ban San Tong

Ban Nakam

2590

Muang Mok

2620

Ban Muangngat

ng

Muang Phoun

Longtiang

KHOANG

Ban Dông
Ban Taviang

2510

2070

ng

1864

2850
Mt. Bia

Songkèo

Muang Thathôm

Ban Vang-An

1803

Muang Mok

viang

Ban Thasi

Ban Houaykap-Lang

2128

BOLI

Ban Houay Pamon

2006

Ban Keo Song Lay

1081

CHAN

Xiangmi

Ban Hatkham

KHAM

2071

Borikhan

Ngm Ngum
Reservoir

XAI

alat

1666

Ban Nongkeun

Muang Pakxan
(Paksane)

Savannakhet

vang

Ban Keun

Na Di

Bung Kan

Ban Thana

Ban Paksa

ical
den

Ban Phnom Kham

Ban Thabôk

13

Mong Mum

Non Sombun

13

Mekong

Vang Xang

92

212

198

Pak Khat

Nong Yao

10

Ban Dong Bang

222

Ban Hatkiang

Ban Nôn

Don Daeng

Don Siat

HON

Ban Thangon

Ban Woen

Na Mahieo

THAILAND

Ban Sôk Kam

ua Khua

VIANG CHAN

Ngum

Phon Phisai

Sophisai

Ban Lao Khram

Temples,
Pagodas

Xiang Khouane
Garden

Kut Khaen

Phon Charoen

Ban Pho Mak Khaeng

VIANGCHAN
(VIENTIANE)

Na Di

Nong Thom

Seka

ang Mai

212

Ban Lao

Ban Pak Suai Noi

Ban Kong Khan

Ferry

Bao Phon Than

Nong Ka

Tha Deua
(Tha Nalang)

16
45

Nong Khai

Sang Khom

Ban Pho Mak

a Bo

211

Chom Si

Ban Nong Kwang

uat

CENTRAL LAOS

0   10   20   30   40 km

205

Above: The black stupa in Vientiane.

halls there are sections for clothing, fabrics, shoes, stationery, sculpture, crockery, jewelry, antiques, washing machines, radios, televisions, clocks, imported drinks and cigarettes. There is less and less room for Laotian crafts, woven materials and basketwork, ceramics and silver jewelry. Many goods have to be paid for in US dollars or in *baht*, the Thai currency. Because of the Laotian customs regulations, many Thai imports are cheaper here than in Thailand.

In Thanon Khu Veng, early in the morning, fresh bread, vegetables and fruit are on sale. The wheat flour for baking white French bread is imported from Thailand. In the market called *Thalat Khua Dinh*, in Thanon Mahasot, flowers, fruit and vegetables can be bought, as well as fresh meat and groceries. The *Thalat Thong Khan Kham* is bigger and is situated in Ban (village) Thong Khan Kham to the north of the town. It is also described as an evening market but is in fact open throughout the day.

The **Post Office**, with a counter for special-issue stamps for collectors, is near the Market Hall. The Laotian stamp series, picturing anything from butterflies to space capsules, are always popular.

Wats and Thats: Although the monasteries and stupas in Vientiane have foundations that go back many centuries, they are all reconstructions. There is scarcely a temple in Laos that has not at one time or another owned a monastery, and so they can be called *Wat* (or *Vat*).

Many monks were quick to give their allegiance to the rebel Pathet Lao movement, thus increasing its prestige among the population. This attracted censure from devout Buddhists; but it helped to ensure that Buddhism, with its philosophy of classlessness, could easily be incorporated into communist ideology. It was tolerated in Laos and suffered little persecution.

Of the two original sects, which leaned to the Thai hierarchy, the Tammayuth

more the government undertook to supply the monasteries with rice.

In Laos today the monastic community, the *sangha*, once again has a fivefold task: to expound the faith, to educate the people, to serve the health of the community by making herbal medicines, to maintain the temples, and to play a part in the international peace movement. However, the monks have to accept political instruction and are supervised by the Ministry of Religion.

The markets: The Morning Market, *Thalat Sao*, is on the east side of town on the corner of of Thanon Lan Xang (Lan Xang Street) and Thanon Khu Vieng. The Evening Market, *Thalat Laeng*, in the western district of Ban Nong Duang, was burnt down in 1987. The Morning Market now stays open all day. It clusters around a multi-storey shopping mall with an inner courtyard and is called "the Supermarket" by the Laotians. In the

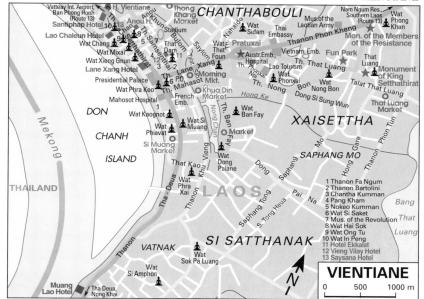

School was close to the royal house of Thailand, though the rules of its order were stricter. It was banned in Laos, as were all Buddhist scriptures in the Thai language.

Before 1975 there were approximately 15,000 monks in Laos, of whom more than 12,000 have stayed on; others have changed their profession or have fled to Thailand. In Laos any man may enter a monastery as a monk. As in most Buddhist countries, he must produce an official document showing that he has no criminal record. This is to prevent criminals from trying to escape the law by entering a monastery.

Recently many monasteries have been restored by the monks with donations from the faithful, but also with assistance from the state. In Laos monks are not exempt from physical work. Today the Laotian United Buddhist Organization, Sang Lao, works alongside the local administration at different levels.

The **Wat Phra Keo**, Pha Kaeo in Laotian, is situated on Thanon Settha-thirat; it has been turned into a museum and is no longer used for worship. It was built in 1565 by King Setthathirat to house the Phra Keo, the Emerald Buddha, which was carried off by the Siamese in 1778.

The temple stood within the palace grounds which extended beyond what is today the main street of Vientiane. The whole temple complex was destroyed by the Siamese in 1828, except for two doors and a side entrance of the *sim (vihara)*, which was reconstructed between 1937 and 1942.

It was built in the Vientiane style, that is to say on a high platform and surrounded by a gallery and a peristyle. Each of the gable sides of the complex has six portals. The red and black lacquer decoration on the doors of the front façade has been lost, but that on the rear façade has survived. The side walls are divided up by ten windows.

Statues of the Buddha from the Dvaravati period, and Laotian Buddhas, are displayed in the gallery. In the garden be-

207

hind the *sim* stands one of the smaller urns from the Plain of Jars.

The interior of the *sim* consists of a single large space. Towards the back, on a high altar, stands the reliquary shrine with a replica of the Emerald Buddha. On display are a golden throne and other memorabilia from the royal palace, statues of the Buddha, including a replica of the Phra Bang from Luang Prabang, as well as valuable woodcarvings and palm-leaf manuscripts.

Wat Si Saket was consecrated as recently as 1824. It was the only building to have survived the destruction of 1828 and thus today is the oldest monastery in Vientiane. It is conceivable that it was deliberately spared by the Siamese since it was built in the Bangkok style. Wat Si Saket is also a museum and is situated on Thanon Settathirat, opposite the Presidential Palace, which is not open to the public. The temple complex gives a good introduction to the design of a Laotian *wat.* It is surrounded by a wall. On the inner side of this a gallery runs round its circumference, in which are displayed hundreds of Buddha statues made from stone, bronze, wood and other materials. The faces and stature of the Laotian Buddhas from various periods, whether seated, standing, or writing, make an indelible impression on the visitor. Most of the statues come from temples in Vientiane and Luang Prabang, but some were made in villages round about; a number of these are in the Khmer style. Wat Si Saket can boast no fewer than 6,840 statues of the Buddha. Fragments have also been preserved, but so far these have not been evaluated.

The *vihara* in the Bangkok style, from which the Vientiane style ws derived, has a veranda all round it and a colonnaded porch in front. Original 19th century murals have been preserved in its niches, de-

picting themes of the Jataka, stories from Buddha's earlier lives. Others were restored in 1913. The floral pattern on the ceiling shows French influence, which was picked up through the decorative art of the Thai kingdom of Ayuthia. The standing Buddha, at the left, on the upper altar, bears the features of the man who endowed it, Prince Chao Anou of Viang Chan (1805-1828). The gilded wooden candleholder dates from 1819.

There is a water dispenser (*hang song nam pha*) on the veranda, which is used for washing the statues of Buddha at festival times.

The library in the courtyard has a roof in the Burmese style. The *tripitaka*, or Pali scriptures, which it used to house, were taken to Bangkok in 1828. One of its three doors is original.

The **That Dam**, or Black Stupa, stands in the middle of Thanon Bartoloni. It is reminiscent of the stupa in Chieng Saen, northern Thailand, and may date from the early years of the Lan Xang empire. There is a legend that a seven-headed dragon sleeps in the *that*, which wakes if the city is in danger.

Pratuxai – the Victory Gate, also known as the triumphal arch or independence monument, stands at the end of Lan Xang Avenue. It was built in imitation of the Arc de Triomphe in Paris, but decorated in Laotian stryle, to commemorate those who died in all the wars before the revolution. For this reason it is also named *Anusavari Kao*, or the Old Monument.

Beyond the *Pratuxai* is the beginning of Thanon Phon Keng (street). On its left-hand side is the Museum of the People's Army of Laos, and a little further on, the **Monument to the Resistance Fighters**. Called the New Monument, it is dedicated to those who died in the revolutionary struggle of the years 1964 to 1973. It is in the form of a *that*.

Wat Phong Khan was completely destroyed and only one large Buddha sur-

Right: Monks taking part in a religious festival in Vientiane.

vives, for which a new *sim* has been built. This is on the left side of Thanon Phon Keng, beyond the New Monument.

The **Monument to King Setthathirat**, the founder of the city, stands at the southern end of the square in front of the That Luang.

The **That Luang** was built in 1566 by King Setthathirat, on the site of an older stupa. According to legend, King Ashoka, the great patron of Buddhism in India, sent a relic of the historic Shakamuni Buddha, and a stupa was built for this in the third century. The Khmer are thought to have erected a stupa on this site in the 11th or 12th century. A model of the first building, the one from the 3rd century, can be seen behind the *that*. The original was discovered when the stupa was being restored.

That Luang, the national shrine and also the emblem of Vientiane, is a large golden stupa, built on the highest of three tiered, square terraces. The design of the towers is based on the architecture of Sukothai, in Thailand. Travellers from Europe in the mid-17th century reported that the *that* was covered with almost half a ton (500 kg) of gold leaf. Like so much else, the That Luang was destroyed in 1828 and not rebuilt until 1900.

There is some dispute about who carried out the work and what models they were following. It is true that the Ecole Française de l'Extrême Orient played a significant part. Opinions also differ as to the artistic value of the reconstruction, but at least it pleases the Laotians, who regard it not merely as a testimony to Buddhism, but also as a national shrine and a symbol of their independence.

The gallery which surrounds the building is 280 ft square (85 m by 85 m). It only has small windows and was added to the building at the beginning of the 19th century as a defense against invaders. Statues from Laos and Cambodia stand at the entrance. At the time of the That Luang festival, visitors stick small rice-balls to the walls in memory of King Setthathirat. Flights of steps lead up over the three square terraces to the foot of the stupa. The first terrace measures 226 ft by 226 ft (69 m by 69 m). It is set with 323 ordination stones, called *sima*, which mark the boundary of the sacred precinct. On each side is a prayer gate, *hao wai*, with an arch above it, through which steps lead up to the second terrace, which is 157 ft square (48 m by 48 m). It is decorated with 120 lotus leaves, and has 288 *sima* and 33 small stupas, each of which once contained a smaller golden stupa, but these were stolen by bandits in the 19th century. On each of 33 stone tablets is inscribed one commandment in the sacred Pali language. Whosoever observes all these, it is said, will be born again as Bodhisattva. This terrace is where processions take place during the spring and autumn festivals.

The next flight of steps leads through arched prayer gates to the third terrace, 98 ft square (30 m by 30 m). The hemispherical stupa, reminiscent of early Indian examples, stands on this terrace. It culminates in an arrow-like spire, with clean, harmonious contours, like a lotus flower rising from its leaves.

The *that* was surrounded by four monasteries. Two of these have been preserved, **Wat Luang Neua** to the north and **Wat That Luang Thai** to the south, today the residence of Pha Sangharat, the patriarch of Laotian Buddhism.

Pah Vet, the Festival of That Luang, combined with a week-long fair in the pagoda, takes place at the time of the full moon in the last lunar month, at the end of November, and at the same time honors every *that* in Laos. The three-day festival begins with prayers and donations at six o'clock on the Sunday morning. In the evening, as a climax to the festival, a candle-lit procession makes its way around the *that*. The monks fire off small home-made rockets into the sky to begin a firework display. Thousands come to the fair and watch games, like the kind of polo without horses, in which one team is dressed in red with a fixed number of players, while the other side can have any number and wear anything.

The That Luang market is held every day near the stupa. The Thanon That Luang leads directly to the Pratuxai.

Wat Si Muang, the Monastery of the Sacred City, also called Wat Phya, was built by King Settathirat in 1563 as the first temple for the guardian spirit of his new capital. The *sim* is a reconstruction, dating from 1915. In the middle of the altar stands a stone column of the Khmer period, draped in cloth. It is said to have been saved from the original temple. In front of it is a wooden stele. The column is the symbol of the city *(luak muang)* and legend has it that when it was erected, a large hole was dug, and a volunteer was required as a human sacrifice. A young pregnant woman finally jumped into the hole and the pillar was dropped on top of her.

A simple stone Buddha, which survived the destruction of 1828 with only slight damage, stands on the altar. It is now regarded as a Buddha to whom one can make wishes, and is surrounded by flashing colored lights. If your wish comes true, you must offer coconuts and bananas to the Buddha. In this temple – and in a number of others – elemental spirits are worshipped as well as Buddha.

The monument in the small park in front of the *wat* represents the last king but one, Sisavang Vong.

At the **Wat Sok Pa Luang** (Wat Mahaphutthavongsa Pa Luang Pa Yai) nuns administer herbal saunas and massage. A monk who came from Thailand in 1932, leads groups in meditation exercises, known as *vipassana*. The monastery stands in Thanon Sok Pa Luang, south of the Morning Market.

Wat Si Amphon, in the street of the same name, close to Wat Sok Pa Luang, is also famous for its herbal saunas.

Right: A collection of Buddhas at the Wat Phra Keo.

The **Museum of the Revolution** in Thanon Samsenthai can only be visited by prior appointment. In the garden behind the museum three large urns are displayed. They came from the Plain of Jars and are of particular interest, as are the enormous ironwood tree trunks from the Laotian mountains.

The **Wat Ong Tu** is situated on Thanon Settathirat on the way to the airport. Its name, which means Heavy Buddha, refers to the large seated statue which, according to legend, is one of the three oldest in Laos. Like so many others, this *wat* was founded by King Settathirat, destroyed in 1828 and rebuilt in the later 19th century. The woodcarvings inside, and those on the gables, exhibit outstanding craftsmanship.

The *wat* is the seat of the second patriarch of Laotian Buddhism, Houng Sangharat. It also provides a school for 300 monks from all over Laos.

Wat Hai Sok stands opposite Wat Ong Tu. It is in the process of restoration, but the seven-tiered roof is of interest.

Wat Mixai is in this area, on the same side of the street as Wat Ong Tu. There is a public school in its grounds.

Wat In Peng (Wat Oupmuong) is a small monastery on Thanon Luang Prabang, beyond the road that branches off to the airport. It was rebuilt in 1940. The frescoes, which have also been restored, are an example of Laotian native art and depict scenes from the Indian Ramayana epic.

Wat Chang, in Thanon Fa Ngum, beside the Mekong, has a bronze Buddha around which the *sim* has been rebuilt. The woodcarvings on the gable are of high quality.

THE AREA ROUND VIENTIANE

The **Nam Ngum Dam** can be reached by two roads. The new and longer, but faster eastern route, Highway 10, turns off beyond the airport and runs for 58 miles (93 km) through a sparsely populated region. There are plans to cultivate sugar cane and cotton here.

In the village of Ban Phnom Kham, 38 miles (62 km) north of Vientiane, you will find a footpath going off to the right, which runs through varied countryside to a small lake, called **Vang Xang**, or Elephant Pool. It is a 25-minute walk. In the 10th to 12th centuries, there were Buddhist shrines on the shores of the lake. You can still see statues of the Buddha carved into a rock-face. It is advisable to take someone with you from the village, who knows the area.

The Nam Ngum reservoir can be crossed by a car-ferry. During the Second Indochinese War, refugees from the Plain of Jars established a settlement about 9 miles (14 km) from the dam. About one-third of the population fled to escape American bombing.

Salt is processed at the village of **Ban Keun**. A small wildlife park has been created not far from the road. **Ban Thalat**

Above: The Garden of Khouane was laid out in 1970 with donations from the Buddhist community.

is an important market-town, lying at the confluence of the Nam Nugung and Nam Lik rivers. There is a road from here to the reservoir.

There are countless islands in the artificial lake. One of them is called Done Nang, Island of the Men, another Done Nang, Island of the Women. It was here that the re-education camps (euphemistically called "seminaries") were located. Another island is named Done Santhiphap, Island of Peace. It is possible to swim in the reservoir, and there are boat-trips.

The older, shorter, western route, along Highway 13, though only 51 miles (82 km), is in poor condition and the journey takes longer. However, it takes you through many villages.

About 12 miles (20 km) from Vientiane on Highway 13, just before the bridge on the way out of the village of Ban Hua Khua, an unsurfaced track branches off to the left. It passes through the villages of Na Sone and Nagang and after nearly 4 miles (6 km) reaches the hill named **Dau Song** (Flat Stone), over-looking the Mekong. To the right, a path leads for a few hundred yards to a recently built pagoda. Buddhist caves and statues of Buddha are concealed in a fantastic landscape of cliffs and forest. From the cliffs you can see across to the Mekong. In the village of Ban Phong Hong a road branches off to the east, to Ban Thalat and to the Nam Ngum dam.

In the region of **Tombok**, the road is unsurfaced and dusty, but it takes you through an unspoilt landscape of tropical forests and to the temple which stands on a hill, 50 miles (80 km) south of Vientiane. This is one of the four most important places of pilgrimage for the Buddhists of Laos, who come to see a *phrabat,* a footprint of Buddha. The place is well worth a visit, especially for the temple festival on the seventh day of the second lunar month, which draws pilgrims from far and wide.

A road named Thanon Tha Deua follows a wide bend in the Mekong southwards, and takes you through Vientiane's developing industrial area.

From the frontier post at the river port of **Tha Deua** (Tha Nalang), a fleet of ten boats run at five-minute intervals, carrying passengers and freight across the Mekong to Nong Khai in Thailand. The crossborder traffic comes to a halt in the middle of the day and on Sundays. At this point, about 6 miles (10 km) south of Vientiane, a bridge is being constructed across the Mekong into Thailand.

Two rows of red and white painted pylons, about 600 yds (0.5 km) apart, carry powerlines over which electricity is exported from Laos to Thailand. Silkworms are bred in the villages and the silk thread is spun and woven. Breeding the highly sensitive silkworms is tricky work.

The **Xiang Khouane Garden** is 16 miles (26 km) from Vientiane in a wood beside the Mekong. It was laid out in 1970 by a monk, with donations from Buddhists, and contains many statues.

VIENTIANE

Arrival and onward travel

Flights: Vientiane's international airport at Vatteay is served from Bangkok and Hanoi by Thai Airways, from Phnom Penh by Lao Aviation and from Hanoi and Bangkok by Vietnam Airlines. The taxi ride from the airport into town (2.5 miles / 4 km) costs about US $ 5; You should agree the fare before you start. Airport Tax: US $ 6.

Ferry: From Nong Khai in Thailand across the Mekong to Tha Deua (Tha Nalang), 6 miles / 10 km from Vientiane. The fare is 30 *baht;* dollars or Laotian *kip* are not accepted. The ferries run daily except Sunday from 8am-11.30am and 2pm-4.30pm. The border-crossing must be entered in your visa. Complete the journey to Vientiane by car, bus or taxi.

Tours in Laos for groups or independent travellers can be booked through travel agents in your home country, or through Diethelm Travel in Bangkok, Saigon Tourist in Saigon or Lao Tourism in Vientiane.

Independent travelers must report within three days at the Immigration Office, Thanon Lane Xang, near the Morning Market.

Accommodation

FIRST-CLASS: **Lane Xang Hotel**, Thanon Fa Ngum, beside the Mekong, Tel. 3672, 5346.

MID-PRICE: **Ambassador Hotel**, Samsenthai Road near the center. **Asian Pavilion Hotel**, Samsenthai Road, Tel 16-9036/7. Restaurant with European, Chinese and Thai cuisines, pub und café. **Le Parasol Blanc**, Nahaido Road, Tel. 3287. Restaurant with international cuisine, café, swimming pool.

Hospital / Embassy

Australian Embassy Clinic, Thanon Phonxai Noi, Vientiane, Tel. 2477, 4691, in emergencies outside normal hours, Tel. 2183.

Clinic of the Swedish Embassy, Thanon Phonxai Noi, Tel. 4641.

United States Embassy, Thanon Bartolini, Tel.3570/2357.

Shopping

Silverware: In Thanan Talat Bao and in the Morning Market. Gold and silver are sold by weight.

Jewelry, handicrafts, antiques: The best opportunities for buying are in Thanon Samsenthai.

Ceramics: There is a state-owned sales center in Thanon Luang Prabang.

Textiles: A state-owned textile center for female Laotian weavers is being run in the Thanon Luang Prabang.

SPLENDOR AND DECLINE OF THE THRONE

THE ROYAL CITY OF LUANG PRABANG
THE AREA ROUND LUANG PRABANG

THE ROYAL CITY OF LUANG PRABANG

The royal city of Luang Prabang, the country's capital until 1975, lies 228 miles (367 km) northwest of Vientiane on the upper reaches of the Mekong. Where the Nam Kane (Nam Khan) river flows into the Mekong on its left bank, a narrow tongue of land is formed. Here at an altitude of about 2,600 ft (800 m) and surrounded by wooded hills, the principality of Muong Swa (Muong Chawa) grew up on the flat land between the rivers, blessed with all the imaginable beauties of nature. In 1353 Fa Ngum founded Lan Xang, the empire of "a million elephants," on this site, having united Muong Swa with the principality of Vieng Chan.

The history of the city and of the kingdom is closely linked with a golden statue of Buddha, the Pha Bang (Phra Bang) about which the British historian, D.G.E. Hall, has written at length. This statue was greatly revered as it was considered to be very sacred, and had been known since the 8th or 9th century in Sri Lanka. It appeared in Cambodia in the 11th century, presumably as a gift to the king, and

Left: The view over Luang Prabang from the hill of Phou Si.

from there came into the possession of Fa Ngum in 1358 as a gift from his father-in-law, the king of the Khmer, when he embraced Hinayana Buddhism. The statue is then thought to have been kept in Vieng Chan. It was not until 1489 that King La Nam Sene Thay took it to Muong Swa and built the Wat Kang to house it. In 1491 the statue was taken to the Wat Manorom and the name of the capital, Muong Swa, was changed to Muong Louang Phra Bang (the modern Luang Prabang). From that time on Luang Prabang was the secular and religious center of the Lao kingdoms. The Phra Sangharaja, spiritual leader of the Laotian Buddhists, had his residence in Luang Prabang until 1975, initially in the Wat Aham and later in the Wat Mai. King Vixun Harath had the Phra Bang taken to the newly built Wat Maha in 1513, and when King Setthathirat established his capital in Vieng Chan in 1560, he took the Phra Bang with him.

The Siamese stole the statue in 1779, but returned it four years later. Following the destruction of the city of Vieng Chan in 1828, which also marked the end of the kingdom of Vieng Chan, the Phra Bang was taken to Bangkok, but in 1839 – or, according to other reports not until 1867 – it was restored to the King of Luang Prabang and set up once again in the Wat

Vixun. In 1894 it was taken to the Wat Mai and remained there until independence in 1947. After that it went to the royal palace. Construction of the Wat Ho Phra Bang was started in the grounds of the palace, but the turmoil of war has meant it has remained unfinished.

Time stands still in Luang Prabang and the past seems more alive than the present. Wars and destruction, the attacks suffered at the hands of powerful neighbors and marauding Chinese, French colonial rule and American bombers – amazingly, none of these have left any visible trace. But the peace and harmony of the place are deceptive. Rebellions and unrest break out repeatedly among the mountain tribes, and today marauding gangs still occasionally make towns, roads and waterways unsafe. Until a few years ago there was a nightly curfew.

Luang Prabang lives on its memories of the splendor of the kingdom, the monasteries and the temples, and waits in an-

Above: A girl of the Meo tribe

ticipation for the the New Year festival (*pimai*), when the guardian spirits emerge from their temples.

The hill of Phou Si (Phusy) rises up in the middle of the town and at its foot stands the Royal Palace. A golden *that,* built in 1804 and restored in 1914, towers up from its wooded summit. It belongs to the **Wat Choum Si**, which was founded in 1774 and renovated in 1962. A flight of 328 steps leads up the hill. They were built in 1936-37. The wearisome climb is rewarded by the views over the Mekong and Nam Kane rivers, the town lying between them, and the broad landscape of hills. To see the sunset from Wat Choum Si is an unforgettable experience.

Four times a day, at 9am, midday, 3pm and 6pm, thirty-three beats on the great drum used to echo across the city, announcing the time and simultaneously reminding people of the thirty-three commandments of Buddha. The drum has fallen silent because, they say, the drummer has died. For many years martial music and the slogans of the Party reverberated morning, noon and night across the town from loudspeakers, but now they too are silent.

Monks live on Phou Si, keeping company with the *phi* and the *naga*, the elemental spirits which still dominate the daily thoughts and actions of the people.

There used to be many temples on the wooded hillside, but most have disappeared. Halfway up the hill a banyan tree from Myanmar (Burma) was planted to mark the 2,500th anniversary of the birth of the Buddha. On the south side stood the Wat Thay Phou and in 1895 the little Wat Chi temple was built, but neither have survived.

From the **Wat Tham Phou Si**, which has a large statue of Buddha, a flight of steps with handrails on either side in the form of *nagas* (serpents) lead up to the **Wat Phrabat Neua**. This temple was built to protect a footprint of Buddha, and was renovated in 1965.

Map labels:
Xieng Mene · Wat Xieng Mene · Wat Comphet · Wat Hath Siao · ★ Caves · Wat Long Khoun · Wat Tham · Wat Khok Pab · *Mekong* · Wat Phone Xay · National Museum (King's Palace) · Wat Choom Khong · Wat Sieng Mouane · Wat Nong · Wat Si Moung Khoun · Wat Xieng Thong · Wat Sop · Wat Si Boun Heuang · Post Office · Wat Mai · Wat Ho Sieng · Thanon · Wat Pha Houak · Photisarat · Wat Pa Phay · Wat Sene · Sakkarine · H. Villa de la Princesse · Wat That · Phousy Hotel · Wat Choum Si · Wat Phrabat Neua · *Nam Kane* · Wat Khili · Wat Pak Kane · Wat That Luang · O Market · Phou Si · Wat Tham Phou Si · Wat Pakha · Wat Phrahouttabat That Phralak, That Luang Market · Wat Aham · Wat Vixun, Museum · Wat Aphay · Wat Phan Luang · Hospital · Kitsarat · Th. Setthathirat · Wat Manorom · Rama Hotel · That Mak Mo · Wat Phone Xang · Pak Ou · Th. Phu Wao · Wat Mune Na · Airport → · Th. · Wat Tao Hai · **LUANG PRABANG** 0 100 200 m · Vientiane · Mittaphab Hotel · Ban Phanom · Wat Pa Nha Thup

Temples and monasteries

The following description of a number of *wat* is only a selection; many of the monasteries are neither works of art in themselves, nor do they possess any, but they allow one an insight into the history of the town and its province, of Buddhism and of the spirit cults. The main streets are lined by one monastery after another, separated by walls and connected by gates. Others are situated on the hillsides on the far side of the Mekong, or further along its banks. There are monks living in nearly all the monasteries. There are said to be about 350 in the town and as many as 1,500 in the province as a whole, but precise figures are hard to come by.

The description below lists the important *wats* first, together with a few lesser ones, if they happen to be close by.

Wat Xieng Thong was founded by King Setthathirat in 1560. Its name means: The Monastery of the City (Xieng) with the Bodhi-Tree (Thong),

the *ficus religiosa*, or Buddha Tree. It lies on the Mekong and the Nam Kane rivers. The road to the *wat* runs along the river bank. In the dry season, the receding water leaves the ground free for growing vegetables. After the rainy season the river rises and the water rushes and gurgles in the narrow valley. There is a beautiful view from a pavilion from which the king used to watch the boat races on the Nam Kane.

The Wat Xieng Thong is enclosed by a wall. A steep flight of steps leads up from the Mekong to the main entrance. The second gate on the opposite east side, is nearer the town. The *sim*, or shrine, was built in 1561 and most recently restored in 1968. On its rear façade is a mosaic depicting the Bodhi-tree from which the temple derives its name. It was 88 ft (27 m) high and its trunk had a circumference of 23 ft (7 m). It stood behind the so-called Red Chapel (library) and a second library. In the latter there is a reclining Buddha dating from the building of the temple.

217

The outside back wall of the library was decorated with a mosaic in 1957 to mark the 2500th anniversary of the birth of Buddha, and the scenes of village life which it depicts are particularly interesting. The small building in front of the *sim* is a burial place for statues. A white *kouty,* a meeting room for monks, occupies the other side of the courtyard, with the monks' accommodation adjoining it.

The building at the east gate was erected in 1961 for the burial of the last king but one, Sisavan Vong, and it contains a funeral bier 40 ft (12 m) high, in the form of ship, and other accoutrements for the royal burial. The double doors and the outside walls are decorated with scenes from the Ramayana epic. On the west side of the courtyard, set a little way back, is an old drum tower, with burial stupas in front of it.

Above: Door to the funeral chapel of the Wat Xieng Thong. Right: Temple complex in Luang Prabang.

The **Wat Pak Kane** is situated on the path to the Wat Xieng Thong, at the mouth of the Nam Kane. It was built in 1737 and visited by the kings at festival times.

The **Wat Mai,** which means New Monastery, was the seat of the leader of the Laotian Buddhists before he moved to the new capital of Vientiane in 1975. The monastery was built as a replacement for the Wat Si Phoum. As early as 1796 King Anourouth expressed the wish that his temple should be the most beautiful in the land. In fact, work did not start until 1821 and was finally completed in 1891. Three stupas have survived from this period. The *vihara* is built in the Luang Prabang style with a five-tiered roof. The rich ornamentation of the doors and columns show not only scenes from the Ramayana epic and the Jatakas, but also of village life. The monastery owns rowing-boats, which take part in boat-races at festival times. The New Year festival, *pimai,* takes place in the Wat Mai, and during this time, the Phra Bang

Buddha is set up in the monastery court-yard.

The **Wat That** was built by King Set-thathirat in 1548, before he moved his capital to Vieng Chan. In 1900 it was destroyed by a storm. Reconstruction began in 1907, with financial contributions from the Buddhist community, and was completed in 1964. It plays an important part in the celebration of the New Year festival.

The **Wat Ho Sieng** was built in the 16th century next to a pavilion dating from 1548. The present building was erected by the royal family in 1705.

Wat Vixun (Wat Visunarath), was built in 1512 by King Vixun Harath, and housed the Phra Bang Buddha from 1513 to 1560. The wooden *wat* burned down in 1896 and was rebuilt two years later in brick and stucco, with stone imitations of the wooden baluster-windows. This use of stone to reproduce wooden elements, though common among the Cham and Khmer, is extremely rare in Laos. Wat Vixun became a museum in 1942. It con-

tains a collection of statues of the Buddha as well as ordination stones (*sima*) from the 16th century, which are frequently set up in Laos to mark out sacred precincts. On the altar there is a large seated Buddha. Devout Buddhists, mostly of the older generation, come here for morning and evening prayers. The That Mak Mo and the Wat Aham stand in the same temple complex.

Wat Mak Mo (That Pathoum) today forms part of the Wat Vixun, and only the stupa survives. The Wat was built in 1514 by the consort of King Vixun Ha-rath, but was damaged in 1914 by Me-kong flood waters. Only the *that* was renovated in 1932. The monastery treas-ures are to be seen in the palace museum. The stupa was so named because it re-sembles a watermelon, or *mak mo*. Its shape recalls early Indian stupas.

Wat Aham was founded in 1818, together with the **Ho Seua Mong**, the temple for the two guardian-spirits of the city: the male Phou Nheu and the female Gna Gneu. The Ho Seua Mong is not

open to the public. In the house of spirits are kept the dance masks for the guardian spirits and the lion, Sin Khao, which until 1975 featured in the New Year festival. (See p. 237). Wat Aham owns boats, which take part in the regattas. They are about 80 ft (25 m) long and are propelled by 48 oarsmen.

Wat Khili was built in 1773 by a prince who hailed from the province of Phouane. The people of this province have erected a temple to their local god on a small mound in the courtyard. By the road stands the little library, a wooden building on piles.

The **Wat Sene** (Wat Sene Soukharam) is one of the four temples which line the main street. It is the seat of the Chief Bonze of the province of Luang Prabang. Built in 1718 on the site of an older temple, it was renovated in 1932. The most recent renovation took place in

Above and right: Luang Prabang, the royal city, is also the city of Buddhas and monasteries.

1957 to mark the 2500th annivaersary of Buddha's birth. On the 7th, 8th, 14th and 15th day of each lunar month, the faithful, mainly women, come to pray in the temple. The Wat owns two 89-foot (27 m) racing boats built of *khene* wood.

Wat That Noy, the Little That, was built by Buddhists from the province of Xieng Khouang.

The **Wat Sop**, beside the Wat Sene, was founded in 1481 by a prince in memory of his father and was originally called Wat Sop Xieng Khane. In 1485 he had a second one built, Wat Xieng Thong, but died in the following year. The two monasteries were combined in the 18th century under the name Wat Sop. The present *sim* dates from 1909. In a building from 1933, north of the *vihara*, there are two Buddhas from the Wat Nak, which was founded in 1768 and destroyed at the end of the 19th century. The monastery runs a school for monks.

The **Wat Si Moung Khoun** lies to the east of the Wat Sop at the end of the main street. It is said to date from 1763.

The **Wat Si Boun Heuang**, also on the main street, was founded in 1758 and boasts some frescoes. It was renovated in the 1950s.

The Wat That Luang is in the south of the city. There is a legend which tells that the Buddhist King Ashoka sent orders from India for it to be built.

The group of buildings we see today date from 1818 and were renovated by Sisavang Vong, the penultimate king of Laos. The Wat is the place where the urns containing the royal ashes are laid. The urn of King Sisavang Vong was placed in the great stupa.

The valuable exhibits in the Wat That Luang come from the little That Nhi Nhong, which is all that survived into this century of the Wat Phone Keo. The French used it as a school and in 1963 a hotel was built on the site. During construction work, three golden Buddhas, precious stones and relics were found in a stone jar. Some were taken to the Wat That Luang and the rest to to the National Museum.

The **Wat Phraphoutthabat Tha Phralak**, west of the Wat That Luang, is said to date from the 15th century and possesses a footprint of Buddha. Renovations took place in 1959 and 1970. The temple stands beside the Mekong, and the best time to visit it is at sunset.

Wat Phone Xay (Wat Phone Xaysana Songkhama), whose name means Monastery of the Hill of Victory, was built in 1791, though the present fabric dates from 1970. The name comes from the great Buddha statue, Phra Xaysana Songkham, the Buddha of Victory.

Wat Manorom was built on the site of an older temple dating from 1375, and was renovated in 1972. The great Buddha had lost both arms, but these have been replaced by ones made of cement. There is a school for monks in the Wat.

Wat Nong (Wat Si Khoum Muong) was built in 1729 on the site of a dried-up lake (*nong*). It was renovated in 1804 and

1888 and is the seat of the Chief Bonze of the city.

The **Academy of Arts** is housed in the former residence of the Queen Mother.

The **Wat Pha Houak**, built in 1861, contains the library of the Ministry of Culture, with valuable old books and manuscripts. To visit it, you must obtain a permit from the Ministry.

The **Wat Pa Phay**, founded in 1815, and restored in 1967 and 1969, is now the offices of the city school authority.

Royal palace, National Museum

There are no official opening-times and you must apply in advance if you want to visit the building. Photography is not permitted in the rooms.

The new palace, with its landing stage on the Mekong, was built in 1904 and used by the royal family until 1975. It is surrounded by a high fence and extensive gardens with old trees from which orchids hang down. There is a pond covered with water lilies and a memorial

to the builder of the palace, King Sisavang Vong. On the right as you enter stands the unfinished Wat Ho Phra Bang, which was to have been built after 1947 to house the Phra Bang Buddha.

On the gable over the entrance to the palace the former emblem of Laos can still be seen: Erewan, the three-headed white elephant symbolizing the three kingdoms of Laos. He is surrounded by dragons, bringers of rain and fertility.

The palace is built on a cruciform plan and, especially in the private appartments, is furnished in a simple, modern manner. In the center, beyond the entrance hall, is the official audience chamber with the throne and a display of the king's robes, weapons and saddlery, as well as a valuable collection of Buddhas, including items from the Wat That Mak Mo and the Wat That Bhi Nhong.

On the right is the reception room for private audiences with the king. It is dec-

Above: A Lao-Theung woman working at a hand-loom.

orated with a scene from the Ramayana epic and a display of statues of the kings. The murals showing scenes from the life of the Laotian people were painted in 1930 by the French artist, de Fauterau. In a further room, on the right, along with other statues and temple accoutrements, is displayed the **Phra Bang Buddha**, a staute of gold 2 3/4 ft (83 cm) high.

On the left of the entrance hall you can see gifts from foreign countries. Beyond is the queen's reception room, with portraits of the last king, Savang Vathana, the queen and the crown prince, painted by a Russian artist. In the private rooms there is a remarkable collection of musical instruments and dance masks for the Ramayana plays.

The markets in Luang Prabang

There are several markets in Luang Prabang, of which the largest, **Thalat That Luang**, lies beyond the That Luang temple and runs down to the Mekong, where boats from the surrounding villages land their produce. Around a smaller market on Thanon Kitsarat, in the town center, there are shops selling antiques and silver jewelry made by the mountain tribes. In all the markets you will see the Hmong (Meo) and other minorities in their traditional costumes.

THE AREA ROUND LUANG PRABANG

It is worth visiting the temples on the other bank of the Mekong just to see the lovely countryside there and to enjoy the view of the two rivers and the city.

The **Wat Xieng Mene** was founded in the 14th century. However, the present buildings only date from the end of the 19th. They stand at the eastern end of the village of the same name. From here a footpath leads up to the **Wat Hath Siao** and **Wat Tham**, a cave-temple with statues brought here from *wats* that no longer exist. There are other caves nearby.

Wat Khok Pab lies further to the east. **Wat Comphet** is the temple situated highest up and enjoying the finest view. It is a 20th century building. **Wat Long Khoun** was twice destroyed, and the present building dates from 1937. It was used by the kings when preparing for the coronation ceremony.

Ban Phanom, or Phanom village, on the far side of the river Nam Kane, is inhabited by the Lu, a Lao-Theung tribe, who provided the servants for the royal court. In 1947 the women went back to their earlier occupation, weaving. Their looms are underneath the stilt houses. They work for a co-operative but are also allowed to sell their work on their own account, at a market held every Sunday. Their cotton and silk fabrics have traditional patterns. The men work in the rice fields run by the co-operative.

Wat Sangkhalok, 3 3/4 miles (6 km) from the village, was built in 1527 for the protective spirit of the city, on the site of an older temple. It was destroyed by a storm in 1883 and rebuilt in 1904. The king would visit the temple at the time of the New Year festival in order to sprinkle the Buddha with holy water in a solemn ceremony. The Nam Dong river flows nearby and Luang Prabang's power station is 9 miles (15 km) upstream.

The **Lao-Lum** village of **Ban Xom** and the Lao-Theung village of **Ban Thapene** lie on the way to the Khouang Si waterfall, which is 15 miles (25 km) from Luang Prabang on Highway 13, towards Vientiane. The road has been improved on this stretch and by 1994 should be repaired and open for tourist traffic the whole way to Vientiane.

The **mountain villages of the Hmong** can only be reached in the dry season, and then only in 4-wheel-drive vehicles. A narrow, rough track, that gets washed away by rain, leads to the village of **Long Lanh.** The journey of about 19 miles (30 km) takes at least two hours and the last stretch has to be covered on foot. But it is well worth the effort if only for the views over the mountains and the glimpse of life in a Meo village.

Up the Mekong to the Caves of Pak Ou

It takes a day to cover the 19 miles (30 km) up the Mekong to Pak Ou, where the Ou flows into the Mekong. The time taken depends on the water level and the power of the boat's engine. There are a few modest rapids to be negotiated. The navigation channel has been signposted as part of the Mekong Project. When the water level is normal the trip takes two hours upstream with a powerful motor, and a good hour back downriver. The boats are very basic, but the boatmen are highly skilled.

When the water level is low, the villagers work in their vegetable plots planted on the riverbanks where the water has receded. Gold is panned on a sand bank which is only exposed in the

dry season. It is worth getting out of the boat to watch. Gold-panning brings an additional income for local people, mainly women, who come from the surrounding Lao-Lum villages. Any profit they make results from a combination of good luck and hard work. The grains of gold are taken home and processed.

The river banks sliding past present an ever-changing scene, and boats drift by laden high with goods for the market. On the right hand side as you go upstream the mountains are higher, and the villages cling to the steep slopes. The left bank has only gentle hills. In the high, forest-clad mountains there are bare patches where the trees have been cleared by burning. In several places the boats glide over rapids. Spray can splash into the boats, so keep your cameras covered. Grotesquely shaped mountains tower above you and seem to bar the narrowing course of the river. The village of **Ban**

Above: In the Pak Ou caves. These Buddha statues have been donated by the faithful.

Xang Hai is worth visiting in order to get an impression of the simple life of the villagers, who live from distilling a kind of alcholic spirit called *lao lao*.

Facing the mouth of the river Ou, in the limestone cliffs, you will see the caves. Steps lead up from the landing stage to the lower cave, **Tam Ting**, then a further flight of steps on the left leads to the higher cave, **Tam Phum**, which runs deeper into the mountain. (Don't forget to bring a flashlight/torch). The innummerable Buddhas in it have been donated by believers and set up whever room could be found. Here and there one may see an attractive little work of art, but on the whole the statues are very unsophisticated. The view down to the Mekong and the Nam Ou and over the mountains is a reward for the exertion of the climb. In the pre-Buddhist era serpent spirits, *naga,* were worshipped in the caves.

On the steep shore opposite, the village of **Pak Ou (Baku)** nestles behind tall clumps of bamboo. The men catch fish to sell in the markets of Luang Prabang, cultivate their dry rice fields some distance away, or sit on the river bank and mend their nets. A water pipe leads from the mountains on the other side of the Nam Ou, high across the river, to a cistern which supplies the village with fresh water. The houses are built on stilts. There is a village shop on a small square, and a *wat*.

About half a mile (1km) further upstream on the Ou some rocky cliffs called **Pha Hen** soar vertically up from the river, and the calm, clear pools at their foot are full of fish. Further upriver, in the dry season, there are small islands where you can enjoy a cool, refreshing bathe (so bring a swimming costume).

Excursions into the territory of the minority peoples

Xayabouri (Xaignaboury), the province and the town, are a one-day trip from Luang Prabang, assuming you return by road. By boat they can be reached in 3 or 4 hours depending on the water level. The swift journey down the Mekong passes through a virgin mountain landscape where the minority peoples have settled and elephants bring tree trunks from the teak forests to the river. There are several temples to see in the town.

Houayxay (Houeixay, Houei Sai) lies at the westernmost point of Laos, to the south of the triangle formed by Laos, Burma and Thailand, known as the Golden Triangle. The region is mountainous and traversed by several rivers which flow east to west, at right angles to the Mekong. There is an air connection from Luang Prabang, and the outward journey can, with permission, take you over the Mekong to Xieng Khong (Chiang Khong) in Thailand.

On a hill above Houayxay stands **Wat Chom Kao**, from where you can look over the town and its surroundings. In the mountains around the town are the villages of the Lantene and Nong Thane mi-

norities. **Ban Poung** is a village of the Lu, a tribe of the Lao-Theung group. **Ban Lentene, Ban Tom Lao, Ban Saohonghinh** and **Ban Nong Thane** are also minority villages. Round here gold is panned and sapphires and rubies found. Goldsmiths and other craftsmen have workshops in the town.

Louang Namtha, the northernmost mountain province, bordering China, is also called Sip-Song Pannas. It figured in the disputes between France and Siam about the north of the kingdom of Luang Prabang, which was terrorized by Chinese bandits.

Surrounded by mountains 6,500 ft (2,000 m) high, it lies on Highway 3 and on the Nam Tha, which flows through the mountains into the Mekong south of Houayxay. Recently it has become possible for foreign visitors to fly from Luang Prabang to Louang Namtha, where very basic accommodation has been provided. Trips are arranged to visit the mountain tribes, hitherto hidden from the outside world.

THE PLAIN OF JARS

XIENG KHOUANG

THE TOWN AND PROVINCE OF XIENG KHOUANG

On the high plateau in the northeast of the country lies the province of Xieng Khouang with its former capital of the same name. The flight from Vientiane leaves the plain of the Mekong, crosses some hill country and is soon taking you over an endless region of forest-covered mountains. When you land, you are 3,000 ft (900 m) higher than Vientiane.

The Xieng Khouang plateau looks as though it were burrowed by gigantic moles. These mounds of earth were thrown up by bombs. The deep craters are close together, and rice grows only sparsely. After two decades, it is still a constant reminder of the Second Indochinese War.

The airport of the new provincial capital, Phone Savanh is called Xieng Khouang in the timetable, and since it is situated in the prefecture of Muong Pek (which means "palmtree district") it is sometimes also called Muong Pek.

The plateau enjoys a pleasant climate all year round. It has hot sulphur springs, caves and the urns or jars of all sizes, which have hardly been studied yet.

Left: Laotian women enjoy a good smoke.

Two-thirds of the inhabitants abandoned the densely populated plateau during the bombing, between 1964 and 1973. Only 120,000 people are currently living in these fertile uplands. Not a town or village was left unscathed by the bombing; everywhere houses, monasteries and temples were destroyed. Rebuilding is only proceeding slowly.

In a small area you will come across groups of Lao Lum and Lao Theung, and at higher altitudes, two tribes of the Lao Soung, the Hmong Khao and Hmong Lay. Women of the Thai Dam, or Black Thai tribe of the Lao Lum group, wear a turban round their hair tied in a bun. Over it they wrap an embroidered cloth.

Phone Savanh (Paradise Hill), the new capital of Xieng Khouang province, lies about 4,000 ft (1,200 m) above sea level. Surrounded by mountains, and with its houses set far apart, it looks like a pioneer settlement. So far it has no "downtown" area, but one is beginning to grow up around the marketplace.

The **Plain of Jars** (Thong Hai Hin) begins 4 1/2 miles (7 km) east of Phone Savanh, near Lat Huang, on the road to Muong Khouane. Southwards stretches a hilly, treeless landscape, which is named Ban Nakam after a village nearby. For quite a distance around, earthenware jars or urns are scattered over the land, for no

Above: Urns on the Plain of Jars.

recognizable purpose. Even by climbing one of the hills, you cannot see them all. Many of the urns seem to be placed in groups, some stand close together on a hilltop, others singly, at varying distances from one another.

The bombing destroyed many of them, leaving shattered fragments and craters. This field of urns is nevertheless a fascinating sight. It stretches as far as Lat Sene, 19 miles (30 km) to the south, where the last seven urns can be found. At the edge of this site, not far from the road, there is a hill with a cave.

Nearby, a few hundred yards (about 1 km) north of the road to Luang Prabang, is a hill with two caves, one above the other: **Tam Kap** and **Tam Mat**. They once contained valuable statues of Buddha, but these were stolen in 1911.

The second and larger site where urns are found, in the Muong Sui district, stretches in a semicircle around two lime-

stone hills, near the road to Luang Prabang by kilometer-stone 27. There is a third site near the Meo village of San Tio, between Muong Phan and Muong The.

There is a legend about a Chinese general who defeated a cruel local ruler and to celebrate his victory ordered rice wine to be fermented in these jars. People like to tell the story, but it should not be taken seriously.

Archaeologists nearly all agree that these vessels were made by a megalithic Austronesian people related to the Lao-Theung. Their purpose was either for burial or for containing burial gifts. But no one is really clear about the period or indeed the people or the tribe to whom these urns are attributed. At all events they belong to a widespread megalithic culture which covered large parts of Indochina and can be traced in Burma (Myanmar), Malaya and Indonesia. It is connected chronologically and culturally with the Dongson culture of the Bronze Age in South-East Asia, whose most important archaeological sites are near the

Vietnamese village of Dong Son, in Thanh Hoa province, south of the Red River delta.

The urns show very considerable differences in size, shape and the material they are made of. There are large ones, some very large, and many smaller ones. The largest can be as much as 10 ft (3 m) high, with a diameter of 1 foot (30 cm). Many are straight-sided, with rounded edges and corners. Others are oval or cylindrical. Nearly all are taller than they are wide and have flat bottoms. Domed lids lie scattered around. Many of the vessels appear to have been chis-elled from granite or porphyry, slate or limestone. Others consist of a mixture of stones and were probably moulded.

French archaeologists have put forward two theories:

1. The urns were created at the place where the stone was quarried, and then brought to their present site.

2. They were moulded from a limestone cement to which various stones were added, then fired in caves. The second hypotheses has led to them being described as earthenware jars.

Muong Kham (Golden District) is the name given to this locality, because of its particularly fertile fields. The town of the same name is 32 miles (51 km) away and can be reached in 1 1/2 hours along a relatively good road.

On the way you pass through the Hmong village of **Ban Tha Chock**. A few miles away in the mountains, there are many caves of historic importance, in which resistance fighters lived, and where the rest of the population came to seek shelter during air raids.

In the **Tam Peaw Cave**, in 1969, 650 villagers were killed when an American bomb exploded at the mouth of the cave. Their village, Ban Nam Eun, was also destroyed. After 1975, it is said that the caves were used as re-education camps.

About two miles (3 km) from Muong Kham, in **Bao Nam Haon,** there are hot

sulphur springs, which have a healing effect on skin diseases.

Nong Het, on Highway 6 going southeast, is a town on the border to Vietnam, which is to be opened in the near future. At present, however, tourists can only visit the district of Nong Het, near the border.

Xieng Khouang, a town lying 4000 ft (1200 m) above sealevel, was formerly the capital of Xieng Khouang province, but has lost that status and been renamed **Muong Khoun**. The journey of 22 miles (36 km) over a bad road, takes an hour and a half. The name Xieng Khouang is explained by a legend: a white elephant (*xieng*) stopped at this spot, turned round in a circle (*khouang*) and could not be persuaded to walk any further. On that spot the town grew up.

There were once many temples in Xieng Khouang. Two of them, the most famous and most beautiful, **Wat Siphon** and **Wat Xieng Khouang**, both built in the style of Xieng Khouang, were destroyed but are currently being rebuilt.

MOUNTAIN AND WATER

SAVANNAKHET / SARAVANH CHAMPASAK

SAVANNAKHET AND SARAVANH

The province of Savannakhet is the most populous in Laos, with about 330,000 inhabitants, and, lying in the fertile plain of the Mekong, is one of the most prosperous parts of the country. Its capital, also called Savannakhet, lies at a height of of 975 ft (300 m) and is the fourth largest town in Laos, with a population of about 45,000. It has nothing to offer the sightseer, but the festival of the That In Hang is one of the four largest temple festivals in Laos, and is attended by the faithful from all over the country. In **Ban Nateuy** there is a salt mine.

The border-crossing at Lao Bao, between Savannakhet and the town of Mukdahan in Thailand, can be used by tourists with a special permit.

The population of **Saravanh,** the capital of the province of the same name, has once again returned to its pre-war level of around 42,000. The town was destroyed in the war and has been rebuilt as a plain and sober administrative center. Part of the Boloven Plateau belongs to the province of Saravanh and the other part to the province of Champasak.

Left: Buddhas in the Wat Phu temple near Champasak.

From Saravanh a road leads across the Boloven Plateau to Tha Teng and Pak Song. From Pakse onward the road connections are better.

CHAMPASAK

This province, whose capital, **Pakse**, lies 975 ft (300 m) above sea level, has had a turbulent history. From the 10th to the 13th century it was the northernmost province of the Khmer empire of Angkor. After the fall of Angkor the empire of Lan-Xang extended its sovereignty to include this region during the 15th century. The kingdom of Champasak came into being around 1800. More recently, during the 1960s and '70s, Champasak played a role in Laotian politics, when its prince, Boun Oum, opted for co-operation with Thailand and the USA.

The name of Pakse means the mouth, *pak*, of the river Se. With a population of 60,000 it is the second largest town in Laos. It did not grow up until 1905, as a center of French colonial government. Not far from the airport the scattered buildings become more densely spaced, to form a town center, but the rest of the town consists of houses on stilts.

Pakse has no buildings of interest, and its temples date from this century. Its markets display the rich produce of the

Above: Selling vegetables, Pakse.

countryside. The town lies in an enchanting mountain landscape on the Mekong, surrounded by fertile rice fields. The most striking mountain is the cone-shaped **Ma Long**, close beside it is the **Bassak** and a little further away the **Batiang**, the elongated **Sa Laou** and the **Nang On**, which resembles a reclining woman. Many legends are woven around these mountains. One version relates that a rich and beautiful young woman, Ma Long, loved a poor boy, Ba Thieng (Batiang), who came from the people of Kha. But Ma Long was also loved and wooed by Bassak, a wealthy member of a royal family. When the poor Batiang brought all the necessary bridal gifts to the girl's parents, including, as was the custom, liquor, they threw these away with scarcely a glance. This is the origin of the mountain Sa Laou, whose name means: "where one throws liquor away." Batiang's courtship was rejected, but on an

island in the Mekong, Ma Long brought his child into the world and died in labor. When the rich Bassak learned that Ma Long did not love him, he killed himself beside her. Nor did Batiang survive the loss. Over the bodies of the dead, mountains grew; close to Ma Long lies Bassak, and a little further away, Batiang.

From Pakse there are excursions to be made, including a boat trip to **Khong Island** and the **Khon Phrapheng Waterfall** near the Cambodian border. In small boats the journey takes 5 to 6 hours depending on the state of the river. Alternatively you can take Highway 13, though this is still in poor condition. Whether or not the border is open depends on the political situation in Cambodia. The regular ferry service is due to be restored soon between Vientiane and Pakse.

Visitors leaving Laos for Thailand may, with a permit, use the frontier station at Chongmek and cross to the Thai town of Ubon-Rachathani.

The fertile highlands of the **Boloven Plateau** have an area of about 3,900 sq. miles (10,000 sq. km), at an altitude of about 4,000 ft (1,200 m). The highest mountain, **Phiamay**, reaches 5,650 ft (1,716 m). The climate is pleasant all year round, favoring the cultivation of coffee, tea, cardamom and vegetables. The plateau is inhabited by the minority Lao Theung and Lao Soung peoples.

Because the Ho Chi Minh Trail ran through the eastern part of the plateau, the area was subject to heavy bombing by the American air force.

From Highway 13, which runs from Vientiane to Cambodia and Vietnam, a road branches off 8 miles (13 km) beyond Pakse, over the Boloven Plateau to **Pak Song** (Paxong). Until the end of the 5th century the plateau was settled by the Chen La, the predecessors of the Khmer.

The town of **Tat Lo**, in Saravanh province, is approached from Pakse, and lies in a wooded region beside the waterfalls of the Nam Se river. Its dam and power

station provide the south of the country with electricity. A good way to explore these attractive surroundings is on the back of an elephant. Near Tat Lo there are villages of the Alack minority, and to the northeast, on the way to Tha Teng, you will pass Kalum villages. Returning to Pakse you go through Katou villages and coffee plantations. Most of the minorities on the Boloven Plateau belong to the Lao-Theung people, the so-called Indonesian group, who have preserved an ancient Austronesian custom, the annual sacrifice of a buffalo.

Champasak and Wat Phu can be reached either by boat along the Mekong, or by road, a distance of 30 miles (48 km). On Highway 13 to Cambodia and Vietnam, 6 miles (10 km) from Pakse, you will see the **Hona Se Waterfall,** on the Nam Se river. About 8 miles (13 km) further on, a road branches off to the left for Pak Song on the Boloven Plateau.

The journey to Champasak takes you through teak forests and past Lao-Theung villages. After 21 miles (34 km)

you reach the village of **Tha Muong** on the Mekong, with a fine view of the the cone-shaped mountain, **Phi Kao**. A car-ferry operates across the Mekong, which is about 3/4 mile (1,200 m) wide at this point. Two islands lie in the river. **Don Kam**, Island of Birth, is where Ma Long is said to have borne her child. Downstream, **Don Deng**, Red Island, is stained with her blood.

Champasak, once a royal capital, is today a sizeable district capital, with a population of about 20,000. The last ruler of Champasak was the conservative Prince Boun Oum, and today his residence is called the **Great House**. The small palace is said to contain a collection of golden Buddhas and other valuable objects from Wat Phu. However, to see them you must obtain permission from Vientiane.

The road from Champasak to the Wat Phu (5 miles / 8km) is bad. It leads to Thailand through the villages of **Ban Phan Non** on the Houai Sa Hua, the "River of Hair-washing," and **Ban**

233

Thanh Kop, the "Village at the Cross-roads." Near the temple there is a turning off the road, which leads up to it.

Wat Phu

On the Phu Pasak, a hill about 230 ft (70m) high, a spring bubbles out of the ground. The combination of hill and water was, from the very earliest times, considered sacred. We learn from Chinese sources that the Chen La, who were forerunners of the Khmer, occupied the hill from the 6th century onward and built shrines to the water spirits and mountain gods. In the 6th and 7th centuries a temple in the form of a *lingam* stood on the rocks. The town at the foot of the hill and the temple on its summit formed a single entity, which has been retained in the later buildings which have survived.

Above and right: The lower temple grounds of Wat Phu.

Wat Phu was built as a shrine to Shiva by King Jayavarman IV in the 10th century, in the style of Koh Ker (921-944), the early Angkor period. It is thought to have been linked with Angkor by a road 60 miles (100 km) long, marked out with stones.

The temple complex is surrounded at a distance by an outer wall and consists of a hilltop shrine and the temples at the foot of the hill, which are connected by a staircase. In the plains, irrigated rice fields stretch away to the Mekong. On the flat ground within the wall is an ornamental pool. At the foot of the hill, the ruins of two temples have been preserved. On the way up to the principal shrine is the statue of the king. A flight of more than 90 dilapidated steps leads to the hill-temple. On one side of them is a low wall behind which frangipani grow. The Laotians call them temple-trees. Very few of the *naga* balustrades have survived on the staircase.

The hill-temple is protected by walls. A further twelve steps lead to the princi-

pal shrine. The tower-shrine rests on a cruciform base. The three-naved interior is entered through a large vestibule. When the king visited the shrine of Shiva, he drank from the spring which flows from the hillside.

The *linga* has disappeared from the main temple, but reliefs of Hindu gods and goddesses still decorate the façades and portals.

Today Wat Phu is a Buddhist monastery and a few monks live in this otherwise deserted place. Only for the annual temple festival do many faithful come from southern Laos, and, since the opening of the frontiers for local people, also from Thailand and Cambodia. Below the statues of Buddha is a "wishing Buddha," which answers the prayers of any believer who manages to touch it with his outstretched hands. The view from the hill-temple over the Mekong valley is magnificent, but the whole temple complex is in a sorry state.

On the day of the full moon of the third lunar month, a three-day Buddhist festival called *Boun Wat Phu* is held. It includes a pagoda market, competitions and games and is one of the four largest temple festivals in Laos. In the temple, cults dating from before the era of Indianization are used in the worship of nature spirits, which have become mixed with the gods of the Hindu pantheon. It is true that the worship of spirits has been officially banned in Laos since 1975, but this does not stop it going on.

At the full moon of the 7th lunar month, on the so-called Crocodile Stone near Wat Phu, a water buffalo is sacrificed to the local earth spirit, Chao Tengkam. Buffaloes remain part of the tradition of the Indonesian Lao-Theung. Centuries ago they replaced human sacrifice. With Hinduism they were taken over by all the Indianized people of Indochina, but in fact belong to the pre-Hindu fertility cults of Aryan tribes who occupied northern India. The earth spirit reveals itself through a priest in a trance. The blood of the sacrificial victim is scattered over the fields with prayers for rain.

LAOTIAN FESTIVALS

The international New Year's Day on 1st January, the Laotian New Year festival from 13th to 16th April, Labor Day on 1st May and the Day of National Celebration on 2nd December, are all public holidays. But the Laotians are also happy to recognize the festivals of their minorities, the Chinese and Vietnamese New Years and Christmas in its commercialized American "Xmas" form, when chains of colored lights are hung in tropical trees.

The traditional festivals, known as *Boun*, are connected with Buddhism. However, they have their roots in pre-Buddhist spirit-worship. *Boun pimai*, the Laotian New Year festival is also a celebration of the the coming of spring and a waterfestival. It used to begin as a celebration of the year's end, on the last day

Above: New Year festival (pimai) in Luang Prabang. Right: A "mohpohn" at the celebration of Raising of Souls (baci).

of the waning moon in the fifth lunar month (April) and lasted 14 days until the end of the waxing moon. Since 1975, however, it has been fixed from 13th to 16th April. At the same time spirit-cults were banned and *pimai* now gives the impression of being a Buddhist festival.

In the royal city of Luang Prabang the guardian spirits of the city and the country once used to take part in the processions and celebrations. Even today *pimai* is celebrated more festively in Luang Prabang than in other places. At the head of the procession walk the local dignatories, holding votive offerings of flowers and fruit in front of them, followed by monks with little buddhas in miniature temples. The showpiece of the procession is a man-made elephant on a cart, accompanied by young girls in traditional costume.

In Wat Mai the golden Phra Bang Buddha is enthroned on a high structure beneath a *hang song nam pah*, also called a *hangling*, which is a serpent, into whose tail the Buddhists pour holy water, which then pours out of the serpent's mouth and over the Buddha. This ritual washing takes place in every temple in the country. *Naga,* the serpent has the function of rain-bringer in South-East Asia, just as the dragon does in East Asia. The participants spray each other liberally with the beneficent water.

In the afternoon, even today, young people especially like to to cross the Mekong in boats to the island of Xieng Meng, a sand bank which appears in the dry season. The new arrivals are greeted with a shower of water. On the island and in the temples little votive mounds, called *that,* are erected. Those who build them may expect health and happiness in the new year.

In the markets one can unburden oneself of sin by purchasing small creatures, especially birds locked in cages, and then giving them their freedom. All over the country races are held. Spectators wait expectantly for the fast serpent-boats, crewed by 25 to 30 oarsmen, on every river in Laos. These recall the invoking and dances of the rain-bringing serpents, who are summoned up at the end of the dry season and driven out again at the end of the rainy season.

One day, perhaps, *Phou Gneu* and *Gna Gneu*, the guardian spirits of the city, will once again take part in the festival, as they did up to the end of the monarchy in 1975. On the second day of the waxing moon the start of the New Year was announced to them and then wearing terrifying masks and accompanied by a small lion, they would leave their dwelling in the Wat Aham, to demonstrate their ritual dances in the Wat Vixun, Wat Xieng Thon and Wat That Luang.

Legend tells that *Khoun Borom* was sent down from heaven to bring order to the world. A huge liana had grown so tall that it cast a shadow over the earth and robbed Man of warmth and light. *Khoun Borom* commanded it to be felled, but noone dared to. *Phou Tao Gneu* and Me

Ngam, an old couple, finally said they would be willing, provided that after their death mankind would offer sacrifices to them and pray to them before every meal. For three days they chopped at the mighty trunk with their axes, then the liana fell and buried both of them. Light and warmth returned and ever since then *Phou Gneu* and *Gna Gneu* have been worshipped as the *Tevoda Luang*, or guardian spirits of the city.

When a dangerous monster in the shape of the lion, *Sin Khao*, threatened the population, the spirits tamed him by teaching him to dance. Since then he has lived with them in their spirit-temple, *ho phi*, and accompanied their dances. Similar legends about the lion, called *singha* in Sanskrit, are told in many countries of Asia.

Then perhaps the conjuring-up of souls will be performed once again, for human beings, animals, plants and even for inanimate objects like the kettle and the rice pot, the *sou khuan*. *Naga*, the serpent king, guardian spirit of the country, will

237

leave his cave on Mount Phousi and come wriggling down in the shape of the giant fire serpent, whose tail is still curled up in the cave when his head has reached the city. There he will unite with his *nagi*, who lives in the sacred pool of the royal palace. This union, the Laotians believe, guarantees the continuation and good fortune of the nation.

Lak Man, a very powerful and dangerous spirit, a *phi*, who manifests himself in a tree and whose spirit-home is not far from Wat Vixun, used to be worshipped on the eleventh day of the seventh month and is also considered to be one of the protecting spirits of Luang Prabang.

The *Festivals of the Rain and Fasting Season*, between the full moon of the eighth month (July) and the eleventh month (October), are Buddhist festivals, at which time pagoda markets usually take place.

Above: "Baci" at a wedding celebration in Luang Prabang.

At the festival of *boun ok pansa*, at the end of the rainy season, boatraces are held on the Mekong and its tributaries.

Boun kao padabdin is the Festival of the Dead, when villagers lay sacrificial gifts for the departed at the walls of the monasteries. At *boun kao salak*, devout Buddhists present gifts of food and clothing to the monks.

BACI – THE SUMMONING UP OF SOULS

A *baci* (or *bassi)*, though organized for tourists these days, can, if the participants are prepared to join in and show some understanding, provide a glimpse of the ancient ritual of summoning up souls. There are many occasions when a raising of souls, *sou khuan*, can be held. After the birth of a child, on the occasion of a wedding, when starting a journey, or returning safely home, in the case of illness or recovery, to celebrate passing an examination, being awarded some honor, or to honor a respected guest – on all these occasions, the souls, which are often floating far away, are summoned back to their owners, in order to bring them strength and happiness. The Laotians believe that not only humans, but also the whole of nature, animals, plants and lifeless objects have souls, and that they are endangered if their souls leave them.

For a *baci*, family and friends foregather, or the employees of a factory, or everyone living in an urban or country neighborhood, or indeed any other group. Sacrifices to the soul-spirits must be carefully prepared. In earlier times, and even today in country districts, a piglet is slaughtered and its boiled head is placed as a sacrifice on a bed of rice, and surrounded by rice brandy and candles. This ceremony can admittedly take many different forms, but the ritualistic purpose remains the same.

Pa khuan, the sacrifice, is placed on a silver platter, *khan*, on a stool in the center of the room. If foreign visitors are present, an artistic structure is made from banana leaves firmly pressed into the shape of a lotus bud, into which are stuck flowers, candles, and little wooden splints hung with short, white cotton threads, and the whole thing is surrounded by eggs, sweets or cakes.

The guests are then invited into the darkened room where they sit on the floor on one side, close to the *pa khuan*, while the hosts sit on the other three sides and along the walls. In Laos it is considered insulting to turn one's feet toward a respected or sacred object or towards any person. For foreigners, therefore, it is necessary either to squat or else to tuck one's legs to the side and behind; neither of which is very comfortable.

When everyone is assembled, the *mohpohn* appears, who is to conduct the summoning. These days he is usually a man who is known to be learned, because he has spent some time in a Buddhist monastery. But in earlier times he was a

moh, a magician. He takes his place facing the guests, and also directly in front of the *pa khuan*. Over his chest and shoulders he wears a white silk scarf. The candles are extinguished, the *mohpohn* places the palms of his hands together in font of him and begins the long, formal, monologue, which grows ever faster and more intense, in a mixture of Lao and Pali, the language of Buddhism – a kind of singsong recitative which can induce a trance-like state.

The hosts place the palms of their hands together in front of them, while the guests touch the *pa khuan* with the tips of their fingers. When the *mohpohn* has finished, they also place their hands together in thanks, then they raise their left hand level with their cheek and extend their open right hand, into which a small portion of the sacrificial gift is placed.

With that the first formal part of the *baci* is completed. The *mohpohn*, and after him first the oldest and most respected male and female hosts approach the guest or guests on their knees, take a cotton thread from the *pa khuan*, murmur a short incantation, tie the white thread around the wrist of the guest and rub his pulse to reinforce the blessing. By touching the one who is blessed by the soul-spirit, they can share in his good fortune. When each participant has tied a *phouk khene* round the wrist of each guest, the informal and more cheerful part of the ceremony begins.

The *choum*, or rice brandy, also called *lao lao*, begins to circulate. Anyone who manages to empty their glass in one gulp is the object of admiration. Everyone present wants to drink to the health, *seun*, of the guest and to dance a *lam vong*, the Laotian "circle dance," with small steps and economic movements. In this the individual, the couples and the whole party dance in concentric circles. The *baci* can be combined with a meal for the guests, and dancing girls may appear, who will perform classical dances.

Nelles Maps

... get you going.

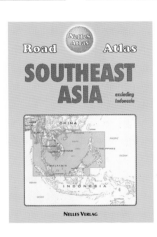

- Afghanistan
- Australia
- Bangkok
- Burma
- Caribbean Islands 1 / Bermuda, Bahamas, Greater Antilles
- Caribbean Islands 2 / Lesser Antilles
- Central America
- China 1 / North-Eastern China
- China 2 / Northern China
- China 3 / Central China
- China 4 / Southern China
- Crete
- Egypt
- Hawaiian Islands
- Hawaiian Islands 1 / Kauai

Nelles Maps

- Hawaiian Islands 2 / Honolulu, Oahu
- Hawaiian Islands 3 / Maui, Molokai, Lanai
- Hawaiian Islands 4 / Hawaii
- Himalaya
- Hong Kong
- Indian Subcontinent
- India 1 / Northern India
- India 2 / Western India
- India 3 / Eastern India
- India 4 / Southern India
- India 5 / North-Eastern India
- Indonesia
- Indonesia 1 / Sumatra
- Indonesia 2 / Java + Nusa Tenggara
- Indonesia 3 / Bali
- Indonesia 4 / Kalimantan

- Indonesia 5 / Java + Bali
- Indonesia 6 / Sulawesi
- Indonesia 7 / Irian Jaya + Maluku
- Jakarta
- Japan
- Kenya
- Korea
- Malaysia
- West Malaysia
- Manila
- Mexico
- Nepal
- New Zealand
- Pakistan
- Philippines
- Singapore
- South East Asia
- Sri Lanka
- Taiwan
- Thailand
- Vietnam, Laos, Cambodia

GUIDELINES

TOURISM IN CAMBODIA

As everywhere else in South-East Asia, tourism in Cambodia started in the 1960s. Initially, tourists came mainly from France and from the United States, whose attention had been drawn to the region by the crisis in Indochina. The principal destination was Siem Reap, the base for Angkor Wat. There were good, fast roads from Saigon and Phnomh Penh, and you could fly in a DC3 Dakota from Phnom Penh to Siem Reap. On the way lay Battambang, the second largest city, with its good hotels and many temples, which could be reached by train either from Phnom Penh or Bangkok. Both road and rail journeys had to be broken at the Thai border, since relations between the two countries were bad. Travellers had the tedious task of walking with all their luggage across more than half a mile (1 km) of no-man's-land.

Immediately opposite Angkor Wat there was a French bungalow-hotel, which was burnt down during the Indochinese War. A couple of miles away in Siem Reap was the Grand Hotel, which-still exists and is being renovated. The Great and Small Circuits, which had been laid out by the French at the beginning of the century, provided access to the temples.

Due to the Indochinese War, the civil war from 1970 onward and the regime of the Khmer Rouge, who for a time had an ammunition dump in Angkor Wat, tourism in Cambodia ceased completely for many years. Not until 1983 did a few sporadic charter flights start bringing small, hand-picked groups of tourists, who were prepared to pay a lot of money for a few hours at Angkor Wat, and soon were also able to visit Bayon. The state-owned travel organizations, transport and hotels were not able to handle larger numbers of tourists until 1990, and then largely thanks to help from Thai and Vietnamese tour operators.

The acid-test, which did not prove entirely trouble-free, was the invasion of journalists and tourists who arrived to witness the return of Prince Sihanouk in 1991. Since then it is true to say that there has been a steadily growing stream of tourists.

In the meantime, foreign investment, mainly from Thailand, has gone into the building of hotels, restaurants, shopping-centers and bars, and the establishment of air and road transport services. This process has been accelerated by the presence of 22,000 well-paid UN peace-keeping troops. How many of the bars and restaurants, in particular, will survive the withdrawal of the boys in blue helmets and manage the switch to tourist custom, remains to be seen.

Even more difficult to predict is when the whole country, and especially the north, will become accessible again. This all depends on the political situation, the security of roads and waterways and the restoring to a usable state of at least a basic tourist infrastructure.

TRAVEL PREPARATIONS

The following information refers to Cambodia. General hints relevant to both Cambodia and Laos can be found on pages 248-250.

Travel season and climate

Cambodia has a tropical monsoon climate with two rainy seasons. In summer, from June to October, the south-west monsoon blows, bringing high humidity. Isolated heavy rainstorms occur, especially in the afternoons. The wettest months are August and September. The winter monsoon only brings occasional rain showers.

As early as March the temperature can climb to well over 30° C. The hottest month is April. Apart from some cooler mountain and coastal regions, the climate is equally hot wherever you go. In Phnom Penh and in the temple district of Angkor, the temperature hardly falls below 26° C. at any time of year, and only drops a few degrees lower at night. The best months for visiting the country are from November to March.

Medical care

Tourists who intend to spend more than a few days in Cambodia are strongly urged to get vaccinated against typhus, cholera, hepatitis and tetanus! The country is totally lacking in adequate medical care. In the case of serious illness, especially if an operation is needed, you should endeavor to fly to Bangkok.

Clothing and equipment

At all times of year you need light cotton clothing (no synthetics), and things to protect you from the sun and rain. For visiting temples stout shoes and long trousers are recommended, for women as well as men. A light woollen jacket should be brought all year round, as the air-condtioning can be very chilly in hotels, aircraft and coaches. If you are travelling into the country you should take a light linen sleeping-bag.

Entry documents

All foreign nationals need a visa to enter Cambodia. However, Cambodia currently has no diplomatic representation in London. Individual travellers arriving by air can obtain a visa at Phnom Penh airport for a fee of US$ 20. You must provide 3 passport-size photos and the visa is only valid for one week, though an extension can be obtained for a further fee. Visas for group travellers will be obtained by the tour operator and are valid for 4-6 weeks.

Travel agents in Bangkok can obtain visas at short notice but for a steep fee.

If you are in Vietnam you can obtain your visa from the Cambodian Embassy in Hanoi, at 71 Tran Hung Dao St, tel. 53788. Office hours are Monday to Saturday, 8 am to 11 am and 2 pm to 4 pm. Alternatively you can apply to the Cambodian consulate in Ho Chi Minh City, at 41 Phung Khae Khon St, Tel. 92751, 92744. (Same office hours).

In Laos visas are issued by the Cambodian Embassy in Vientiane, at Thanon Saphan Thong Neua, Tel. 2750 and 4527.

In every case you have to fill out an application form in triplicate and provide a valid passport and three photographs.

The address of the British Embassy in Phnom Penh is: 29, 75th Street, Tel. (23) 27124.

Currency and exchange

The unit of currency in Cambodia is the Riel (r.). One Riel = 10 Kak = 100 Sen. You are not allowed to take Riel notes or coins into or out of the country, but an unlimited amount of foreign curency can be brought in. To do this you must complete a currency declaration. You may take out again the amount declared on the form, less any sums that have been exchanged for local currency, or spent on items for which you must show receipts. Since air-tickets, hotels, tours and many other things can only be paid for in US dollars, it makes sense to bring only US dollars with you. They should be in low denominations including a sufficient number of $ 1 bills for small purchases, drinks and tips. Cashing travellers cheques is only possible in banks in Phnom Penh, where a high handling-charge is imposed. You will always receive the cash in Riel.

Some hotels in Phnom Penh accept Visa and Mastercard.

Due to devaluation it is not possible to give a precise rate of exchange. However in 1993 the rate for US$ 1 ranged between 2200 and 2500 Riel.

Customs regulations

Customs regulations follow the international pattern and the importing of firearms, drugs, etc, is strictly forbidden. Cameras, electrical and electronic equipment must be declared.

Tobacco products and alcohol may be imported in small quantities.

Important: When travelling from Cambodia to Vietnam it is in your interest to draw up a detailed list of all goods you have bought in Cambodia, especially antiques (or what might be considered as such), and to get it stamped by the Vietnamese customs when you enter the country. This will prevent any difficulty when you come to leave Vietnam, since exporting Vietnamese art and antiques is strictly forbidden.

Arrival

By air: Information can be obtained from airline offices and tour-operators in Europe, North America and Australasia.

In Bangkok: Diethelm Travel, Kuan Gwan Building II, 140/1 Wireless Road, Bangkok 10330.

In Phnom Penh: Booking office of Cambodian Airlines (Département de l'Aviation Civile du Cambodge) 62 Tou Samouth Boulevard, Mon-Sat 7 am-11 am and 2 pm-5 pm.

By road: From Ho Chi Minh City (Saigon) to Phnom Penh, via the border crossing at Moc Bai, the journey takes about 6 hours by car and 10 hours by bus. The border is open from 6.30 am to 6 pm. The border-crossing must be entered in your Vietnamese visa. Your visa for Cambodia must specify Bavet as the crossing point. There is a public bus service in both directions but this is not available to tourists.

By ship: From My Tho in Vietnam, on the Mekong Delta 50 miles (80 km) to Phnem Penh there is a steamer service, but it is not available to tourists.

From overseas: Ships arrive at Sihanoukville (Kompong Som). We have no information on passenger service and cruises for tourists.

The crossing for road and rail on the **border with Thailand** is at Poipet, but this lies in the area still controlled by the infamous Khmer Rouge and is currently not open to tourists.

TRAVELLING IN CAMBODIA

Tours can be booked in Europe, or at Saigon-Tourist in Saigon, Vinatours in Hanoi and Diethelm Travel in Bangkok.

Information and reservations in Cambodia: *Diethelm Travel Cambodia Ltd.*, 8 Saigon Blvd, Phnom Penh, Tel. (00855-23) 23930 or 24930. *Phnom Penh Tourist*, 313 Vithei Karl Marx, Phnom Penh, Tel. (00855-23) 24095, Fax 26043.

Internal flights by Kampuchea Airlines, 206a, Tou Samouth Blvd, Phnom Penh Tel. (00855-23) 25105.

There are 2 flights a day from Phnom Penh to Siem Reap. Air-tickets can be obtained at Pochentong Airport. (One-way flight costs US$ 43 plus airport-tax of US$ 3. Luggage up to a limit of 10 kilos goes free on internal flights.)

There are two flights a week to Battambang. Find out the day and time of departure in advance. You can fly by helicopter several times a week to Koh Kong and Sihanoukville.

Overland excursions can be made from Phnom Penh to Tonle Bati and Oudong (Udong). Other excursions depend on current political conditions and you should find out about them from tour organizations. The journey to Siem Reap via Battambang can be undertaken **by car** when political conditions are stable.

Train journeys on alternate days to Sihanoukville and to Battambang, with onward road connection to Siem Reap, can be made by tourists but are not without danger.

Steamer trips on the Mekong and Tonle Sap rivers: short excursions are possible from Phnom Penh. Steamer trips to Kratie and Stung Treng are not yet available to tourists.

Taxis: These are available at the airport and the big hotels. The fare to your destination should be negotiated before you start the journey. The same is true for rickshaws, known locally as *cyclos*.

The major national highways:
Currently, certain stretches may not be used by tourists for security reasons; all the roads are in very bad condition and many bridges have been destroyed.
Highway 1: Phnom Penh – Saigon (Vietnam) via Svay Rieng, border crossing at Moc Bai (open to tourists).
Highway 2: Phnom Penh – Takeo – Chau Do (Vietnam). Border closed.
Highway 3: Phnom Penh – Kampot (on the Gulf of Siam), open.
Highway 4: Phnom Penh – Sihanoukville (seaport), open.
Highway 5: Southern route to Angkor: Phnom Penh – Kompong Chhang – Pursat – Battambang – Sisophon – from here to the north-west and to the Thai border, and east to Siem Reap.
Highway 6: Northern route to Angkor. Phnom Penh – Skun – Kompong Thom – Siem Reap.
Highway 7: Skun – Kompong Cham – Memot – Kratie – Stung Treng – and the border with Laos (closed to tourists).

Banks

The **Foreign Trade Bank of Cambodia**, 24 Tou Samouth Blvd, Phnom Penh, Tel. (23) 22466 cashes cheques drawn on corresponding banks, which include the Midland Bank in London, the Commonwealth Bank of Australia (Sydney), and the Banque Nationale de Paris (BNP), which has branches in Montreal and New York as well as in France.

At the Bangkok Bank, 26 Tou Samouth Blvd, Tel. (23) 26593, you can draw cash using a Visa credit-card.

Post, telephone, telex, fax

Air mail takes a long time to reach Europe and the USA. It should only be posted in Phnom Penh at the reception desks of large hotels or at the main post office near Wat Phnom Penh.
International telephone calls, and telex and fax connections are only possible from Phnom Penh. Waiting for a connection does not usually take very long. A reliable job is done by the service bureau in the Hotel Cambodiana Sofitel.

Office hours and opening times

Offices, public service counters and ministries are officially open from Monday to Saturday, from 7.30 am to 11.30 am and from 2.30 pm to 5.30 pm. Shops are open from early morning until late in the evening, but often close for a long lunch-break in the middle of the day.

Tipping

This is admittedly not obligatory, but in view of the very low wages, tips are always gratefully received.
There can scarcely be another country that has so many beggars. These are usually people who have had one or both legs blown off by a land-mine and who receive absolutely no assistance from the state. Sometimes they form organized gangs and try to extort money from shopkeepers by force, or rob buses and trucks on the overland highways. Up to now, however, tourists have hardly been troubled by them.

TOURISM IN LAOS

In Laos, too, tourism only began in the 1960s and was limited to the capital,

Vientiane, and the royal city of Luang Prabang, which were connected by Highway 13. The journey by car took about six hours. There was also a steamer service on the Mekong between the two cities.

From 1972 onward the Second Indochina War led to a suspension of tourism.

Between 1975 and 1983 travel to Laos was impossible. Thereafter, Diethelm Travel, based in Bangkok, supported the build-up of tourism in Laos and became the leading organizer of tours to that country. Their tours include visits to minority tribes in the remote mountain regions of northern Laos, with departure over the border into northern Thailand.

The Laotian government has so far not shown much enthusiasm for tourism, least of all for independent travellers. When making reservations you will encounter the following problem: in order to leave Vientiane and visit other regions even groups require special permits which have to be collected in Vientiane. An application form has to be submitted, with a photograph.

TRAVEL PREPARATIONS

Travel seasons and climate

In Laos the dry season runs from November to April and the rainy season from May to October. The winter monsoon from the northeast does not reach Laos. The southwest monsoon in the summer months brings heavier rains to the plains in the southern part of the country than to the mountainous north. The highest rainfall is on the west side of the mountain range which separates Laos from Vietnam.

Temperatures depend both on the season and on altitude. In the plains along the Mekong the temperature starts to rise in late February and reaches 38° C, as high as in neighboring Thailand and Cambodia. But on the high plateaus and the mountains temperatures are 10°C lower all year round. In December and January temperatures in the mountains can be as low as 15°C and can even drop to zero for short periods. The best time of year for visiting Laos is from November to March or April.

Clothing and equipment

Light cotton clothing is the most suitable for travelling. The differences in temperature between the plains and the mountains, for example between Vientiane and Luang Prabang, make it necessary always to take some woollen clothing with you as well. In the cool season you will also need an anorak. For cold nights in the mountains, cotton long-johns are a good idea, for women as well as men. Always take a waterproof jacket and something to protect against the sun.

A flashlight is essential when visiting the cave-temples and should always be kept handy after dark as power-cuts are quite common.

Entry documents

To enter Laos you have to have a visa. These are issued for a maximum of 15 days but can be extended in Vientiane. (Application with 3 photographs). For group tours, the visas are normally obtained by the tour operator.

In theory, it is possible to obtain individual visas from the Laotian Embassy, if there is one, in your own country. It is worth enquiring, but be prepared to wait for many weeks for it to come through.

Alternatively, visas can also be obtained from Diethelm Travel, Kian Gwan Building II, 140/1 Wireless Road, Bangkok 10330. However, this takes approximately 4 weeks. You can also apply direct to the Embassy of the Laotian Democratic Republic in Bangkok, whose address is 193 Sathorn Tai Road, Bangkok 10120, Tel. 286 0010.

Arriving by air or road

Vientiane's international airport is at Vattay, 2 1/2 miles (4 km) from the city. The taxi costs about US$ 5 and should be negotiated before you start. An airport tax of US$ 6 is payable on departure.

You can also enter and leave Laos by taking the ferry across the Mekong from the town of Nongkhai in Thailand to Tha Deua (Tha Nalang), 6 miles (10 km) from Vientiane.

Other border crossings can only be used when leaving Laos and then only as part of an organized tour. Further information from Diethelm Travel.

TRAVELLING IN LAOS

Tours for individual travellers or groups are organized in Britain by Regent Holidays (UK) Ltd, 13 Small Street, Bristol, BS1 1DE, Tel. (0272) 211711 and also by Diethelm Travel in Bangkok, Saigon Tourist in Saigon, Vinatours in Hanoi or Lao Tourism in Vientiane. When you have made your reservation, the tour organizer handles the official registration of the tourists on arrival (for this you need to complete an application form with 1 photograph). Individual travelers must report within three days to the Immigation Office (Ministère de l'Intérieur) in Thanon Lan Xang near the Morning Market.

Group tours can be booked to the following towns and regions:

Vientiane – Nam Gnum Dam (bus or car and boat).

Vientiane – Luang Prabang with excursions (either by air or by boat along the Mekong, then car, bus or jeep).

Vientiane – Luang Prabang – Houeixay (Air journey, trip along the Mekong). Departure to Xieng Khong in northern Thailand.

Vientiane-Luang Prabang – Xayabouly (By air, boat along the Mekong).

Vientiane – Savannakhet – Pakse – Champasak – Tat Lo – Boloven Plateau (by air, boat along the Mekong, bus or car). Departure via Chongmek to northeastern Thailand.

Information from Diethelm Travel Laos, Setthathirath Road, Namphu Square, Vientiane, Tel. (010 856 21) 4442; Fax (010 856 21) 5911; Telex 804-4351 Diet Lao LS.

Starting in 1994 Highway 13 from Vientiane to Luang Prabang will be open, and the passenger steamer service along the Mekong from Vientiane to Pakse is due to start up again.

Currency and exchange

In Laos the US dollar, the Thai *baht* and the Laotian *kip* are all accepted. The Laotian unit of currency is the kip (K) and there are notes of 1, 5, 10, 20, 50 and 100 K. Coins, called *aat*, are very rare. (The current exchange rate is approximately 900 K to 1 US dollar).

In hotels, shops restaurants and even in markets, you will often find that only US$ or Thai baht are accepted, so that you only need to change small amounts into Laotian currency. Neither travellers cheques nor credit cards are accepted. The only place you can cash dollar travellers cheques is at the Banque pour le Commerce Extérieur Lao, near the Lane Xang Hotel in Thanon Pang Kham. The best thing is only to bring cash with you.

Customs regulations

As well as personal effects you are allowed to bring in small amounts of alcohol, tobacco products and photographic equipment. Importing firearms and drugs is strictly forbidden.

Post, telephone, fax, telex

Mail to Europe takes a long time to arrive. However, provided it is handed in at the main post office in Vientiane or at the reception desk of the Lane Xang Hotel, it might reach its destination. Posting mail outside Vientiane is not advisable.

International telephone calls can be made from the International Telephone Office in Thanon Settathirat. The main post office provides fax and telex services. Outside Vientiane it is still not possible to receive phone calls or telex messages from abroad.

Diplomatic representation, tourist information

Britain has no embassy or mission in Vientiane, and diplomatic affairs are handled by the British Embassy to Thailand, in Wireless Road, Bangkok, Tel. (010 66 2) 253 0191.

The following are some of over 20 countries represented in Vientiane:
Australia: Thanon Phonxai Noi (Tel. 2477). **India**: Thanon That Luang (Tel. 2410). **Japan**: Thanon Dong Si Sun Wun (Tel. 2584). **Thailand**: Thanon Phon Kheng (Tel. 2508). **USA**: Thanon Bartolini (Tel. 3570/2357).

Tourist information can be obtained from the **Direction Nationale de Tourisme,** Thanon Settathirat, Boîte Postale 122, Vientiane, Tel. 3627.

Laotic diplomatic representation abroad

USA: 2222s St, NW., Washington DC, 20006, Tel. (202) 6670058. Also responsible for Canada. **Australia**: 1 Dalman Crescent, O'Malley A.C.T. 2606, Canberra, Tel. (06) 2864535, 2866933. Also responsible for New Zealand.

TRAVEL TIPS FOR CAMBODIA AND LAOS

Electricity

In both countries the electric current is 220 volts. Power blackouts are frequent, even in the capital cities. In smaller towns

the current is switched off for long periods. Hotels keep candles for these occasions. After dark you should always keep a flashlight handy. Batteries can be bought. In many hotels adaptors are necessary for French and American sockets.

Food and drink

If you follow a few basic rules you should be able to avoid gastric or intestinal troubles.

1. Water from the taps is not intended for drinking. Make sure that the the the vacuum-flask in your hotel room has been freshly filled with drinking water. However, you can never be quite sure that it has been boiled and is germ-free.

2. As far as possible stick to hot drinks such as coffee or tea; but cold beer is all right. It is the only cold drink that has to be boiled as part of the brewing process. Be careful with fruit juices and other iced soft drinks.

3. Avoid ice cream, fruit salad and green salad. If you eat fruit, peel it yourself.

4. Heavy European dishes are not suitable for the tropics. Local food goes down more easily, and the spices prevent it from going bad. However, you should not inflict large quantities of strongly spiced food on your stomach. Meals served fresh from the pan are more digestible than a cold buffet that has been prepared some time ago.

5. If, in spite of your caution, you fall victim to tummy-troubles, you should eat nothing at all, or just plain boiled rice, and drink a lot of liquid, especially tea.

Gifts

Small gifts in recognition of some service give a great deal of pleasure. They must always be presented with the right hand (since the left is considered impure). Small, practical items such as a sewing kit, cosmetics or pens and paper, are very welcome. Things you no longer need, including clothing, are best thrown in the waste-basket, so that no one thinks you have "forgotten" them and comes chasing after you. Hotel staff sometimes ask you for a written confirmation that an item is no longer required.

Insects

A regular intake of vitamin B reduces the danger of insect bites. Cockroaches are at home in tropical climes and reach a handsome size. They are harmless, but if you want to avoid seeing them, do not keep fruit or other food in your room and have your dirty plates and cutlery taken away. These can also attract rats.

Laundry, dry cleaning

In nearly every hotel you can get your laundry washed and ironed in a few hours. Articles of cotton or silk are given the proper treatment. To date there are no dry cleaning services in either country.

Medicines to pack

Your first-aid kit should include surgical dressings and plaster, elasticated bandages, and remedies for diarrhoea, constipation, temperature and infection.

It is essential to bring sufficient quantities of the usual medicines with you. Medicines, if available at all, are usually badly stored and in poor condition.

Photography and photographic supplies

You should bring all your own film with you. Although it is possible to buy film in these countries it will often have been kept in poor condition.

There is an absolute ban on photographing airports, military installations and soldiers. You should only photograph local people with their permission. Some mothers will object if you try to

photograph their little children, but others are obviously pleased to be photographed. Provided you use the required tact you can take some lovely pictures.

The mountain people are often camera-shy. You should always be reticent in dealing with monks. In pagodas and temples you should obtain permission.

Security

Local people imagine that a tourist's suitcase and bag contain untold treasures. So to avoid offering temptation you should keep everything zipped up and, where possible, locked. In the larger hotels valuables can be kept in a safe free of charge. Do not leave passport or air-tickets in your suitcase. Expensive jewelry is better left at home.

Vaccinations

The only obligatory vaccination is against yellow fever, if the visitor has, in the last six days prior to entering Cambodia or Laos, been resident in or has passed through an affected country.

Throughout Laos and Cambodia (except in the capitals) there are outbreaks of malaria all year round, in its virulent form *(plasmodium falciparum)*.This strain is resistant to many treatments. Ask your doctor or health center about appropriate preventive medication against this and other tropical diseases. A tetanus injection is a sensible precaution, for those small scratches and wounds that are often overlooked.

ETIQUETTE

The feet, which come into contact with the dust of the street, are considered impure, whereas the head is so pure and highly regarded that it should not be touched at all. This means that you should not even stroke a child's head. To do so causes great embarassment both to the child and the mother, since politeness prevents them from daring to stop you.

If a small child looks at a foreigner laughing and then suddenly turns away in tears, this is because it has been frightened by the person's light-colored eyes. All Asiatics have dark eyes. Many travellers like to give a sweet or other small present to a child. But children can make themselves unpopular with tourists by aggressively demanding sweets, pencils or coins. Maybe they have only just discovered that foreigners have these desirable objects to give away!

If you want to call someone over to you, there is a right way and a wrong way to do it. The right way is to use the whole hand; turn the palm inwards and move your hand towards you. Any other hand-gestures are liable to be misinterpreted.

Polite Asians have learned that Europeans shake hands when they meet, and attempt to do the same to you, but the women do not like doing it. The Cambodians and Laotians greet each other by putting the palms of their hands together in front of their chest, or, if showing particular respect, at head height, and bowing from the waist.

Asians try not to display annoyance, dislike or dissatisfaction. They look on aghast when a foreigner indulges in a loud and voluble outburst of anger, whether he has any justification or not – their view is that anyone who has to shout must be in the wrong.

A Cambodian or Lao who is the cause of such a scene loses face – but so does the person making all the fuss. It is not easy for a European who arrives at the airport only to see his plane taxiing down the runway, to smile calmly and say: *mai pen rai*, it really doesn't matter. But will losing his temper make the plane stop? The English-speaking Khmer or Lao will say "No problem," and by that he means that the other person should not worry about it any more, as he will make the problem his.

Mai pen rai, don't worry about it, there's nothing you can do about it!

Temples and pagodas

Both the Cambodians and the Laotians are devout Buddhists. One should not hurt their feelings by behavior which infringes their religious laws. Shoes must always be removed before you enter a pagoda. You must not point at a holy object with the hand or finger, and when seated you must not point the toes or soles of the feet towards the altar, a statue of Buddha, a monk or any other person. One either has to squat or else sit with the legs tucked away to the side so that the soles of the feet point backwards.

If you give a present to a monk you must not put it into his hands. It should be placed on a tray or cloth in front of him, or on the altar. Women should behave with reticence towards monks.

There are no definite rules about clothing but wearing shorts and low-cut tee-shirts or blouses in a pagoda can seem like an insult to a devout Buddhist.

GLOSSARY

Cambodia

angkor (Sanskrit), *nokor, nagara*: capital, royal city
apsara: semi-divine dancing girls
ba (ba yon, ba phuon): father; in connection with shrines: the earth
banteay: fortress, fortifications; temples and monasteries with surrounding walls are also called *banteay*
baray: reservoir for irrigation purposes
beng: marsh
chau: lord
damrei: elephant
prasat damrei krap: shrine of the kneeling elephant
devajara: god-king
garuda: bird-man, steed of Vishnu
Harihara: Vishna and Shiva represented and worshipped in one person

kompong: town by water
kompong preah: kompong of the holy men
kulen: lychee-tree
maha (Sanskrit): great
me: mother
me bon: in connection with shrines: of the water
meru: the Indian mountain of the gods with 7 terraces, upon which 33 gods are enthroned, surrounded by the ocean of the world
neak pean: the curled-up snake
prasat: (tower-) shrine
Prasat Neang Khmau: Shrine of the Black Lady
prea, prah: holy
prei: forest
prei monti: forest of the palace
pteah: Cambodian house built on stilts
sri, srei: glorious, fortunate man
stung: river, tributary
ta, ta keo: ancestor, venerable man
thom: large, great
wat, vat: Buddhist monastery

Laos

maha: great
nam: river
Nam Khane: the river Khane
pak: mouth, estuary
Pak Ou: where the Ou joins the Mekong
prang: (tower-)shrine
sima: stones which fence off a sacred area
that: stupa (burial shrine)
vihara, vihan, Laotian *sim:* temple which houses the image of a god or Buddha; can also bemean the whole monastery.

AUTHOR

Annaliese Wulf, the author of the Nelles Guide to Cambodia/Laos, has been travelling around South-east Asia, including Cambodia and Laos, since 1964, and before the 2nd Indochinese War spent a long time among the temples of Angkor. Her descriptions of the art of the country are based on first-hand knowledge and on standard French research works. The more recent facts and figures on economic and political developments were taken from publications by Dr Oskar Weggel, Institute of Asian Studies, Hamburg, whom we would like to thank here.

PHOTOGRAPHERS

Archiv für Kunst und Geschichte, Berlin 33
Beck, Josef 1, 45, 50, 55R, 65, 66, 68, 70, 78, 90, 91, 127R, 128, 134, 142, 148, 160/161, 178, 200/201, 202, 209
Deichmann, Günther (Mainbild) 97,236
dpa 36, 39, 44, 182, 183, 184, 185, 186, 187, 188, 189
Evrard, Alain (Mainbild) 117
Gradnitzer, Sybille 16, 53, 58, 88, 95, 108/109, 121, 123, 124, 131, 132, 144, 146, 156, 179, 194, 199, 216, 220
Hellige, Wolfgang cover, 2, 12, 20, 21, 22, 24, 29, 57, 60, 61, 62, 64, 67, 72/73, 74, 96, 103, 110, 119, 120, 129, 135, 138, 147, 150, 162, 198, 218, 224, 230, 232, 234, 235
Hinz, Hans 69
Höbel, Robert 23, 83, 89, 33, 141, 151, 154, 157
Janicke, Volkmar E. 174
Keller, Hans-Jörg 8/9, 10/11, 28, 31, 41, 42, 43, 46, 85, 99, 102, 104, 114, 115, 127L, 155, 158/159, 167, 169, 170, 172, 175, 176, 191, 192, 193, 214, 221, 222, 226, 238
Röhl, Wolfgang (Mainbild) 173, 212
Saxer, Lili (Diethelm Travel) 79
Schneider, Hilde 106, 137
Simmons, Ben (Mainbild) 19, 32
Bildarchiv Verlagsburo Simon & Magiera 34, 38
Wulf, Annaliese 17, 35, 48, 55L, 84, 86, 87, 125, 136, 166, 180, 181, 196, 197, 206, 211, 219, 228, 237